Dr. Marsha Rano is a winner. All she does has a touch of excellence about it. This book is no exception. She was a model student and an honor graduate of Beacon University in 2009. I had the pleasure of reading her dissertation. I recommend this book for any thinking Christian interested in confronting error among Christians throughout the Body of Christ. She is not on a witch-hunt in this book. She is laying out strong, clear principles for maintaining strong doctrine and hence right thinking and rewarding living. Her case study interview of *The Secret* is fascinating. From that study she has laid out principles that will enable the average Christian to overcome humanistic and immoral influences that abound today. I recommend this book to every thinking Christian and especially those in ministry today.

—Ronald E. Cottle, PhD, EdD, Founder / President,
Christian Life School of Theology

In this book Dr. Marsha Rano reveals how easily we as Christians can buy into non-biblical aspects of our culture if we compromise truth and honesty in our daily life. A must-read for every Christian!

—David W. Balsiger, LHD, Executive Director / Producer,
Balsiger Media Enterprises

This book is long overdue! People don't reject God's Word because "right answers" don't exist to the difficult problems it deals with. They reject it because of lack of exposure and engagement to that evidence. This timely resource confronts and calls ministry leaders to action—understand genre analysis and then apply good hermeneutics—today … for the sake of His Church.

—Reverend Rick Wulfestieg, MA, Director,
Foursquare Media, International Foursquare Churches

Few Christian authors understand the intricate web of deception surrounding *The Secret* as Dr. Marsha Rano. Her expertise at exposing the dark side of this popular, trendy brand of spirituality is commendable. Her insights on the necessity of truth are desperately needed in the body of Christ in this hour. I heartily recommend her book.

—Dr. Mike Shreve, Author of *In Search of the True Light*, CEO, Deeper Revelation Books

Dr. Rano's very well researched book shows us how to avoid the pitfalls of confusing biblical fact with man's fiction. Remember, Satan quoted scripture to Jesus BUT he twisted it. This is a must read book to help keep each of us from falling prey to Satan's manipulations.

—Charles E. Sellier, Founder / President, Grizzly Adams Productions

For centuries, people have wrestled in trying to discern truth from lie. Dr. Marsha Rano has done a superb job examining the subject of truth and exposing the essential elements of God's truths and the world's lies. The best seller, *The Secret, promotes ideas that seduce people into believing those lies.* Rano explains and gives illumination for those looking for truth.

—Dr. Stanley Fleming, President / Founder, Gate Breakers Ministries

To Don & Cheryl -

TRUTH WAR

Discerning Truth From Error

Every Lie Has Truth as Its Starting Place

Buy the truth, and sell it not!
Prov 23:23

Dr. Marsha Scudder Rano

Marsha Rano

CROSSBOOKS
PUBLISHING

CrossBooks™
A Division of LifeWay
1663 Liberty Drive
Bloomington, IN 47403
www.crossbooks.com
Phone: 1-866-879-0502

First published by CrossBooks 10/31/2013

ISBN: 978-1-4627-2780-3 (sc)
ISBN: 978-1-4627-2782-7 (hc)
ISBN: 978-1-4627-2781-0 (e)
Library of Congress Control Number: 2013908230

Printed in the United States of America.
This book is printed on acid-free paper.

Author's note: Names and some locations have been changed to protect identities. Some fiction included.
Author's note: For the sake of brevity, in some instances the author employs terms like "man" or "men" or "mankind" to refer to all of humanity.

Dedicated to the memory of our precious grandson
Anthony Todd Biaśo Jarrett
and
To my husband and life partner, Tom,
an example of a life lived in Truth
in the form of integrity, humility, and meekness
before God and men.

Every Lie Has Truth as Its Starting Place

Truth stands alone.
Therefore truth requires nothing beyond itself to exist—
Deception is nothing beyond a distortion of truth.
Therefore deception requires truth even to exist—
Anything beyond truth IS deception.

TABLE OF CONTENTS

FOREWORD

This book by Dr. Marsha Rano contributes greatly to the desperate need of the church to practice biblical discernment. More than a plea for discernment, it is a workbook that provides practical lessons in cultivating discernment in the Christian life. The teachings that the author presents will equip serious readers with a foundation for biblical discernment that will enable them to make careful distinctions in their thinking about truth.

Truth is a precious commodity that should be handled carefully, but today's culture teaches otherwise in one form or another. Relativism claims that truth is always changing. Morality is by majority. If everyone says something is good, then it simply becomes good. Subjectivism suggests that something may be true for you, but not necessarily for me. Existentialism argues that the only truth is that which you can experience. Rationalism makes a god of logic, allowing the individual to decide what is true or untrue. Pragmatism forgets all about truth and simply searches for what works.

These and similar philosophies teach that there is no absolute truth relating to morality or doctrine, allowing for no definitive standards of belief or behavior. It is no surprise that secular society values pluralism and diversity higher than truth, but the same attitude has sadly infected an increasing segment of the church. Ours is an open-minded age that prefers tolerance to truth and compromise to orthodoxy. Those who insist on adhering to rigid biblical morality and doctrine are branded as narrow-minded, judgmental, intolerant, bigoted, outmoded, and discourteous. As a result, many individual believers, churches, and denominations as a whole have forfeited biblical clarity in favor of moral and doctrinal error. For example, leaders of some denominations have appointed committees to study certain moral issues and to recommend what the church's stance should be. Why do we need ecclesiastical committees to investigate and rule on matters that God has already decided?

The temptation to embrace deception is great, and believers often accept it too much with too little discernment. There is a definite attraction to the deception, especially when an immensely popular television personality may subscribe to it and promote books that teach it. The deception often supports its claims by quoting the Bible and talking about Jesus. Many non-discerning people, in their efforts to be nonjudgmental, think that since a renowned celebrity embraces the teaching and since Jesus and the Bible receive mention; then it must be acceptable. However, individuals or churches that fail to discern between sound doctrine and false teaching, between good and evil, and between truth and lies set themselves up for all kinds of error. A compromising church may be a popular church, but it is a powerless church. Only as the church maintains a passionate love for truth and an intense hatred for error will it manifest its power in society.

In 1 Thessalonians 5:21–22 the apostle Paul issues an unmistakable call to discernment. We are already witnessing the disastrous results of the indifference of the church in the face of the current trend toward moral, doctrinal, and political corruption. This book by Dr. Marsha Rano contributes greatly to the desperate need of the church to practice biblical discernment. More than a plea for discernment, it is a workbook that provides practical lessons in cultivating discernment in the Christian life. The teachings that the author presents will equip serious readers with a foundation for biblical discernment that will enable them to make careful distinctions in their thinking about truth.

—Dr. Jerry Horner, founding dean of the School of Divinity,
Regent University, and former dean of the School of Theology,
Oral Roberts University

A WORD FROM THE AUTHOR

Did You Know?

- Over 60 percent of those who fall into spiritual error are professing Christians?
- Over 50 percent of senior Protestant pastors believe there is no such a thing as absolute moral truth?
- Over 60 percent of students from religious schools admit to cheating, and nearly 85 percent confess to lying regularly?
- Only 32 percent of all Americans believe the Bible is true, 67 percent deny there is such a thing as truth, and 70 percent do not believe in moral absolutes?

What's in It for Me?

As you glance through this book, you may be musing: "Why do I need this book; why do I need to read a book on truth, of all things?" You may be saying to yourself, "I'm a fairly honest person. Sure, I may tell an occasional lie, but only to spare someone's feelings or protect my family or myself against harm or embarrassment. But I'm most certainly not a pathological liar. So why is this book on truth important to me?" Allow me to encourage you that these are valid questions, and I will attempt to answer them now!

The Red Thread
How to Discern Truth from Error

The "Red Thread" throughout this study on Truth is this: when we choose to walk in truth and honesty as a daily commitment, we exponentially increase our ability to discern Truth from error. Our safeguard against error is to be honest in all our dealings with man and with God: "The eye is the lamp of the body. So if your eye is sound, your entire body will be full of light. But if your eye is unsound, your whole body will be full of darkness. If then the very light in you [your conscience] is darkened, how dense is that darkness!" (Matt. 6:22–23, AMP). The Gospel of Luke warns: "Make sure that the light you think you have is not actually darkness" (Luke 11:35, NLT). Honesty and truthfulness in our daily life enables us to have light, clarity, and clear vision to discern what is true from what is false. It is then that we are able to allow the Holy Spirit to effect authentic spiritual growth and development in us and ultimately impact the world through us with the Truth of God. Our newfound appreciation of the necessity of truth allows us to discern Truth from error and so walk in the fullness and purpose of God through truth and honesty in the form of integrity, humility, and meekness.

Truth and Honesty or Deceit and Dishonesty

Most of us, if we are honest with ourselves, would agree that being truthful and honest is one of the biggest challenges we face and one of the hardest to acknowledge. Nobody wants to think of him- or herself as dishonest. Yet this is one of the biggest struggles we all face in daily life. How many of us can identify with the following scenario?

> I took the day off from work for a dental appointment, but I would really rather go to the beach with my friend. I think I'll just call the dentist's office and tell them I'm sick and can't make my appointment today. After all, I work hard so I deserve a day off to have some fun.

Sound familiar? Each of us needs an exercise in Truth to recognize and comprehend the import of truth and honesty to reveal the Truth of God and expose the Lie of Satan in our life. This study will impart Biblical principles to help each of us safeguard against deception through discerning Truth from error. My prayer is that every person who desires to do so will walk fully and without reservation in the will and purpose of God.

The Truth of God

Plato, one of the great philosophers of all time, makes this observation about the God of the universe: "God is truth and light his shadow."[1] The Truth of God is that God the Father is above all other gods. He is the Creator of the universe, and all that is in it (see Genesis 1:1–31). He is the "Alpha and Omega; the Beginning and the End … who is and who was and who is to come, the Almighty" (Rev. 1:8). According to W. E. Vine, "He fulfills the meaning of His Name; He is 'very God,' in distinction from all other gods, false gods… He cannot lie." Vine continues, "'The truth of God' is indicative of His faithfulness in the fulfillment of His promises as exhibited in Christ."[2]

The Truth of God is that He cares deeply for each of us—so much so that He sent His only begotten Son to die the death of a criminal in our place for our sins (John 3:16). Jesus, God the Son, says of Himself, "I am the way, the truth, and the life. No one comes to the Father except through Me" (John 14:6). He is altogether Truth. Truth begins and culminates in Him and through Him. Vine has this to say about truth: "'The truth of the Gospel' denotes the 'true' teaching of the Gospel, in contrast to perversions of it … 'The truth of God … even as truth is in Jesus,' gives the correct rendering, the meaning is *not merely ethical 'truth,' but 'truth' in all its fullness and scope, as embodied in Him; He was the perfect expression of the truth*"[3] (author's emphasis).

The Truth of God is that He never leaves us or forsakes us (Deut. 31:6) and He "is our refuge and strength, A very present help in trouble" (Ps. 46:1). His love for us attends to our every need. He sends to us His Spirit—God the Holy Spirit, His Spirit of Truth, who will lead us into all

Truth: "When He, the Spirit of truth, has come, He will guide you into all truth; for He will not speak on His own authority, but whatever He hears He will speak; and He will tell you things to come" (John 16:13).

The Lie of Satan

Absent of the effective equipping of the foundational truths of Christianity, the Church is left without the means to defend against the onslaught of New Age philosophies and other false teachings and is thus frequently drawn into all forms of error. Christian leaders of necessity must equip their constituents to confront false teachings—also known as false doctrines or doctrines of error or spirits of error—directly and specifically with the Biblical principles of the foundations of truth to distinguish and discern between Biblical Truth and doctrines of error.

The Secret—a contemporary New Age philosophy—typifies the Lie, which is the very lie Satan propagated against humanity from the beginning—in the Garden when he tempted Eve and convinced and deceived her into thinking that God was holding out on the first couple. Satan has employed this stratagem to deceive humanity down through the ages. Contrast and comparison of the Truth over against the Lie among members of the local church today reveal a lack of comprehensive teaching of the foundations of Christianity as leaders and laypersons continue to fall prey to Satan's cunning query "hath God said" (Gen. 3:1, KJV). Over 56 percent of leaders and lay leaders surveyed from local churches across the country have a secular worldview of truth, and over 66 percent of those interviewed see no danger with incorporating New Age philosophies into their faith.[4] The following notes on the New Age Movement and *The Secret* verify Satan's ploy to lead us away from Truth and into error:

> The New Age Movement is a modern revival of very old ancient, divergent, religious traditions and practices. The actual original root is squarely centered in Genesis 3:1–5, and reverberates throughout the movement's continued historical expressions. In the original lie, Satan questions God's word, His authority and benevolent rule (v. 1),

> disputes that death results from disobedience (v. 4), and claims that through the acquisition of the secret or Gnostic wisdom man can be enlightened and can be 'like God' (v. 5).[5]

> [The New Age philosophy *The Secret* asserts], the real secret is you. It's your true identity. And, like a good author, Rhonda Byrne saves that part of the secret to the very last section [where she avers] the sacred secret is that you are God.[6]

The Research

The research for this book includes interviews, surveys, and a workshop to gather data and information to investigate and assess the necessity of truth and honesty and the Truth of God in the life of the believer to discern Truth from error and thus avoid the Lie of Satan and his deceptions. The data and statistics in this book were gathered from the interviews and surveys and a test in the form of a workshop, the results of which determine the need for truth and the Truth of God in the life of the believer to avoid the Lie of Satan and his nefarious doctrines of error.

The interviews of adults with firsthand knowledge of *The Secret* book or DVD who profess to be Christians and a survey of adult Christian leaders and lay leaders from diverse backgrounds provided crucial data that determined the need for this teaching in the Church. A survey of the workshop participants at the conclusion of the test provided data that determined the viability of this teaching and revealed the need for education on truth and the Truth of God specifically targeting the adult Christian leader as well as lay leaders and persons in the pew.

The results of the research reveal the veracity of this teaching on discerning truth from error for effective ministry in the Body of Christ and demonstrate the significance of understanding the Truth and the Lie in the life of the believer and its respective impact on the life of the believer, on the Church, on education, on society as a whole, and subsequently on all the people of God.

ACKNOWLEDGEMENTS

This book is dedicated to the many friends and family to whom I owe a debt of gratitude for their unwavering support of me and this work. They have been my cheerleaders and sounding boards. Thanks to Dr. Stanley Fleming, president of Gate Breakers Ministry, for sharing his expertise and his plethora of knowledge on the subject of Truth versus false religions. To Pastor Bill Kline, senior counseling pastor of Resurrection Fellowship, for his constant input and availability throughout the creation and administration of the work. To my dear friends and co-laborers in Christ at Christian Life Educators Network, whose gracious endorsements of this book I so humbly appreciate. To my friend and colleague, Dr. Jerry Horner, for whose poignant and compelling words in the foreword of this book I am grateful. To the late Chuck Sellier, founder and president of Grizzly Adams Productions, who gave permission to use excerpts from *The Truth is No Secret* Workshop Curriculum. To my friends and editors, Diana Richardson and Steve Parolini, whose keen eyes and expertise helped to refine the message contained within the pages of this book.

A special thanks to my two daughters, my two sons-in-law, and my five grandchildren for their phenomenal input and support throughout the writing of this book, and to my dear husband and life partner since 1965 for his unrelenting patience, encouragement, and support without which this book would not have made it to pen and paper.

Finally, it is to the God of all Truth that I am eternally grateful for His prompting me to research and write this most-needed book on Truth and Error, for without His coaching, this book would never have seen the light of day.

INTRODUCTION: TRUTH THAT SAFEGUARDS

> There is a way which seems right to a man and appears straight before him, but at the end of it is the way of death.
>
> —PROVERBS 14:12, AMP

At first glance, this book might appear to be an exposé of *The Secret*—a contemporary New Age philosophy leading many unwary Christians astray. While I will address that philosophy—for it is one of the more popular examples of distorted truth in our culture today—the book is far more than an exposé. It is a commentary on the import to recognize Truth and confront un-Truth in a post-Christian, post-Truth culture. *The Secret* is just one tangible example of how Satan works in our lives to lead us away from the truth of God and into countless doctrines of error that can rob us of our peace, our joy, our purpose, and much more.

"And you shall be as gods" (Gen. 3:5, AKJV) is the lie Satan has leveled against man since time immemorial. Knowing God chooses to give man free will to love Him and obey Him, Satan appeals to man's pride and his ego to draw him away from the Truth of God and into the Lie of Satan. Pride is the very offense that beset Satan leading him away from God and to his own downfall. Satan seals his own fate when he rejects God and succumbs to his own pride. In Isaiah 14:12–14 God articulates Lucifer's rebellion against God and his subsequent fate as a result, "How you have fallen from heaven, [Lucifer], son of the dawn! ...You said in your heart, 'I will ascend to the heavens; I will raise my throne above the stars of God; I will sit enthroned on the mount of the assembly, on the utmost heights of the sacred mountain. I will ascend above the tops of the clouds; I will make myself like the Most High'" (NIV).

The Lie of Satan is that we can successfully be god of our own life—that we can make decisions for ourselves and effectively determine what is in our own best interest and in the best interest of others—without God. This age-old lie is the same lie Satan propagates against humanity to this day.

The Truth of God is we have a God-given ability to make our own decisions as to whom we will serve—whom we will make god (or God) of our life—and those decisions come with life-altering ramifications, for good or for evil. Joshua challenges us, "Choose for yourselves this day whom you will serve" (Josh. 24:15, NIV). Thus God sets before us the choice between life and death—the Truth of God and Lie of Satan—and He beseeches us to "choose life" (Deut. 30:19).

In these pages, I will examine truth and error from a Biblical context to help readers discern between the two in their own life and learn how to walk in Truth and truthfulness. As repetition is an effective teacher, throughout the book I will employ the repetition methodology by examining numerous facets of truth and error to help drive home the point of *The Red Thread* for the readers.

While truth is at a premium as the primary subject taught in the classrooms or the pulpits of the Church today, Charles Stanley understands the import of Truth in the life of every believer; and in his recent sermon "Building Truth Into Your Life," he challenges us with the following questions on Truth and truthfulness in daily life:

A. Do I consider myself to be a truthful person?
B. Do I have a tendency to slightly alter the truth?
C. Do I sometimes feel threatened by the truth?
D. Do I think it's acceptable to lie as long as I don't hurt anyone?
E. How do I feel when I don't tell the truth?
F. How do I feel when I know someone isn't telling me the truth?
G. Do I want people to be honest with me?[7]

In this book I will examine Biblical and theological principles, and provide Biblical and theological tools to help readers differentiate—or discern—between the Truth and the Lie, and thereby facilitate Truth in their lives to safeguard against deception. While it would be a significant study and a fascinating topic for a book in its own right, this book does not address in detail the theological aspects of such accounts as that of Rahab whose selfless act to hide the messengers of God saved the lives of such men of God as Joshua from certain death (Josh. 2:4, 6), and that of Corrie ten Boom whose heroic act to hide persecuted Jews in Nazi Germany rescued innocent lives from the same fate.[8] Rather, this book addresses the theological aspects of deception in our everyday life and how it can rob us of our ability to discern truth from error. To that end, I pray these words will help readers grow and develop in their understanding of the necessity of Truth and truthfulness—or honesty—and that through the application of Truth in the form of integrity, humility, and meekness, they will walk in the will and purpose of God for their lives (see glossary for definitions of the Truth, the Lie, and truth and lie, etc.).

The intent of this book is to edify and encourage you and free you in areas of need of which you may not even be aware. Please consider the following Scripture before determining whether or not you would profit from this study on discerning truth from error. The prophet Jeremiah warns, "The heart is deceitful above all things, and desperately wicked: who can know it?" (Jer. 17:9, KJV).

Learn vital information in this book to discern truth from error in your own life, or to help a friend or family member struggling in this area of need. There is a short test on the following page to help determine your current level of understanding of the import of Truth and truthfulness in your daily life and your potential vulnerability to deception.

So, hold on to your seat because we are about to embark on a journey of truth in every area of life!

An Exercise in Truth
The Dress; The Credit; The Windfall

Answer these questions according to what you would do in each scenario. It's important that you search your heart and be completely honest with your responses.

The Dress

A friend asks how you like her new dress. In your opinion, her new dress is unflattering to her, but you don't want to hurt her feelings by telling her so. Do you lie and tell her she looks great in her new frock, or do you kindly and tactfully give her your honest opinion? What would you do?

____

____.

The Credit

Your boss credits you and gives you a bonus for the success of a recent project. The problem is you—and only you—know that the credit for the success of this project belongs to a co-worker and not you. There is no way anyone else would know of this error in credit unless you tell. Do you give credit where credit is due, or do you keep the secret and the bonus? What would you do?

____

____.

The Windfall

The bank teller inadvertently forgets to post your $2000 withdrawal, and you notice on your next bank statement the $2000 is still in your account. Do you call the bank and tell them of their $2000 error in your favor, or do you praise God for the much welcomed windfall for your much needed family vacation? What would you do?

____

____.

Part I
TRUTH OR CONSEQUENCES

The Red Thread
Discerning Truth from Error

The television commercial captivated Jeremy's attention. It was an ad for a product that promised to restore an auto's old vinyl top to new. Jeremy gazed out the living room window at his 1960s classic car sitting in his driveway that he had just spent hours scrubbing and polishing to ready it to sell. But nothing he tried would revive its tired old vinyl top. As he glanced at the "For Sale" sign he had placed in the window of the car, he sadly sighed to himself, **"How can I sell a car that look like this?"**

Thinking back to the commercial he had just watched on TV, Jeremy had an idea! He would purchase the magic solution and see if it would clean up the dilapidated vinyl top enough to attract a buyer for his albatross of an auto. Jeremy went directly to the local auto store and purchased the *liquid gold in a bottle*. Upon returning home with the magic solution, he immediately applied it to the decrepit vinyl fabric atop his undesirable possession and—to his amazement—the solution immediately began its work to restore the luster and vitality to the weather-worn, sun-beaten top!

Within minutes the old deteriorating vinyl top had been restored to a brand-new luster. Jeremy, beaming over how good his 1960s classic looked, promptly reached inside his car and removed the "For Sale" sign from the window, remarking with glee, **"How can I sell a car that look like this?"**[9]

As is the case with many of us, Jeremy uses the exact words in both scenarios, but his meaning behind each instance is antithetical to the other; and yet the readers of this anecdote perceive both meanings. In this same way, others perceive the meaning behind our words far beyond the words we speak. Thus, in our daily communications with others, *let us say what we mean and mean what we say*!

Chapter 1

AND YOU SHALL BE AS GODS: THE LIE OF THE AGES

> But let your "Yes" be "Yes," and your "No," "No." For whatever is more than these is from the evil one.
>
> —Matthew 5:37

Truth vs *Isms*

In a post-Christian post-Truth culture where *isms*—from relativ*ism* to existential*ism*—permeate every corner of society and where believers and unbelievers alike consider truth archaic and implausible—secular-human*ism* aggressively attacks the underpinnings of the Christian faith ... which is Truth. Because of this phenomenon we have little awareness of or education about the import of truth at every level in our daily lives; the spirit of this age seduces and leads many into embracing dangerous doctrines of error.

This particular trend engenders in us a *self*-serving desire to be god of our own life—to determine for ourselves what is right or wrong—and this trend renders us vulnerable to every wind of doctrine that promises power, purpose, and peace. This problem crosses all demographic lines, including: race, gender, age, education, marital status, socioeconomic background, and denominational affiliation. What leads us away from Truth? The deceitful "lusts and desires that spring from delusion" (Eph. 4:22, AMP). The writer of 1 John 2:16 identifies these as "the lust of the flesh [craving for sensual gratification] and the lust of the eyes [greedy longings of the mind] and the pride of life [assurance in one's own resources or in the stability of earthly things]," and concludes that "these do not come from the Father but are from the world [itself]" (AMP).

Our rejection of Truth leaves us susceptible to doctrines of error that endorse *self*-reliance, *self*-importance, and *self*-deification. Some no longer avow, "I can do all things through Christ" (Phil. 4:13); rather they now avow, "I can do all things—period." The spirit of this age engenders *self*-sufficiency and exalts material*ism* and *self*-gratification, yet Jesus cautions, "You cannot serve God and mammon (deceitful riches, money, possessions, or whatever is trusted in)" (Matt. 6:24b, AMP). Adam and Eve fall prey to deception in the Garden when they succumb to the serpent's malevolent drivel, "You will be like God, knowing good and evil" (Gen. 3:5b); that is to say, "You don't need God; you can be god of your own life—you can choose for yourself what is good and evil—right or wrong."

> Now the serpent was more subtle and crafty than any living creature of the field which the Lord God had made. And he [Satan] said to the woman, Can it really be that God has said, You shall not eat from every tree of the garden? And the woman said to the serpent, We may eat the fruit from the trees of the garden, Except the fruit from the tree which is in the middle of the garden. God has said, You shall not eat of it, *neither shall you touch it*, lest you die. But the serpent said to the woman, You shall not surely die, For God knows that in the day you eat of it your eyes will be opened, and you will be like God, knowing the difference between good and evil and blessing and calamity.
>
> —Genesis 3:1–5, AMP

The Dilemma

When we reject the Truth of God, God renders us vulnerable to the Lie of Satan, which is every form of deception that hails us god of our own life. The prophet Jeremiah declares deceitfulness rules in the heart of humanity: "The heart is deceitful above all things, And desperately wicked; Who can know it?" (Jer. 17:9). Eve demonstrated this in the Garden when the devil engaged her in a conversation over God's actual command concerning the Tree of the Knowledge of Good and Evil. In Genesis 2:17 God instructs Adam, "But of the tree of the knowledge of good and evil you shall not eat, for in the day that you eat of it you shall surely die." Yet Genesis 3:3 reveals Eve's heart concerning the same: "But of the fruit of the tree which is in the midst of the garden, God has said, 'You shall not eat of it, *nor shall you touch it*, lest you die'" (author's emphasis). Her insertion of the words "nor shall you touch it" into God's command concerning the Tree of Knowledge of Good and Evil reveals the process of deceit already beginning in Eve's heart as she perverts God's one and only requirement.

When truth and integrity are not the motivating factors in the workings of our conscience, then lies and deceptions and untruths become acceptable. Jesus—the absolute paradigm of truth and integrity—exhorts, "Let your 'Yes' be 'Yes,' and your 'No,' 'No.' For whatever is more than these is from the evil one" (Matt. 5:37). He warns,

> The eye is the lamp of the body. So, If your eye is sound, your entire body will be full of light. But if your eye is unsound, your whole body will be full of darkness. If then the very light in you [your conscience] is darkened, how dense is that darkness!
>
> —Matthew 6:22–23, amp

The absence of truth and integrity darkens our conscience—the seat of truth and integrity—and renders us incapable to clearly distinguish and discern truth from error. The writer of Luke admonishes, "Make sure that the light you think you have is not actually darkness" (Luke 11:35, nlt). When we walk in dishonesty and deceitfulness, we are easily led away from truth and into error where we are "tossed to and fro and carried about with every wind of doctrine" (Eph. 4:14). Paul instructs us to walk in "true righteousness and holiness" and in truth and honesty with all people in all circumstances (see Ephesians 4:21–25). This requires abandoning the old nature of lusts and desires that stem from delusion and deception—rejecting all falsity and lying (v. 22b), and embracing the new nature of truth and truthfulness in every situation (vv. 23–24).

Jesus does not just say, "The truth shall make you free," rather He prefaces it, saying, "*You shall know the truth*, and the truth shall make you free" (John 8:32, author's emphasis). Truth has little effect without the knowledge and recognition of the reality of truth. More than 60 percent of those who fall into error claim to be Christians.[10] Today's post-Christian, post-Truth culture prefers tolerance to truth. The secular-humanist worldview postulates there is no absolute truth, only truth as each sees it. This leads its adherents to say, "Your truth is not my truth." Yet Jesus—the quintessence of truth—demonstrates truth at every point in His life—never counting the cost. The writer of 1 Peter pens,

> He was guilty of no sin, neither was deceit (guile) ever found on His lips. When He was reviled and insulted, He did not revile or offer insult in return; [when] He was abused and suffered, He made no threats [of vengeance]; but he trusted [Himself and everything] to Him Who judges fairly.
>
> —1 PETER 2:22–23, AMP

Jesus—the supreme archetype of Truth—refuses to alter His testimony but speaks only truth even to the pouring out of His own blood. Therefore, let Jesus be our model as we pursue truth and trust everything "to Him Who judges fairly." Let us have the mind of Christ in all things and pattern our lives according to His example. Let us follow Him.

> Then God spoke all these words: "I am the Lord your God, Who has brought you out of the land of Egypt, out of the house of bondage. You shall have no other gods before or besides Me."
>
> —Exodus 20:1–3, AMP

The Standard

Without the foundational truths of Christianity,[11] the Church is defenseless against New Age philosophies and other false teachings[12] and is thus vulnerable to all forms of spiritual error. Christian leaders must equip their parishioners to recognize and confront false teachings—also known as false doctrines, doctrines of demons, or doctrines of error—directly and specifically with the Biblical principles of the foundational truths of Christianity. This will enable them to discern between Biblical Truth and doctrines of error.[13] Consider one example of how this works in practice. The New Age philosophy espoused by *The Secret*[14] is a prototype of the Lie that Satan propagates against humanity[15] whose tenets diminish the necessity of the Truth essential to the foundations of Christianity, and distorts the outcome of its absence in the beliefs of members at the local church.

Whether or not New Age philosophies such as *The Secret* work is inconsequential; the issue *is not* whether they work, rather the issue is whether they violate God's eternal laws and God's eternal Truth. New Age philosophies do indeed violate God's Holy selfless Truth of Biblical Christianity and His eternal universal laws as this book reveals. New Age philosophies such as *The Secret* are counterfeits, perversions, and substitutes of God's Truth and of truthfulness in the form of integrity, humility, and meekness and of God's eternal laws or principles.

Chapter 2

INDUCTION TO TRUTH: EQUIPPING THE SAINTS

> Stand therefore [hold your ground], having tightened the belt of truth around your loins and having put on the breastplate of integrity *and* of moral rectitude *and* right standing with God, And having shod your feet in preparation [to face the enemy with the firm-footed stability, the promptness, and the readiness produced by the good news] of the Gospel of peace.
>
> —Ephesians 6:14–15, AMP

Exchanging the Truth for the Lie

Linda Crawford[16] came from a home where her mother was a devoted Christian. Although her father was a wonderful man who showered her with love and attention, he was not a Christian. At the tender age of eight, Linda invited Jesus into her heart. While she did not understand how vital walking in truth and honesty was to discerning truth from error, Linda faithfully served God and lived a holy life to the degree she understood. She continued in such faithfulness for the next forty years until the death of her father. When he died everything about Linda's faith was challenged as she was met with the dark realization that to her knowledge her father never received Jesus into his life. This brought Linda face to face with the realization that her father might not have gone to heaven and that she, as a Christian whose destiny was heaven, might never see her father again.

The emotional pain from the thought that she might never see her father again coupled with her inability to discern truth from error, steered Linda on a quest for a path that would ease her pain and give her assurance that death ultimately would reunite her with her beloved father. This led Linda unwittingly to a cult religion that allayed her fears with a promise that she most certainly would one day be reunited with her father whether or not he was ever born of the Spirit. Without the ability to discern truth from error, Linda's itching ears (2 Tim. 4:3–4) were sated by this empty promise that inexorably led her away from Truth and into error.

Linda became a member of this cult to satisfy her yearning to one day be reunited with her father. Linda's rejection of God's absolute Truth[17] rendered her vulnerable to the Lie that she could alter the Truth by altering her belief system. In her quest to manipulate and control her own destiny, Linda rejected the Truth and embraced the Lie. It certainly is possible that prior to his departure from this earth, Linda's father may have embraced the Truth of Christ and received Christ as his personal Savior, which would ensure her father's final destiny as heaven. But this, of course, is something only God Himself would know with certainty.

Linda's story is the epitome of how easily man walks away from the Truth[18] and into the Lie[19] that he can solve his own problems—make his own decisions—be the god of his own life—and control his own destiny.[20]

Jesus Is the Paradigm

Jesus is the Truth and is our model for truth and truthfulness. Jesus has no part in deception—all that He is, all that He does, all that He speaks is the embodiment of truth and honesty. Jesus rejects lies and deceptiveness and models truth, truthfulness, and honesty in every aspect of His life at all cost, even to the shedding of His own blood. Clear, honest, truthful communication without skirting the truth is

Christ's example to His followers. Jesus provides manifold examples of what it means to be truthful and honest even in the midst of difficult circumstances and uncomfortable confrontations. Whether we answer like Jesus with, "It is as you say" (Luke 23:3); or with an allegory like Jesus' parable of the sower (Matt. 13:1–9, 18–23); or whether we answer a question with a question like Jesus in Matthew 21:24 where "Jesus answered them, 'I also will ask you a question'" (AMP); honesty and truthfulness remain paramount in our communications to discern and avoid deception. To illustrate: if someone asks a question of us that we would rather not answer, we do not owe that person an answer to that question; we can choose to not answer at all, or we can choose to answer an uncomfortable or inappropriate question *with a question* like, "Why do you ask?" or "How is that your business?"

To fully understand truth requires comparing and contrasting it over and against error. While there are many facets to truth and error, this book hallmarks the underlying thesis of "the truth" and "the lie" as: (1) acknowledge theological Truth which defines Christianity (see chapter 3), (2) embrace truthfulness and honesty on every level of life (Matt. 5:37), and (3) reject falsehoods and lies that lead to deceptions and delusions (Eph. 4:22). Simply put: "Truth is stating what is. Falsehood is stating something to be so, when it is not."[21] The truth in this context is *alētheuo*, which denotes "speaking the truth."[22] The lie in this context is *pseudologos*, which "denotes 'speaking falsely' … and is applied to 'demons,' the actual utterances being by their human agents."[23]

> The Truth: Theological Truth—is *alēthinos* which "refers to 'real, ideal, genuine, it is used of God, John 7:28; 17:3; 1 Thess. 1:9; Rev. 6:10; these declare that God fulfills the meaning of His Name; He is 'very God,' in distinction from all other gods, false gods … signifies that He is veracious, 'true' to His utterances, He cannot lie."[24]

> The Lie: The outcome of pagan religion—is *pseudo*. Its meaning according to 2 Thessalonians 2:9: "'Lying wonders' is, literally, 'wonders of falsehood,' i.e., wonders

> calculated to deceive (cf. Rev. 13:13–15), the purpose being to deceive people into the acknowledgment of the spurious claim to deity on the part of the Man of Sin."[25]

The majority of Christians embrace the Truth of Christ yet few, by comparison, acknowledge the import of honesty and truthfulness in daily communications with others. Nevertheless honesty and truthfulness in daily communications is a foundational key to discern and avoid deception: "Make sure that the light you think you have is not actually darkness" (Luke 11:35, NLT). Because of our naïveté of truth and error, false doctrines like Chrislam[26]—a blasphemous intertwining of Christianity with Islam—creep into the Church at an alarming rate, while some Bible publishers delete references to God as the Father and to Jesus as the Son of God and replace them with terms like Allah:

> First, Wycliffe and SIL (Summer Institute of Linguistics) have produced Stories of the Prophets, an Arabic Bible that uses an Arabic equivalent of "Lord" instead of "Father" and "Messiah" instead of "Son."
>
> Second, Frontiers and SIL have produced *Meaning of the Gospel of Christ*, an Arabic translation which removes "Father" in reference to God and replaces it with "Allah," and removes or redefines "Son." For example, the verse which Christians use to justify going all over the world to make disciples, thus fulfilling the Great Commission (Matthew 28:19) reads, "Cleanse them by water in the name of Allah, his Messiah and his Holy Spirit" instead of "baptizing them in the name of the Father and of the Son and of the Holy Spirit."[27]

The writer of Ephesians 4:21–25 addresses the import to walk in the Truth of Christ in "true righteousness and holiness" (v. 24), and to be truthful and honest in our dealings with everyone in all circumstances (v. 25). This requires abandoning the old nature of lusts and desires that stem from delusion and deception—rejecting all falsehoods (v. 22b), and embracing the new nature of truth and honesty in every situation (vv. 23–24). His admonishment provides insight essential to be honest and truthful in all things. He writes:

> Assuming that you have really heard Him and been taught by Him, as [all] Truth is in Jesus [embodied and personified in Him], Strip yourselves of your former nature [put off and discard your old unrenewed self] which characterized your previous manner of life and becomes corrupt through lusts and desires that spring from delusion; And be constantly renewed in the spirit of your mind [having a fresh mental and spiritual attitude], And put on the new nature (the regenerate self) created in God's image, [Godlike] in true righteousness and holiness. Therefore, rejecting all falsity and done now with it, let every one express the truth with his neighbor, for we are all parts of one body and members one of another.
>
> —Ephesians 4:21–25, AMP

So, how do we put off the old nature of deceit and lust and put on the new nature of truth and substance? We must die to ourselves and live to Christ not through the law but rather through grace,

> So you also must consider yourselves dead to sin and alive to God in Christ Jesus. Let not sin therefore reign in your mortal body, to make you obey its passions. Do not present your members to sin as instruments for unrighteousness, but present yourselves to God as those who have been brought from death to life, and your members to God as instruments for righteousness. For sin will have no dominion over you, since you are not under law but under grace.
>
> —Romans 6:11–14, ESV

We do not accomplish this through keeping the law, rather we accomplish this by walking in grace and in truth through Jesus, "For while the Law was given through Moses, grace (unearned, undeserved favor and spiritual blessing) and truth came through Jesus Christ" (John 1:17, AMP). Thus we walk in truth through God's grace—Heaven's influence on the human heart.[28] Five being God's number for grace,[29] there are at least five requisites to put off the old nature and put on the new—to walk in the Truth and avoid the Lie, to discern truth from error: (1) be honest with God and man, (2) trust God and not self, (3), fear God and not man, (4) walk in God's love, and (5) obey God.

Requisite One: Be Honest with God and Man

We've heard it said, "We're only as sick as the secrets we keep,"[30] thinking our secrets are safe with us. However Scripture warns, "He will both bring to light the secret things that are [now hidden] in darkness and disclose and expose the [secret] aims (motives and purposes) of hearts" (1 Cor. 4:5, AMP). Scripture is replete with examples of man's secrets that God reveals for all to read. It starts with the first couple in the Garden when they try to hide their sin of the lust of their eyes, the lust of their flesh, and their pride of life through which sin is born into the entire human race (see Genesis 3:10). Note that there is no repentance on their part for their sin, only deceit and blame. Their son Cain succumbs to the pride of life and afterward tries to bury the evidence in the dead body of his brother—the result is the loss of his home, his family, and his identity (Gen. 4:8–12). Note again there is no repentance on Cain's part, only arrogance and self pity. Achan hides his sin after he yields to the lust of his eyes, and not only do his kinsmen lose battles because of his secret sin but he and his family pay the ultimate price with their lives over his deceit (see Joshua 7). King David succumbs to the lust of his eyes and his flesh and to the pride of life and murders his faithful servant, Uriah, in an attempt to conceal his dirty little secret about his illicit affair with Uriah's wife, Bathsheba, and the innocent son born of their affair pays for David's sin with his life (see 2 Samuel 11–12).

Our New Testament friends are no different. We read about Judas, whose heart is lead away from Truth by its own deceit and he tries to cloak his sin when he betrays the Son of God with a kiss; his doom is he cannot live with himself after such a traitorous act and he commits suicide (Matt. 26:14; 26:48; 27:5). And we can't forget Ananias and his wife Sapphira who try and hide their secret sin of greed when they surrender to the lust of the flesh and attempt to lie to the Holy Spirit; the result—they both drop dead on the spot (Acts 5:1–11).

"But," some may query, "what about the Biblical account of Rahab the harlot, as mentioned earlier, who hid the messengers of God from the king's men (see Joshua 2); or the modern day account of Corrie ten Boom who hid persecuted Jews from Nazi Germany's Secret Service Soldiers?" First, it's important we realize that accounts like these two are indeed the exception and not the rule—extremely rare occurrences that are few and far between. Second, even as Paul explicates "the letter kills but the Spirit gives life" (2 Cor. 3:6), it is vital we understand that God is more interested in the motives and purposes behind our deeds than our deeds per śe (see 1 Corinthians 4:5). Thus, there might be a rare occasion when the Holy Spirit would prompt us to keep a secret to protect innocent life. But the heroic deeds of these courageous women of God should not become a license to lie to save someone from embarrassment or spare someone's feelings.

On the other side, we read the account of Esther, Queen of Persia, who conceals her identity as a Jew from her king until the Holy Spirit, through a relative, prompts her to do otherwise. Mordechai beseeches Esther to do the right thing and reveal her Hebrew roots to the king and face potential death along with all her countrymen, challenging her with, "Who knows whether you are come to the kingdom for such a time as this?" (Esther 4:14b, KJV). Upon Esther's decision to reveal her secret, she resolves, "If I perish, I perish" (Esther 4:16b, KJV). Esther's decision to speak the truth and let the proverbial chips fall where they may not only saves her life and the lives of all her kinsmen but ultimately changes the course of history for an entire nation. To wit, our resolve to speak truth and trust God with the outcome opens our heart to hear the Holy

Spirit Who is faithful to lead us with that still small voice that says, "This is the way, walk ye in it" (Isa. 30:21a, KJV).

To avoid the pitfalls of our forerunners and walk in honesty with God and man, the imperative is to put off the old nature and put on the new and allow Truth to permeate every part of our being by allowing Him to birth Truth in us and through us. Paul sheds light on how to do this in his exhortation to gird up our loins with truth and to put on the breastplate of righteousness (Eph. 6:14). It is from the heart the issues of life flow, and it is from the loins all life flows. The heart is the seat of our ability to choose to do what is right, and the loin is the seat of our ability to procreate and reproduce Truth and honesty in our lives and in the lives of those near us.[31] The question is will our progeny be the product of Truth or of error? Jesus' legacy in us is Truth and honesty if we allow. Paul instructs, "Let this mind be in you which was also in Christ Jesus" (Phil. 2:5)—the operative word being "let." It is our choice to allow Him to birth Truth and honesty in us. Jack Hayford contends the saddest words in the Bible are in Genesis where the writer announced Adam's son Seth was created in his image rather than the image of God (see Genesis 1:27 and 5:3).[32] Let us allow Him to birth His Image in us and through us.

Requisite Two: Trust God and Not Self

It is imperative to trust God in order to walk in truthfulness rather than deceitfulness. The writer of 1 Peter declares that in the face of all manner of opposition,

> [Jesus] was guilty of no sin; neither was deceit (guile) found on His lips. When He was reviled and insulted, He did not revile or offer insult in return; [when] He was abused and suffered, He made no threats [of vengeance]; but He trusted [Himself and everything] to Him Who judges fairly.
>
> —1 Peter 2:22–23, AMP

What leads us to lie or deceive rather than to speak the truth is our lack of trust in the One who is the very essence of Truth. Therefore, truthfulness and honesty require trust in God.

To trust God requires we abandon our own ambitions and goals and trust God's purpose for our own life. This does not come without a struggle for our propensity to be god of our own life and our own destiny is a mighty force that is self-seeking and insists on its own rights and its own way (see 1 Corinthians 13:4–8). To trust God requires we acknowledge His goodness, believe His thoughts toward us are for peace and not evil, and place our faith in the future and the hope He has for each of us (see Jeremiah 29:4).

It is when we walk away from trusting ourselves and determine to place our trust and faith in a Holy God who knows everything from beginning to end and knows every detail of our own life—past, present, and future—that we are able to truly walk in truth and honesty to the abandon of consequences. Thus, forsaking trust in ourselves and choosing to trust God in our stead is an essential step to putting off the old nature and putting on the new nature of which the writer of Ephesians speaks (4:21–24).

Requisite Three: Fear God and Not Man

To trust God is to fear Him rather than man, "The fear of man brings a snare: But whoever puts his trust in the LORD shall be safe" (Prov. 29:25).[33]

> Fear of man leads to a life weakened with hidden sin. Along with any attempt to break this yoke, the evil one comes and taunts us saying that we have already shown ourselves to be a "good for nothing." Proverbs is right when it says that "the fear of man brings a snare." Once caught, it is hard to get out.[34]

To fear man requires deceptiveness to cloak sin; to fear God requires openness and honesty before God and man. Yet, to fear "the LORD is the beginning of knowledge" (Prov. 1:7). The psalmist warns us,

> The LORD has said to me in the strongest terms: "Do not think like everyone else does. Do not be afraid that some plan conceived behind closed doors will be the end of you. Do not fear anything except the LORD Almighty. He alone is the Holy One. If you fear him, you need fear nothing else. He will keep you safe."
>
> —ISAIAH 8:11–14, NLT

The writer of Proverbs declares, "The fear of the LORD is to hate evil; Pride and arrogance and the evil way. And the perverse mouth I hate" (8:13), and the psalmist definitively identifies whom we should fear with these words, "You, Yourself, are to be feared; And who may stand in Your presence When once You are angry?" (Ps. 76:7). The Hebrew root for the fear of God and for the fear of man are different. The Hebrew word translated "the fear of the LORD" in Proverbs 1:7 is *yirah*, which means "fear, reverence, piety." It also connotes "to respect, to reverence, to be awesome." *Yirah* can also refer to the fear of man in the sense of honor or respect for those in power or authority. Conversely, the Hebrew word translated "the fear of man" in Proverbs 29:25, "The fear of man brings a snare, But whoever trusts in the LORD shall be safe," is *hadarah* meaning "panic, fear, terror, horror." It also connotes a "place of fear, to make afraid, frighten, and make tremble."[35] This kind of fear causes us to stumble and fall when we succumb to the fear of man, while the fear the Lord engenders trust in us toward God where we are able to be open and honest in all our dealings and communications with God and man.

There are promises specific to the fear of the Lord. Two come to mind. The psalmist pens, "The LORD delights in those who fear him, who put their hope in his unfailing love" (Ps. 147:11, NIV); and in Psalm 37:4 he identifies the benefits of delighting ourselves in the Lord, "Delight yourself also in the LORD, And He shall give you the desires of your heart." In the book of Malachi, the writer makes an amazing promise to those who fear God: "Then those who feared the Lord talked often one to another; and the Lord listened and heard it, and a book of remembrance was written before Him of those who reverenced and worshipfully feared the Lord and who thought on His name" (3:16, AMP). Thus the fear of man has torment (1 John 4:18), but the fear of the Lord yields peace and promise and safety.

Requisite Four: Walk in God's Love

To reverently and worshipfully fear and trust God, intrinsically necessitates we love God and we walk in His love. To walk in God's love requires a healthy fear of God. The writer of Matthew warns, "And do not fear those who kill the body but cannot kill the soul. But rather fear Him who is able to destroy both soul and body in hell" (Matt. 10:28).

They who walk in God's perfect love are able to walk in the boldness and confidence of truth, honesty, and justice without fear of consequence or reprisal.

> Fear has no place in love. Bold confidence (1 John 4:17), based in love, cannot coexist with fear. Love, which, when perfected, gives bold confidence, casts out fear (compare Heb. 2:14, 15). The design of Christ's propitiatory death was to deliver from this bondage of fear.[36]

When we walk in God's love, we don't walk in fear for "perfect love casts out fear" (1 John 4:18), and engenders confidence, truth, and justice in us. God's love in us "is not self-seeking … [and] does not rejoice at injustice and unrighteousness, but rejoices when right and truth prevail" (1 Cor. 13:5–6, AMP). In 1 John we read,

> There is no fear in love [dread does not exist], but full-grown (complete, perfect) love turns fear out of doors and expels every trace of terror! For fear brings with it the thought of punishment, and [so] he who is afraid has not reached the full maturity of love [is not yet grown into love's complete perfection].
>
> —1 JOHN 4:18, AMP

To walk in God's love requires that we love our brother. "If someone says, 'I love God,' and hates his brother, he is a liar; for he who does not love his brother whom he has seen, how can he love God whom he has not seen?" (1 John 4:20). We must love our brother enough to walk in truth and honesty at all times and in every circumstance.

Jesus exhorts us to love the Lord our God with all our heart, our soul, and our mind, and love our neighbors as we love ourselves (Matt. 22:37–39). God's love in us is self*less* rather than self*ish*. When we operate in the love of God, we put the needs of others before our own. Jesus tells us the greatest test of love is when the opportunity presents itself that we give up our own life—our life-sustaining requirements—for that of a friend (John 15:13). The writer of 1 John admonishes us,

> This is real love—not that we loved God, but that he loved us and sent his Son as a sacrifice to take away our sins. Dear friends, since God loved us that much, we surely ought to love each other. No one has ever seen God. But if we love each other, God lives in us, and his love is brought to full expression in us.
>
> —1 JOHN 4:10–12, NLT

We cannot separate our love for one another from God's love in us. To do so would no longer be God's love operating in us (see 1 Corinthians 13:4–8).

Requisite Five: Obey God

To walk in honesty and trust and fear and love God requires that we obey God. Jesus makes it clear if we love Him we will keep His commandments (John 14:15). The prophet Isaiah admonishes us that to obey God is better than any sacrifice we can make to Him (1:11; see also 1 Samuel 15:22). Through the prophet Amos we are reminded of our fallen nature and our propensity to do as we choose to the abandon of God's instructions to us: "'My people have forgotten how to do right,' says the LORD" (Amos 3:10, NLT).

We understand the principle of obedience over against sacrifice with our own children when we instruct our daughter, for example, to clean her room and she takes out the trash instead. That she took out the trash is an unacceptable sacrifice on her part in light of her disobedience in not cleaning her room. Our nature since the Fall is not to obey God, rather it is to set our own rules—obey our own inclinations—and reserve sacrificial deeds to worship of God. W. Guy Delaney, explains,

> Obedience is a learned trait. Obedience fights against itself, because there is a human yearning to be free, to live for our self, to do our will and not someone else's. We are obedient, like young children, when we are totally dependent upon someone else. But as we grow to be more independent, like teenagers, obedience is more problematic. We have a yearning to do it our way, to control our own destiny, to prove to the world that we can make it on our own. Being free to worship God takes a lot of practice.[37]

Thus being honest with God and man, trusting and fearing God, loving God and others, and obeying Him from our heart enables us to put off the old nature of deception and put on the new nature of truth. Thereby we are able to discern truth from error. These requisites encompass the virtues of integrity, humility, and meekness which we will examine in depth in another chapter.

The Truth Is

In an age of uncertainty where relativism, situational ethics, and tolerance replace absolutism, moral rights and wrongs, and commitment to truth, humanism challenges Christians at every point to defend and preserve the foundational truths of Christianity.[38] Christians who encounter these deceptions often lack the ability to recognize and discern truth from false teachings and the tools to confront them. Statistics reveal this to be true not only among lay Christians but Christian leaders as well.[39] *The Secret*[40] is nothing more than an extension of age-old New Age philosophies[41] along with other false teachings that are deceptive in their very nature.

Everything about truth and everything that encompasses truth is significant. While there are many Hebrew words for deception, there is only one word for Truth. The Hebrew noun for truth is **אמת**, transliterated *Emet* or *Emeth* and translated *Truth.* Its meaning denotes "*firmness, stability, perpetuity, security.*"[42] Bullinger declares, "*Truth* is found only in the Word of God, in Christ, who says of Himself, the living Word, 'I am the truth' (John 14:6); and the *written* Word, the Scriptures, 'Thy word is truth' (John 17:17)." He continues,

> But a more simple fact concerning this remarkable word is this, that the first letter, *Aleph* (א), is the first letter of the [Hebrew] alphabet; the middle letter, *Mem* (מ), is the middle of the alphabet; while the last letter, *Tav* (ת), is the last letter of the alphabet. As much as to say to us, that the Word of the Lord is altogether truth. From beginning to end every letter and every word expresses, and contains, and is the Truth of God.[43]

The positioning of the letters at the beginning, the middle, and the end of the Hebrew alphabet bespeaks absolute balance.[44]

Conversely, the Hebrew word for falsehood—one form of deception—is שקר transliterated *sheker* and translated *falsehood.*[45] The first letter is *shin* (ש), the middle letter *qof* (ק), and the last letter *resh* (ר). These three letters appear one after the other just before the end of the Hebrew alphabet signifying extreme imbalance,[46] the antithesis of the remarkable balance of the letters for the word *truth* at the beginning, the middle, and the end of the alphabet.

Essentially there are two reasons Christians are ill-equipped to recognize or discern truth from falsehoods: (1) ignorance—*naïveté* of the import of truth in their own life, and (2) idolatry—a quest to be god of their own life. Either church leaders are not teaching their congregants to discern truth from error enabling them to wisely choose to walk in Truth in every aspect of their life, or their listeners are choosing to turn away from Truth and trust their own ability to decide for themselves what is good and evil.

Ignorance

For us to discern error or false teachings we must first discern truth. Ravi Zacharias emphasizes that "truth by definition, will always be exclusive. Indeed Jesus claimed such exclusivity."[47] According to Jesus in John 14:6, truth is absolute and truth is knowable.[48] If someone is driving north on a highway; that same person cannot simultaneously be driving south on that highway. Truth is *either/or* not *and/also*—truth is exclusive. Author, philosopher, and poet Ralph Waldo Emerson makes this observation of truth, "God offers to every mind its choice between truth and repose. Take which you please—you can never have both."[49] To walk in truth is not effortless rather it requires commitment to pursue truth at all cost; the benefits yield the ability to discern truth from error, which is worth its weight in gold.

As we have already determined, Ephesians 4:22, 24, and 25 (AMP) declares man strays from truth when he walks in his old nature "corrupt through deceitful lusts and desires that spring from delusion" (v. 22). Walking in truth requires that we "put on the new nature (the regenerate self) created in God's image, [Godlike] in true righteousness and holiness ... rejecting all falsity and done now with it, let everyone express truth with his neighbor" (vv. 24–25). Paul admonishes, "So ... we may no longer be children, tossed [like ships] to and fro between chance gusts of teaching, and wavering with every changing wind of doctrine... Rather, let our lives lovingly express truth [in all things, speaking truly, dealing truly, living truly]" (vv. 14–15, AMP).

Idolatry

We deceive ourselves when we restrict idolatry—idol worship—exclusively in terms of bowing to false gods such as the golden calf, for we participate in idolatry when we follow after or adhere to any "thing" or any "one" that would seduce us away from the truth of God's

Word. The innocuous can become lethal, like: Our favorite television program; our favorite sport; our pastor; even our children can become idols in our life. Anything that usurps God's place in our life—for all intents and purposes—is an idol. Scripture warns of the Lie and of the father of lies with these words, "He [the devil] was a murderer from the beginning, and does not stand in the truth, because there is no truth in him. Whenever he speaks a lie, he speaks from his own resources [nature], for he is a liar, and the father of it" (John 8:44). According to *Vine's Complete Expository Dictionary of Old and New Testament Words*, "the lie" according to 2 Thessalonians 2:9 is "'lying wonders.' ...Note: In Romans 1:25 the 'lie' or idol is the outcome of pagan religion; in 1 John 2:21–22 the 'lie' is the denial that Jesus is the Christ; in 2 Thessalonians 2:11 the 'lie' is the claim of the Man of Sin."[50]

From the beginning of time to present, Satan deceives man with the Lie that man can be god of his own life (Gen. 3:1–7). Man violates the Law of God when he embraces the Lie of Satan and in so doing he rejects the Truth of God—the Omnipotent, Omniscient, Omnipresent God—the God Who has ultimate control of life itself. Thus, rejection of the Truth renders us vulnerable to the lie, tempting us to embrace every fleeting lie and deception that exalts man and makes him god of his *own* life and destiny.

Idolatry or Ignorance

How are Christians led away from the Truth? How do we go from loving God and serving God to pursuing New Age philosophies and other false teachings? Our desire to set our own standards of right and wrong without being accountable to an absolute standard of truth leaves us defenseless against seductive doctrines of error that allude to a promise of peace, power, and purpose outside of God. In the case of Linda Crawford, we find disappointment, disillusionment, and a lack of trust in God's goodness. That, coupled with her lack of the reverent and worshipful fear of God (see Proverbs 1:7) that yields knowledge and godly wisdom to discern absolute Truth, led her away from truth and on a quest to control her own destiny. And yet those who know Linda would probably characterize her as a strong

Christian with high moral values. Some might even characterize her as one who lives a holy life or one who walks in holiness.

How is it, then, that Linda could be led away from the Truth and on a path to the Lie—a path replete with cunning, deception, and false teaching? Isn't walking in holiness tantamount to walking in truth? Then how is it that Satan is able to deceive Linda? Doesn't living a holy life produce truth in the life of the believer? Where is the fruit of that truth? Linda's friends may attest to the apparent holiness in her life, yet Linda rejects the Truth and subsequently embraces the Lie—which forever alters her life. The answers to all of these questions can be found in the Bible.

From Genesis and Romans we read that man's arch-enemy lured humanity's first parents away from the Truth when he tempted them

> to doubt the goodness of God (Gen. 3:1), to cease practicing continuous thanksgiving (Rom. 1:21–23), and to turn their attention away from God. When he succeeded, Adam and Eve disobeyed their Creator, rejected their creatureliness, and sought … "absolute moral autonomy, a prerogative which the Bible reserves for God alone."[51]

It is apparent that

> Eve was deceived into thinking that she didn't need to obey the God who created her and who loved her; that she didn't need that love relationship; rather that she needed to decide for herself what was right and wrong; that she needed to "take responsibility" for her own life … to "look within" for wisdom … to pursue self-realization … to find her SELF … to be the god of her own life.[52]

R. Paul Stevens confirms these assertions with these words, "Instead of being regents of the creation that bears God's signature, the man and woman begin to manipulate their environment to satisfy their own greed, or contrarily, to worship the created order (Rom. 1:25)."[53]

This penchant appears to cross all demographic lines including race, education, age, marital status, socio-economic background, gender, religious persuasions, even leadership in the Church at large. In his letter to the Ephesians, Paul asserts "deceitful lusts and desires that spring from delusion" (Eph. 4:22, AMP) are the malevolent culprits that lead man away from Truth and into error. The writer of 1 John 2:16, identifies these lusts as "the lust of the flesh, the lust of the eyes, and the pride of life." In short, man's rejection of the Truth of God, his penchant toward idolatry, and his ignorance of the import to walk in truth and honesty in his daily dealings render him vulnerable to every form of deception that endorses self-reliance, self-importance, and self-deification.

Part II
GOD OF ALL TRUTH

The Red Thread
Discerning Truth from Error

The following account of Jack Hayford typifies the import of discerning truth from deception in our daily life:

> When I was a boy, I was introduced early to a means my mother would use in dealing with each of us children—my brother, my sister, and me. Whenever Mamma thought any of us might be tempted to be less than truthful because of the pressure of a situation where possible correction may follow an honest confession, she would take a precautionary step.

Instead of simply asking, "Did you do (such and such) ...?"; she would precede the question with a statement. This statement had a very sobering effect on me, because it so vividly evidenced the reality of my accountability to be truthful in the eyes of God. Mamma would say, "I'm going to ask you a difficult question, Jack. But before I do, I want to say, I'm asking it 'in front of Jesus.'"

She wasn't playing games.

She wasn't threatening.

She wasn't using a religious ploy.

Rather, in our house we took the Lord seriously. Our home was a happy place to live, but we really believed in the genuine things about God's love, His kindness, His blessing, His salvation in Christ, and the beautiful truth of His Word. And when Mamma would say, 'In front of Jesus,' a powerful image would come to my mind.

We all knew God is everywhere, all the time. But there was a unique sense of the immediacy of the Living Lord when those words were spoken. I could imagine Jesus seated on a throne immediately to my left as I stood face-to-face with my mother and prepared to hear whatever question she had.

> Let's live our lives out that way.
> In front of Jesus.[54]

Indeed Hayford's mother had a clear picture of the reality that Jesus is ever present in our midst, whether we are aware of His presence or not. What we say and do—whether behind closed doors or on the world's stage—Jesus is ever present. Let this challenge each of us to live our lives "in front of Jesus."

Chapter 3

MAN EMBRACES THE TRUTH: AUTHENTIC LIFE AND PURPOSE

> Even if not overtly admitted, the search for truth is nevertheless hauntingly present, propelled by the need for incontrovertible answers to four inescapable questions, those dealing with origin, meaning, morality, and destiny. No thinking person can avoid this search, and it can only end when one is convinced that the answers espoused are true. Aristotle was right when he opined that all philosophy begins with wonder; but the journey, I suggest, can only progress through truth.
>
> —Ravi Zacharias[55]

What Is Truth?

There are many facets of truth, including scientific, philosophical, and theological truth. As the scientific, philosophical, and theological facets of truth are germane to understanding truth as I present it in this study, for expediency's sake we will only examine these three.

In the search of truth, Pontius Pilate's rhetorical question "What is truth?" (John 18:38) echoes down through the annals of time from so many centuries ago; Merriam-Webster provides an excellent answer to this age-old question. Truth is:

1. a *archaic*: fidelity, constancy b: sincerity in action, character, and utterance
2. a (1): the state of being the case: fact (2): the body of real things, events, and facts: actuality (3) *often capitalized*: a transcendent fundamental or spiritual reality b: a judgment, proposition, or idea that is true or accepted as true <*truths* of thermodynamics> c: the body of true statements and propositions
3. a: the property (as of a statement) of being in accord with fact or reality b: *chiefly British*: true c: fidelity to an original or to a standard
4. a: *capitalized Christian Science*: GOD—in truth: in accordance with fact b: actually.[56]

As stated, while the categories of truth are numerous, I'll focus on the three most familiar categories of truth relevant to this study: (1) scientific truth (practical application), (2) philosophical truth (absolute versus relative), and (3) theological Truth (the essence of Christ and the essence of truthfulness).

> Truth can never be reached by just listening to the voice of authority.
>
> —Sir Francis Bacon

Scientific Truth

Scientific truth appears to have the potential to change with each new discovery relevant to the contemporary perception of a particular truth. But although scientific truth appears to change, in reality it is man's perception of a particular truth that changes. A great example of this is man's early perception of the world as flat.[57] Columbus' voyage and his subsequent discovery that the world is round scientifically proved the Biblical account of this truth through the prophet Isaiah who declares, "It is He who sits above the circle of the earth" (Isa. 40:22). Some Bible translations refer to earth in this Scripture as a round ball; while still others refer to it as a globe. Merriam-Webster defines science:

1. a: the state of knowing: knowledge as distinguished from ignorance or misunderstanding
2. a: a department of systematized knowledge as an object of study <the *science* of theology> b: something (as a sport or technique) that may be studied or learned like systematized knowledge <have it down to a *science*>
3. a: knowledge or a system of knowledge covering general truths or the operation of general laws especially as obtained and tested through scientific method b: such knowledge or such a system of knowledge concerned with the physical world and its phenomena: natural science
4. a: a system or method reconciling practical ends with scientific laws <cooking is both a *science* and an art>[58]

Hence science is the search for truth through observation and examination to prove or disprove a particular existing theory. Sir Francis Bacon, the English philosopher (1561–1626) whom history esteems as the one to usher in modern science, asserted, "Truth can never be reached by listening to the voice of authority."[59] Accordingly we must explore beyond the contemporary voice to discover scientific truth.

Scientific truth is both repeatable and predictable. It is observable through such discoveries as Sir Isaac Newton's Law of Gravity: "What goes up must come down"[60] and Newton's Third Law of Motion: "For every action, there is an equal and opposite reaction."[61] We encounter scientific truth every day. Mathematics and earth sciences are examples of scientific truth in that they are observable, provable and repeatable, and predictable: Two and two always equal the sum of four, four quarts always equal one gallon, and if the apple comes loose from the limb, it will surely fall to the ground.

> We may agree, perhaps, to understand by Metaphysics an attempt to know reality as against mere appearance, or the study of first principles or ultimate truths, or again the effort to comprehend the universe, not simply piecemeal or by fragments, but somehow as a whole.
>
> —Francis Herbert Bradley[62]

Philosophical Truth

Philosophical truth is more complex than scientific truth in some respects. While scientific truth aligns with knowledge or fact and derives from observation, philosophical truth aligns with hypothesis or conjecture and derives from implication. Some philosophers lean toward unambiguous or absolute philosophical truth, while others lean toward abstract or relative philosophical truth. Merriam-Webster defines philosophy this way:

1. a (1): all learning exclusive of technical precepts and practical arts (2): the sciences and liberal arts exclusive of medicine, law, and theology <a doctor of *philosophy*> (3): the 4-year college course of a major seminary b (1) *archaic*: PHYSICAL SCIENCE (2): ETHICS c: a discipline comprising as its core logic, aesthetics, ethics, metaphysics, and epistemology
2. a: pursuit of wisdom b: a search for a general understanding of values and reality by chiefly speculative rather than observational means c: an analysis of the grounds of and concepts expressing fundamental beliefs
3. a: a system of philosophical concepts b: a theory underlying or regarding a sphere of activity or thought <the *philosophy* of war>
4. a: the most basic beliefs, concepts, and attitudes of an individual or group b: calmness of temper and judgment befitting a philosopher.[63]

In his scholarly journal article "Is Everything Relative, Including Truth?" Ray Bradley, prolific author and professor of philosophy, cites philosopher Aristotle (384–322 BCE) and his definition of philosophical truth that leans toward the unambiguous or absolute. Bradley paraphrases Aristotle, "A statement is true if things in reality are as the statement says they are; otherwise it is false." Bradley expounds on Aristotle's definition, "There is nothing terribly perplexing about this simple definition, which philosophers sometimes call the 'Simple' or 'Realist' or 'Absolute' account of truth."[64]

With abstract or relative philosophical truth, the principal problem lies in the meaning of truth rather than truth itself. Authors Bradley Dowden and Norman Swartz explain, "The principal problem is to offer a viable theory as to what truth itself consists in… The problem is not: *Is it true that there is extraterrestrial life?* The problem is: *What does it mean to say that it is true that there is extraterrestrial life?* Astrobiologists study the former problem; philosophers, the latter."[65] The authors further clarify,

> This philosophical problem of truth has been with us for a long time. In the first century AD, Pontius Pilate (John 18:38) asked "What is truth?" but no answer was forthcoming. The problem has been studied more since the turn of the twentieth century than at any other previous time. In the last one hundred or so years, considerable progress has been made in solving the problem.[66]

> The truth is incontrovertible, malice may attack it, ignorance may deride it, but in the end; there it is.
>
> —Winston Churchill[67]

Theological Truth

In pursuit of truth, scientists, philosophers, and theologians often juxtapose research and discovery of these facets of truth, which leads to hybrids or mutants of theological truth. In his writings, Oliver Wendell Holmes Jr., after studying Herbert Spencer's works on Social Darwinism, concluded the following:

> Evolution applies not only to physical organisms but also to the sphere of beliefs and convictions. The great, towering principles that have shaped civilizations are not transcendent truths ... but simply those that won out in the "struggle for life among competing ideas." These were to become the core teachings of philosophical pragmatism.[68]

In his assessment, Holmes provides the perfect example of how the mixing of philosophy with theology mutates theological truth. Nancy Pearcey expounds on hybrids or mutants of theological truth:

> Modern people tend to place morality and science in completely different categories, but for [John] Calvin both were examples of God's law. The difference is only that humans must choose to obey the moral law, whereas natural objects have no choice but to obey the laws of physics or electromagnetism. If we look at the world through Calvinist eyes, we see God's governing every element in the universe, God's word constituting its orderly structure, God's truth discoverable in every field.[69]

Merriam-Webster on theology:

1. a: the study of religious faith, practice, and experience; *especially*: the study of God and of God's relation to the world
2. a: a theological theory or system <Thomist *theology*> <a *theology* of atonement>[70]

Vine defines theological Truth this way: "refers to 'real, ideal, genuine, it is used of God, John 7:28; 17:3; 1 Thess. 1:9; Rev. 6:10; these declare that God fulfills the meaning of His Name; He is 'very God,' in distinction from all other gods, false gods ... signifies that He is veracious, 'true' to His utterances, He cannot lie."[71]

While it may seem theological truth changes with new discoveries, in reality new discoveries only add a new level of understanding to existing theological truth. Jesus makes this clear in the Gospel of Matthew, "Do not think that I have come to abolish the Law or the Prophets; I have not come to abolish them but to fulfill them" (Matt. 5:17, NIV). Ray Anderson declares, "There is no theological task that has any basis in God's truth other than the task of expounding the ministry of God."[72] He illustrates his claim with the analogy that the Holy Spirit reveals new paradigms of a particular truth over time as circumstances dictate or permit. He likens Jesus' parable of new wine in new wineskins to embracing new paradigms of a particular existing truth, which forms a new theology.[73] This process, however, does not nullify the former paradigm of a particular theology, but rather it provides new insight into existing theology.

The Essence of the Truth

Truth is the essence of God's message to humanity. By definition theological truth is the essence of the Christian faith. Winston Churchill declared, "The truth is incontrovertible, malice may attack it, ignorance may deride it, but in the end; there it is."[74] Truth is a constant, it is what it is; truth never changes. To alter truth is to deceive. Deception is dependent upon truth; truth, however, stands alone. Deception is not the absence of truth; rather truth is the absence of deception. That is to say, there is no such thing as counterfeit money unless authentic money exists first—the authentic can exist without the counterfeit, but the counterfeit cannot exist without the authentic. As the counterfeit requires the authentic to exist, so deception requires truth to exist.

Thus truth exists without deception, but deception cannot exist without truth. Deception requires truth to exist, for at its core deception is a counterfeit, a perversion, or a substitute of truth. Satan is the great deceiver and his greatest ploy is to masquerade as an angel of light (2 Cor. 11:14). He peppers truth with deception, as in the Garden when he said to Eve, "Hath God said," thereby deceiving and leading many astray. Once you add even a little deception to truth, it is no longer truth you have, but deception. It is the little foxes that spoil the vine (Song of Sol. 2:15), and it only requires a little leaven to ferment the entire loaf (1 Cor. 5:6). Even so, a little error—or deception—nullifies truth.

The essence of truth denotes virtues like faithfulness, truthfulness, integrity, sincerity, and transparency. In the book of John, Jesus prays, "Sanctify them by Your truth. Your word is truth" (John 17:17). With these words Jesus demonstrates the purpose of truth is to sanctify its adherents. Vine provides this definition for truth (*alētheia*):

- In Romans 15:8 "the truth of God" is indicative of His faithfulness in the fulfillment of His promises as exhibited in Christ.
- In Ephesians 4:21 … "even as truth is in Jesus," gives the correct rendering, the meaning is not merely ethical "truth," but "truth" in all its fullness and scope, as embodied in Him; He was the perfect expression of the truth.
- This is virtually equivalent of His statement in John 14:6; (b) subjectively, "truthfulness," "truth," not merely a verbal, but sincerity and integrity of character.[75]

Jesus declares, "I am the way, the truth, and the life. No one comes to the Father except through Me" (John 14:6). With this statement Jesus reveals Himself to be the Truth of God.

Jesus identifies integrity as a foundational truth of Christianity when He declares, "The eye is the lamp of the body. So if your eye is sound, your entire body will be full of light. But if your eye is unsound, your body will be full of darkness. If then the very light in you [your conscience] is darkened, how dense is that darkness!" (Matt. 6:22–24, AMP). The author of Proverbs 11:3 gives a strong admonition concerning integrity: "The integrity of the upright will guide them, But the perversity of the unfaithful will destroy them." Truth is the essence of God's message to humanity through His Holy Word. The Psalmist declares God places His Word above everything—even His own name, "I will worship toward Your holy temple, And praise Your name For Your lovingkindness and Your truth; For You have magnified Your word above all Your name" (Ps. 138:2). Following are thoughts from two of the world's foremost philosophers and thinkers on the subject of truth:

> The splendor of truth shines forth in the works of the Creator and, in a special way, in man, created in the image and likeness of God (cf. Gen. 1:26). Truth enlightens man's intelligence and shapes his freedom, leading him to know and love the Lord. Hence the Psalmist prays: "Let the light of your face shine on us, O Lord" (Ps. 4:6).
>
> —VERITATIS SPLENDOR[76]

> Truth provokes those whom it does not convert.
>
> —BISHOP THOMAS WILSON[77]

The essence of truth is reality in its totality—truth never changes and is itself unchangeable. The late Francis Schaeffer defined Christianity as total truth, "Christianity is not merely religious truth, it is total truth—truth about the whole of reality."[78] Pearcey defines total truth as the essence of Christianity and the ultimate reality of life and existence.[79] Thus honesty, integrity, truthfulness, and transparency are hallmarks in the life of one who purposefully walks in truth. Pearcey argues if Christians believe Christianity is truth in its totality, then there must be an integration of their convictions and their actions. The apostle Paul determines it is not *what we say* but *what we do* that convinces others of the truth. In his words, "The only letter of recommendation we need is you yourselves. Your lives are a letter written in our hearts; everyone can read it and recognize our good work among you" (2 Cor. 3:2, NLT). Pearcey writes, "We may do a great job of arguing that Christianity is total truth, but others will not find our message persuasive unless we give a visible demonstration of that truth in action. Outsiders must be able to see for themselves, in the day-to-day pattern of our lives, that we do not treat Christianity as just a private matter, a comfort blanket, a castle of fairy-tale beliefs that merely make us feel better."[80]

To demonstrate truth in our lives is to actively pursue truth. Emerson challenged us to actively pursue truth, "God offers to every mind its choice between truth and repose. Take which you please—you can never have both."[81] With this statement, Emerson asserts that man must actively be on a quest for truth. That is to say, to seek truth is not passive; rather it is an active pursuit. Emerson's findings concur with the writer of 2 Timothy 2:15 (AMP) who admonishes,

> Study and be eager and do your utmost to present yourself to God approved (tested by trial), a workman who has no cause to be ashamed, correctly analyzing and accurately dividing [rightly handling and skillfully teaching] the Word of Truth.

Thus we are to continually pursue truth; whether in science, philosophy, or theology.

Great Wisdom

Christians exercise great wisdom when they walk in the truth. They do this by aligning their will and desires with the Law of God. This alignment requires "truth (*alēthēs*), (*alēthinos*), and truthfulness (*alētheia*)"[82] in every aspect of our life and does not come without a struggle. It requires walking after the Spirit and not the flesh. The apostle Paul expounds on the struggle between the spirit and the flesh in the Book of Romans when he addresses his personal struggle with this dilemma (see also Psalm 1:2):

> For I endorse and delight in the Law of God in my inmost self [with my new nature]. But I discern in my bodily members [in the sensitive appetites and wills of the flesh] a different law (rule of action) at war against the law of my mind (my reason) and making me a prisoner to the law of sin that dwells in my bodily organs [in the sensitive appetites and wills of the flesh].
>
> —ROMANS 7:22–23, AMP

Paul continues his discourse on this seeming paradox, "So then indeed I, of myself with the mind and heart, serve the Law of God, but with the flesh the law of sin" (v. 25, AMP). In the first verse of Romans 8 Paul concludes his discourse on this dilemma, "Therefore, [there is] now no condemnation (no adjudging guilty of wrong) for those who are in Christ Jesus, who live [and] walk not after the dictates of the flesh, but after the dictates of the Spirit" (AMP).

The essence of Paul's message is the Law of God is truth, and we walk in great wisdom when we by God's grace walk in truth and honesty and thereby align our will with the will of God. Jesus exercises this wisdom in the Garden of Gethsemane when He pours out His will before God as He agonizes over His foreboding destiny and yet resolves, "Nevertheless, not what I will [not what I desire] but as You will and desire" (Matt. 26:39b, AMP).

Jessica Foster,[83] a Christian from age six, demonstrated what it means to exercise great wisdom and walk in truth when a fender bender put her integrity to the test. The fender in the accident already had a previous dent in it, and the insurance adjuster included this previous dent in his estimate for repairs. How would Jessica handle this error in her favor? She worked two jobs to put her husband through law school, had two children in school, and had bills piling up. Was God blessing her with extra cash from the accident, or was her faith in God's ability to meet their needs being put to the test? Because Jessica had predetermined to always walk in truth, without hesitation Jessica told the adjuster about the previous dent, and he corrected his estimate accordingly. Jessica rejected the cash windfall for a higher reward—her integrity remained intact, her conscience remained clear, and deception remained far from her door.

To walk in truth is not so much a deed we perform but a decision we make in advance to obey God and align our will with the will of the Father and trust God in His Wisdom to attend to the rest. In his interview in the Grizzly Adams® Productions television special *There Is More to The Secret*, Ed Gungor characterizes the inner-struggle Paul describes:

> The currency at stake here, I think is, who's in control, is it God or is it humans? ...Because of that, we come with ... an attitude of humility, and an attitude of openness, ...to say: "God, I don't want to be the initiator, the instigator of everything that is, I want—as Jesus taught us—to pray: Thy kingdom come; Thy will be done on earth as it is in

heaven—not, Thy kingdom come, my will be done." So, there's a reconfiguring of who's in control.[84]

Biblical Models

The Jacob Model: Encounter God and Engage Truth

"What is your name?" (Gen. 32:27). With this query we find in the book of Genesis, God confronts Jacob with the truth about his own nature, and as a result God is able to radically change Jacob's nature by exposing him to the truth about the depravity of his human condition. God wants to engage His people in truth. Encountering, engaging, and embracing truth radically changes us at our very core. Indeed, it is through Jacob's encountering, engaging, and embracing truth that he comes to terms with his own sinful character teeming with lies and deceitfulness. Subsequently Jacob recognizes and discerns his own lack and God's sufficiency to change him from the inside out.

The truth of God's Word is the mirror that reveals the truth about our own nature to bring us to repentance and restoration (see Genesis 32:22–29). The writer of James compares the truth of the Word with a mirror:

> But be doers of the word, and not hearers only, deceiving yourselves. For if anyone is a hearer of the word and not a doer, he is like a man observing his natural face in a mirror; for he observes himself, goes away, and immediately forgets what kind of man he was. But he who looks into the perfect law of liberty and continues in it, and is not a forgetful hearer but a doer of the word, this one will be blessed in what he does.
>
> —James 1:22–25

During his night-long wrestling match with the *Theophany* of God, Jacob declares that he will not release the Angel of God until He declares a blessing on him (Gen. 32:25–26). The Angel's response to Jacob's demand is revealing. The Angel announces He cannot bless Jacob until Jacob acknowledges who he is—until Jacob comes to terms with his own sinful nature. The writer of the text explains that the Angel "asked him, What is your name? And [in shock of realization, whispering] he said, Jacob [supplanter, schemer, trickster, swindler]!" (Gen. 32:27b, AMP).

The Holy Spirit will always press us to look deep within to examine the motives of our heart and come face-to-face with the truth of our own sinful nature. It is when Isaac's son recognizes and confesses his name is "supplanter, schemer, trickster, swindler" that Jacob is able to acknowledge his complete lack and God's utter sufficiency to transform him from his old nature to a new nature as Jacob surrenders all of who he is to the loving and trustworthy God of all Truth. It is from that recognition and confession that God announces to Jacob, "Your name shall be called no more Jacob [supplanter], but Israel [contender with God]; for you have contended and have power with God and with men and have prevailed" (Gen. 32:28, AMP).

The Peter Model: Acknowledge the Truth of Christ

Jesus asks His disciples, "Who do men say that the Son of man is?" (Matt. 16:13b, ASV), to which the disciples reply, "Some say John the Baptist, some Elijah, and others Jeremiah or one of the prophets" (v. 14). He asks His disciples more explicitly, "But, who do you [yourselves] say that I am?" (v. 15, AMP), to which only Simon Peter—boldly and unashamedly—replies, "You are the Christ, the Son of the living God" (v. 16). In spite of all his impetuousness and double-mindedness, Peter is the only one of Jesus' disciples who acknowledges the only Truth throughout all the ages by which all humanity is saved—Jesus Christ, the Truth, the only begotten Son of God. Only the Spirit of God could reveal this Truth.

In his bold and truthful declaration and humble confession, Peter reveals the very essence of Christ in all His glory and majesty. It is only when we come to the truth of what Peter acknowledges that "there is no other name under heaven given among men by which we must be saved" (Acts 4:12b) than that of Jesus the Christ, the Son of the living God, that we are able to embrace the Truth and receive eternal life.

Chapter 4

GOD'S VERY NATURE: TRUTH

> Cultural norms can often change and settle in precarious ways. Such shifts are currently underway, aided by an explosion of information, images, and technology that have left the mind assaulted by various enticements. In the dramatic displacements that we are witnessing, the question "What is truth?" must be answered if the essence of life is to be guarded.
>
> —Ravi Zacharias[85]

The Essence and Character of God Is the Truth

The essence and character of God—God's very nature—is Truth. Plato describes God's nature in simple terms: "God is Truth and Light is His shadow."[86] Augustus Hopkins Strong (1836–1921) recounts Plato's portrayal of God: "Truth is His [God's] body, and light is His shadow."[87] In his 1907 work *Systematic Theology*, Augustus Hopkins Strong identifies God's nature as truth on every level of His entire Being:

> Truth in God is not a merely active attribute of the divine nature. God is truth, not only in the sense that he is the being who truly knows, but also in the sense that he is the

> truth that is known. The passive precedes the active; truth of being precedes truth of knowing… All truth among men, whether mathematical, logical, moral, or religious, is to be regarded as having its foundation in this immanent truth of the divine nature and as disclosing facts in the being of God.[88]

Strong qualifies the essence of God's nature with a quote from David Hollaz (1648–1713):[89] "Truth is the conformity of the divine essence with the divine intellect."[90]

God is the personification of Truth in the life, death, and resurrection of His only begotten Son, Jesus the Christ. The author of the scholarly journal article "Western Philosophy" cites Augustine of Hippo (354–430) on Truth, who defines God's nature this way: "Beyond the world of the senses there is a spiritual, eternal realm of Truth that is the object of the human mind and the goal of all human striving."[91] The author illuminates, "This Truth he [Augustine] identified as the God of Christianity."[92] Jesus declares this truth, "I am the way, the truth, and the life. No one comes to the Father except through Me" (John 14:6).

Moral Character

Truth stands alone and requires nothing beyond itself to exist, deception is nothing more than a distortion of truth and thus requires truth even to exist; anything beyond truth *is* deception. Truth is at the core of moral character and requires of its bearers truth at every level.

God the Father embodies truth and engenders truth at every level in His people. God is Truth and thus He is wholly worthy of our trust. Absolute Truth is at the very heart of who God is and because of that we can trust Him implicitly to do what He says He will do. What does the essence and nature of God look like in man? God's nature in man necessitates walking in truth and truthfulness, encompassing the manifold virtues of "moral character."

It has been said that *morals* are when the standard sets the behavior and *mores* (pronounced mor'ēz) are when the behavior sets the standard.[93]

Genuine moral character is determined by a preset unchanging standard of behavior predetermined by an eternally existent unchanging Source, Who is the God of all creation. It also has been said the difference between morals and ethics can be summed up this way, "Morals define personal character, while ethics stress a social system in which morals are applied."[94] Thus morals set the standard of behavior and ethics point to that standard as appropriate behavior. To that end, without morals there can be no ethics. Following in this vein, an amoral society—a society lacking moral standards—is an unethical society by definition.

Moral character is the embodiment of truth which produces trust in the bearer of such character. Moral character transcends all social *mores* and all social systems and is the attribute we prize above all else in one another, for without it there can be no trust. What we say and what we do should comport with one another. Healthy relationships require moral character in both parties. We know how important it is to have a trustworthy friend, and it is equally important that our friends can trust us. To be able to place our trust in another person is a priceless commodity, yet we can't have this kind of trust relationship with someone we know does not always walk in truth and honesty. Conversely, if our friends or family can't trust us to be truthful at all times, how then can they trust us to, for example, look after their home while they're on vacation, or pick up their children from school when they're running late, or share with us an intimate or personal issue and trust us to keep their confidence. It is in our telling the truth about the simple things like what time we had dinner last night that this trust is built in one another. It is when we consistently walk in truth and honesty and communicate honestly in all our daily dealings, and when we demonstrate we are wholly trustworthy to do what we say we will do, that our friends and family will recognize our commitment to moral character and they will know they can trust us.

While there are many aspects to moral character, including honesty with God and man, trusting God over self, reverently and worshipfully fearing God, loving God and operating in His love, and obeying His marvelous Word, in this chapter I will focus on three key virtues: (1) integrity, (2) humility, and (3) meekness. Augustine aptly appraises

God's nature in man's character with this: "Moral character is assessed not by what a man knows but by what he loves."[95] Jesus declares, "For where your treasure is, there your heart will be also" (Matt. 6:21). He clarifies, "If you keep My commandments, you will abide in My love, just as I have kept My Father's commandments and abide in His love" (John 15:10). We have a propensity toward disobedience and rebellion, both of which lead to *deception*, *pride*, and *willfulness*—the antitheses of *integrity*, *humility*, and *meekness*. We can't walk in truth and truthfulness without moral character; that is without, in all honesty, trusting, fearing, loving, and obeying God and thus walking in integrity, humility, and meekness.

Moral character agrees with truth at all times—it never bends or twists truth. Ronald Habermas, author of *The Evangelical Dictionary of Christian Education*, cites Augustine: "All truth (*alētheia*) is God's truth."[96] In his article "On Truth," Stanley Fleming imparts this narrative of President Abraham Lincoln: "Lincoln once asked, 'How many legs does a dog have if you call the tail a leg?' His answer: 'Four; calling a tail a leg doesn't make it a leg.'"[97] Fleming explains,

> Lincoln was a pragmatic politician and not a philosopher, but his witty statement reveals one of the definitions of truth: Truth means the real state of things, agreement with fact, or conformity to actuality. The word *truth* is a noun, a thing, as compared to the word *truthful*, an adjective, which would deal more with ideas of honesty and sincerity. At some level, truth is important to everyone. Yet if it were easy to grasp, we wouldn't be discussing it.[98]

Truth and truthfulness are seldom popular and can be of great cost to the bearer of the message or the virtue. Biblical history demonstrates this reality. In Matthew 27 Jesus delivers His message of Truth and pays the ultimate price through the most humiliating form of execution of the day. In Acts chapter 7 Stephen speaks the truth to the Jews and pays for his message with his life. Even foolish Balaam, at great risk to himself, delivers a truthful prophecy with this definitive assertion, "I can utter only the word that God puts in my mouth" (Num. 22:38).

Sound Doctrine
The Tree of Life

The fruit of the Tree of Life is life everlasting (see Genesis 3:22), which comes through faith in Christ and choosing to obey God's Word through the power of His Holy Spirit, for "the mind governed by the Spirit is life and peace" (Rom. 8:6, NIV). To obey Christ is to walk in the Truth of His Word—and in truth and truthfulness.

Along with truth comes liberty through disambiguation. Fear and confusion all but disappear in the light of truth. Remember Jesus' declaration concerning truth: "Then you will know the truth, and the truth will set you free" (John 8:32, NIV). The absence of ambiguity in our communications with others gives us the impetus and freedom to boldly declare truth without fear of reprisal. Thus freedom is a byproduct of truth through disambiguation. It would be rare indeed to find someone who does not appreciate the freedom that accompanies honest and trustworthy communications with others.

Along with truth also comes accountability. Truth at the center of our communications with others produces security in that each knows what to expect from the other as both are accountable to truth and honesty. Indeed truth, by virtue of its very nature, is accountable to truth. Jack Hayford, founding pastor of The Church on the Way, possesses a strong sense of accountability to God and to man. The roots of this accountability extend to his childhood, where in the safety and nurture of his home and family environment truth and honesty were the rule of the day. Hayford recalls, during times of discipline during his childhood, his mother gently confronting him with these words, "Tell me the truth, Jack, in the presence of Jesus."[99] These words resound in Hayford's memory to this day as a constant reminder of an ever-present Savior, who cares deeply about him and how he lives his life. Because of his single-minded commitment to walk in truth through integrity, humility, and meekness, Hayford has *light*, *clarity*, and *clear vision* to help impart and integrate these virtues into the individual lives and the corporate life of the congregation at The Church on the Way. Every facet of his life exudes truth—and people take notice. John MacArthur, senior pastor of Grace Community Church, Sun Valley, California, makes this observation: "Jack Hayford is a model of diligence, faithfulness to the Lord, and enduring integrity and proven character. Many have fallen in the battle. Hayford is still standing—a tribute to God's marvelous grace."[100]

When we commit ourselves to a life of truth through disambiguation and accountability—conscientiously displaying *integrity* in life and in ministry, *humbly* pleasing God rather than man, *meekly* submitting our will to the will of God, and willingly embracing a fresh walk in the Spirit—we establish the strong foundations of sound doctrine that renders a lasting and effective personal life or public ministry. This comes through "God-shaped lessons ... in renewal through repentance; in humbling of self through self confession; and in Holy Spirit-begotten discovery through the Word."[101]

Lives dramatically change as growth and spiritual formation take place corporately and individually through the model of *integrity*, *humility*, and *meekness* in our daily life. Thus when we walk in truth through disambiguation and accountability, our life becomes a living example of sound doctrine that helps initiate openness and candor in the lives of individuals around us, and as a consequence translates into healthy growth and transparency among the brethren.

Virtues of the Truth
Integrity

To understand the true nature of God and walk in the truth and reality of who He is—to know the truth of God's Word and have genuine fellowship with Him—we must live and function from a heart of integrity. Integrity is honesty with God, with others, and with self. Integrity is completeness and wholeness. It is single-mindedness; it is not wavering between two opinions, but with a single mind and a single heart serving one Master. Jesus declares we cannot serve two masters (Matt. 6:24a). We cannot serve *God* and *Self.* We will either conform to God's image or the world's image—one or the other. Each is diametrically in opposition to the other. Paul cautions,

> Do not be conformed to this world (this age), [fashioned after and adapted to its external, superficial customs], but be transformed (changed) by the [entire] renewal of your mind [by its new ideals and its new attitude], so that you may prove [for yourselves] what is the good and acceptable and perfect will of God, even the thing which is good and acceptable and perfect [in His sight for you].
>
> —Romans 12:2, amp

When we walk in integrity, God's truth is able to transform us into the image of Christ by renewing our minds; and through the renewing of our minds, sanctification—set apart unto God that His truth may be manifest in our lives—is the natural outcome. Jesus prays for His own, "Sanctify them [purify, consecrate, separate them for Yourself, make them holy] by the Truth; Your Word is Truth" (John 17:17, amp). Mel Lawrenz, author of *The Dynamics of Spiritual Formation*, asserts that Romans 12:2 is "one of the clearest statements of our choice in the process of sanctification and spiritual reformation. Two ways are clearly, unambiguously, and boldly identified. We may conform to a pattern defined by the world or one designed by God. The results are radically different."[102]

To understand the significance of integrity we must have a grasp of the term. There is no plural form of *integrity*. There is no degree of integrity. Either we walk in integrity, or we don't. Mark DeMoss explains, "We often hear someone described as having 'a lot of integrity,' but to my thinking, that's impossible. If *integrity* means 'completeness'—the Latin *integritas* literally means 'whole'—then the question of completeness wants a yes or no response, not *How little?* or *How much?*"[103] Sid Wadmed qualifies DeMoss' rationale with this rhetorical question, "Would you want to do business with someone 99 percent honest?"[104] What are the hallmarks of integrity? Merriam-Webster defines the hallmarks of integrity this way:

1. firm adherence to a code of especially moral or artistic values: INCORRUPTIBILITY
2. an unimpaired condition: SOUNDNESS
3. the quality or state of being complete or undivided: COMPLETENESS
4. synonyms: see HONESTY.[105]

Integrity is incorruptible, sound, complete, and honest. It encompasses total truth and honesty under all circumstances. Integrity cannot exist without truth in the life of its adherent. Integrity is faithful to do what is right and just, at all cost. Pearcey affirms, "If we stand up for what is right against injustice, we may not be successful in our careers, or win public and professional recognition, or earn as much money as we might have. Those who follow Christ may end up sharing in His suffering."[106] She quotes Francis Schaeffer from his work *True Spirituality*: "Without integrity at the personal level, a Christian worldview easily deteriorates into a lifeless set of ideas or a bare cognitive system."[107] Pearcey explains that "while it is true that Christianity offers the best cognitive system for explaining the world, it is never just a system. Knowing the truth has meaning only as a step to living the truth day by day."[108]

Integrity Is Truthfulness

By virtue of its very nature, integrity espouses truthfulness at every level in the lives of those who subscribe to it. Lawrenz explains, "The way to integrity (wholeness) is integration. It is when we behave the way we believe and our inner and outer lives become congruent. The alternative—contradiction instead of integration, hypocrisy instead of integrity—is the one thing for which Jesus reserved his severest condemnation."[109]

It is impossible to separate truth or truthfulness from integrity. Integrity means saying what we mean and meaning what we say. It is standing for what we believe—even when the stance is an unpopular one. Integrity is speaking the truth at all cost—even in the face of grave opposition. Paul emphasizes the import of truth and truthfulness in Ephesians chapter 4 with this: "Let our lives lovingly express truth [in all things, speaking truly, dealing truly, living truly]" (v. 15, AMP).

Integrity Is Single-Mindedness

Wholeness, healing, and deliverance are byproducts of a life of integrity. Jesus speaks of integrity in terms of single-mindedness. He admonishes us,

> The eye is the lamp of the body. So if your eye is sound, your entire body will be full of light. But if your eye is unsound, your whole body will be full of darkness. If then the very light in you [your conscience] is darkened, how dense is that darkness! No one can serve two masters; for either he will hate the one and love the other, or he will stand by and be devoted to the one and despise and be against the other. You cannot serve God and mammon (deceitful riches, money, possessions, or whatever is trusted in).
>
> —Matthew 6:22–24, AMP

Jesus demonstrates single-minded integrity to us throughout His life, His death, and His resurrection. The writer of Hebrews describes Jesus as the archetype of single-mindedness:

> Looking away [from all that will distract] to Jesus, Who is the Leader and the Source of our faith [giving the first incentive for our belief] and is also its Finisher, [bringing it to maturity and perfection]. He, for the joy [of obtaining the prize] that was set before Him, endured the cross, despising and ignoring the shame, and is now seated at the right hand of the throne of God.
>
> —Hebrews 12:2, AMP

Integrity Is the Antithesis of Duplicity

When we walk in integrity, we won't deceive and neither will we easily succumb to deception for integrity provides a solid platform for discerning truth from error. Paul warns us away from deception and encourages us to walk in integrity—integrating truth into every part of our life—with this,

> We may no longer be ... tossed to and fro between ... gusts of teaching and wavering with every changing wind of doctrine ... of unscrupulous men, ... in every shifting form of trickery in inventing errors to mislead. Rather, let our lives lovingly express truth [in all things, speaking truly, dealing truly, living truly].
>
> —EPHESIANS 4:14–15, AMP

The author of 1 John warns:

> If we say that we have fellowship with Him, and walk in darkness, we lie and do not practice the truth. But if we walk in the light as He is in the light, we have fellowship with one another, and the blood of Jesus Christ His Son cleanses us from all sin. If we say that we have no sin, we deceive ourselves, and the truth is not in us. If we confess our sins, He is faithful and just to forgive us our sins and to cleanse us from all unrighteousness. If we say that we have not sinned, we make Him a liar, and His word is not in us.
>
> —1 JOHN 1:6–10

Duplicity pollutes integrity. In our pursuit of truth it's not enough to have an allegiance to truth. We must exercise caution with openness to new ideas, or we could straddle the line between conventional truth and new ideas to a point where we cross over that line through compromise or confusion and invalidate our very pursuit. Mark Halfon warns that deception pollutes integrity. *The Stanford Encyclopedia of Philosophy* cites Halfon:

- Halfon (1989, p. 54) argues that Socrates had a commitment to the pursuit of truth and knowledge, and he demonstrated his intellectual integrity in the face of attacks on it. Socrates may be an outstanding example of a person of intellectual integrity; nevertheless, there is more to intellectual integrity than having a commitment to truth and knowledge.

- Intellectual integrity is often characterized as a kind of "openness"—an openness to criticism and to the ideas of others. However, if one is too open, one could absorb too many influences to be able to properly pursue any line of thought. So an adequate account of intellectual integrity must incorporate conflicting claims: that one must be open to new ideas but not be overwhelmed by them.
- An account of intellectual integrity should recognize other sources of conflict and temptations that impede intellectual integrity, such as the temptations offered by the commercialization of research, self-deception about the nature of one's work, and the conflict between the free pursuit of ideas and responsibility to others.[110]

The apostle Paul addresses intellectual integrity this way, "Casting down arguments and every high thing that exalts itself against the knowledge of God, bringing every thought into captivity to the obedience of Christ" (2 Cor. 10:5). From this it is clear we either are people of integrity, or we are not. By virtue of the term *integrity*, either everything about us is integrated in truth—including our intellect—or we are *not* people of integrity.

Integrity Is Moral Goodness

Moral goodness is intrinsic in integrity. Integrity is forged in conflict in what one wants to do versus what one should do. There is more to integrity than adherence to a superficial code of ethics. Integrity will always challenge moral goodness. We have a moral compass that we cannot escape. Paul declares in Romans chapter 2 that God writes His moral law in the hearts of man in the form of a conscience which leaves man without excuse when he does not respond according to the dictates of his heart (vv. 14–15). Paul writes, "The essential requirements of the Law are written in their hearts and are operating there; with which their conscience (sense of right and wrong) also bears witness; and their [moral] decisions (their arguments of reason, their condemning or approving thoughts) will accuse or perhaps defend and excuse [them]" (v. 15, AMP).

Halfon describes moral goodness in these terms,

> Persons of integrity embrace a moral point of view that urges them to be conceptually clear, logically consistent, apprised of relevant empirical evidence, and careful about acknowledging as well as weighing relevant moral considerations. Persons of integrity impose these restrictions on themselves since they are concerned, not simply with taking any moral position, but with pursuing a commitment to do what is best.[111]

Self-gratification, self-servitude, and self-promotion are incongruent to integrity. Lynn McFall, in her scholarly journal article "Integrity," argues opposing views on this subject. McFall asks, "Are there no constraints on the *content* of the principles or commitments a person of integrity may hold?" to which she replies, "Sally is a person of principle: pleasure. Harold demonstrates great integrity in his single-minded pursuit of approval. John was a man of uncommon integrity. He let nothing, not friendship, not justice, not truth stand in the way of his amassment of wealth." McFall continues in this vein when she argues the absurdity of integrity without moral goodness:

- A person of integrity is willing to bear the consequences of her convictions, even when this is difficult... A person whose only principle is "Seek my own pleasure" is not a candidate for integrity because there is no possibility of conflict—between pleasure and principle—in which integrity could be lost. Where there is no possibility of its loss, integrity cannot exist.
- Similarly in the case of the approval seeker. The single-minded pursuit of approval is inconsistent with integrity... A commitment to spinelessness does not vitiate its spinelessness—another of integrity's contraries.
- The same may be said for the ruthless seeker of wealth. A person whose only aim is to increase his bank balance is a person for whom nothing is ruled out: duplicity, theft, murder.[112]

She concludes, "Expedience is *contrasted* to a life of principle, so an ascription of integrity is out of place. Like the pleasure seeker and the approval seeker, he lacks a 'core,' the kind of commitments that give a person character and that make a loss of integrity possible. In order to sell one's soul, one must have something to sell."[113]

Humility

Humility cannot exist without truth at its core, for to be humble is to openly and truthfully confront our own inabilities and freely acknowledge our profound need of God and of others. Humility is not weakness; to the contrary, humility displays great strength of character. Humility is an exercise in genuine self-confidence; for it is when we recognize our weaknesses that we can acknowledge our strengths in God. R. C. Sproul depicts humility this way: "The opposite of abrasiveness; this inner mildness flows from a confident strength that is the antithesis of arrogance. The man who is secure in his love for God does not need to intimidate but can be kind and humble."[114]

Some of the great thinkers consider humility the cornerstone of virtue. Augustine writes, "Humility is the foundation of all the other virtues hence, in the soul in which this virtue does not exist there cannot be any other virtue except in mere appearance."[115] Pullias and Cottle expound on humility, "Genuine humility ... is crucial to the most creative self-confidence... No one would consider Albert Einstein, Helen Keller or Abraham Lincoln either proud or groveling; rather they had the incomparable strength of genuine humility and the wholesome awe that accompanies it."[116]

Humility is acknowledging our lack and God's sufficiency to meet the needs of His children. Jesus characterizes the essence of humility with the parable of the man in need in the middle of the night, when he acknowledges his own lack and God's ability to fill it (Luke 11:5–10). Bible scholars and theologians refer to this passage as the prayer of importunity[117] which is the essence of humility. E. M. Bounds describes the prayer of importunity as "the pressing of our desires upon God with urgency and perseverance."[118]

Humility Is Dependence on God

To walk in humility is to depend on God rather than ourselves for wisdom and direction and provision. It is to defer to God for answers to life's most pressing questions. Hayford describes the working of humility in his own life and his dependence on God to work humility in him, "My honest confession of impotence opened the door to omnipotence... Honesty requires acknowledgement of what we aren't. And there's nothing more inherent in human nature than the insistency that we can do it ourselves, and 'I'm going to do it my way, too!'"[119] He employs King David as an archetype of humble dependence upon God: "There is a continual state of dependence that is appropriate even in the most learned saint. David exemplifies it in the words, 'Show me thy ways, LORD; teach me thy paths. Lead me in thy truth, and teach me: for thou art the God of my salvation; on thee do I wait all the day'" (Ps. 25:4–5).[120]

Humility Is the Fear of the Lord

Humility requires that we view God as the ultimate source of and the ultimate authority on all that exists. When we fear God we position ourselves to be secure in Him. To fear God is to trust God—that includes reverence and respect for who He is and acknowledgement that He holds the keys to life and death in His wholly capable hands. The writer of Proverbs exhorts, "The fear of man brings a snare: but whoever puts his trust in the LORD shall be safe" (Prov. 29:25, AKJV). On the fear of the Lord, the writer declares, "The reverent fear and worshipful awe of the Lord [includes] the hatred of evil; pride, arrogance, the evil way, and perverted and twisted speech I hate" (Prov. 8:13, AMP). Pearcey writes, "We must begin by being utterly convinced that there is a Biblical perspective on everything—not just on spiritual matters... Once we understand how first principles work, then it becomes clear that all truth must begin with God."[121]

It is in the posture of reverent fear and deference to God that we open ourselves to hearing His voice in our lives. In his article "Humility or Humiliation," James Robison establishes that prophets of God must humbly walk in the fear of the Lord. Robison asserts, "We will bow before

God, or be broken before God."[122] Dr. Tony Evans iterates this sentiment in these terms, "When we are in the exalting business, we force God to be in the humbling business."[123]

The humble fear of God results in true knowledge and wisdom to discern truth from error and walk in truth. Many of us have knowledge; but when we have a reverent fear of God, He fills us with *HIS* knowledge, which includes wisdom—the ability to effectively assimilate and apply knowledge in truth and humility. In Proverbs 1:7 the writer proclaims, "The fear of the LORD is the beginning of knowledge, But fools despise wisdom and instruction." Founder of "Constant Encouragement" Gwen Shamblin has this to say about humility and the fear of God:

> Pride produces disgrace; humility produces wisdom. You will not be disgraced if you find true humility. It involves fear of God where you don't want to do wrong. Look to Jesus, he walked humbly among men and only boasted of God. Even when someone tried to call him good, he stopped the person and said, "Only God is Good."[124]

She concludes, "Pray that we can understand this level of humility."[125] The interconnection between humility and the fear of the Lord is abundantly apparent, and many Biblical scholars and philosophers recognize this interconnection and attest to it. W. T. Jones writes, "Humility is this, to escape destruction by keeping ever before one's eyes the fear of the Lord, to remember always the commands of the Lord… To not delight in doing his own will and desires, but … be subject to his superior in all obedience for the love of God, imitating the Lord."[126]

Humility Is Renewal Through Repentance

Humility is opening our hearts to the truth of our own sin and shortcomings, admitting and confessing our sins to our Heavenly Father, and allowing Him to help us change that behavior through the act of repentance. To repent is to have another mind—to have the mind of Christ, which requires a conscious decision to turn away from sin and walk in the light of God's Holy Word. Repentance carries the connotation of making a 180-degree about-face and going in the opposite direction. The New Testament Greek word for repentance is *metanoia*, which means to have "a change of mind and purpose and life."[127] In the book of Philippians the apostle Paul identifies the essence of the mind of Christ, which is the aspiration of every believer in Christ through the renewal that comes from humble repentance:

> Let this mind be in you which was also in Christ Jesus, who, being in the form of God, did not consider it robbery to be equal with God, but made Himself of no reputation, taking the form of a bondservant, and coming in the likeness of men. And being found in appearance as a man, He humbled Himself and became obedient to the point of death, even the death of the cross. Therefore God also has highly exalted Him and given Him the name which is above every name, that at the name of Jesus every knee should bow, of those in heaven, and of those on earth, and of those under the earth, and that every tongue should confess that Jesus Christ is Lord, to the glory of God the Father.
>
> —PHILIPPIANS 2:5–11

Hayford explains there are "God-shaped lessons ... in renewal through repentance; in humbling of self through self confession; and in Holy Spirit-begotten discovery through the Word."[128]

The renewal of the hearts and of the land of the children of Israel as a result of their repentance at God's bidding in 2 Chronicles is a great example of renewal through repentance: "If My people who are called by My name will humble themselves, and pray and seek My face, and turn from their wicked ways, then I will hear from heaven, and will forgive their sin and heal their land" (7:14). As a result of their humble repentance, the Israelites established the synagogue in locations like Masada and Herodium,[129] and ultimately the synagogue school, which built its curriculum around the Mosaic Law and eventually becoming mandatory for Jewish children ages five years old and older.[130]

Humility is pride's polar opposite. King Hezekiah is a prime example of humility bringing renewal through repentance. Shamblin reminds us that

> King Hezekiah did not respond to the kindness given to him from God, and so wrath was about to come upon the whole city. Then Hezekiah repented of his pride, and the city was spared. It was pride that kept him from giving thanks to God. Look at your life and everything that God has given and done for you; do not forget to continually send up praise to God for it all![131]

Humility Is Deeper Revelation of God

It is when we humbly submit ourselves to a Holy God and seek to know Him more intimately and desire to understand His ways more clearly that He shares with us deeper revelation into His character and into His plans and purposes for us and through us. This is where the creativity of God flows toward us and we are its humble beneficiaries.

History documents that as the prophets of God humbly sought "a deeper understanding of God and His revelation"[132] than that which the synagogues schools provide, God gave them the wisdom and means to establish the first schools for the "sons of the prophets"[133] whose curriculum was "based upon inducing prophetic utterance, instruction in the Law, prayers, meditation, and rituals of worship."[134] After the seventy-year exile in Babylon, the "prominent scribe [Ezra] would be seen as the religious leader of his school and was referred to as a rabbi, meaning 'master.' These rabbinical schools were a powerful force in postexilic Judaism for the duplication and interpretation of the Hebrew scrolls."[135] "The prophet Samuel is believed to have founded such a school at Ramah."[136]

Meekness

Meekness is submission to God; it is yielding our own will to the will of God; it is placing His will and purpose for our lives above our own. Meekness goes hand in hand with integrity and humility. It is virtually impossible to walk in truth and not function in one of these three virtues. Though meekness encompasses gentleness, meekness is not weakness. Genuine meekness displays great strength of character. Genuine meekness carries the connotation of a powerful stallion submitting to its rider's slightest movement of the reins.[137] Meekness opens *our* hearts to hear *God's* heart and aids us in discerning truth from error—the hallmark of prophets of God. The nature of God's prophets is meekness for their hearts are right before God and their ears listen for His voice. Fletcher Seift pens, "They [God's prophets] were the public conscience of Israel, the soul of its religion, the creators of its public opinion, its most conspicuous, its most revered, its most convincing teachers."[138] The writer of 2 Peter 1:21 reveals a similar line of thinking: "For prophecy never came by the will of man, but holy men of God spoke as they were moved by the Holy Spirit."[139]

Meekness is humbly placing our confidence in God rather than ourselves. Through faith we place our trust in Him to accomplish through us those things we otherwise could not accomplish by ourselves. John Ritenbaugh depicts faith and confidence as a part of meekness, "God desires more of us: 'Now the just shall live by faith; but if anyone draws back, My soul has no pleasure in him' (Heb. 10:38). Faith—confidence—is part of meekness, and thus the meek are not timid."[140] Scripture depicts Moses as the meekest man in human history. Numbers 12:3 declares, "Now the man Moses was very meek (gentle, kind, and humble) or above all the men on the face of the earth" (AMP).[141] When we walk in meekness we exercise great strength of character, "The meek … shall inherit the earth" (Matt. 5:5). Wilbur Dunkel poses the question, "For the Christian man of today, has meekness ceased to be a virtue?" to which he replies, "It certainly has if we think of meekness in the unfavorable sense of submissive, spiritless, and easily cowed." He continues, "But in the positive meaning of 'meek,' … being gentle, courteous, kind, merciful, free from self-will, and humble are attributes of Christ Jesus."[142]

Meekness Is Teachable

When we walk in meekness we are open and teachable—testing everything over and against the Word of God, embracing what is good and profitable according to His Word and rejecting that which stands in opposition to His Truth. To be teachable is to be open to new methodologies and amenable to change, to reform, and to renewal. During Carole Novak's interview of John Goodlad, she queried Goodlad on reform and renewal in the classroom. Novak asked, "What advice would you give to educators—classroom teachers, administrators—and others interested in expanding their efforts in the area of school reform?" Goodlad responded, "The first thing I would say is, you have a moral responsibility as a steward of the school to participate in school renewal. You cannot be an observer; you have to be a participating member... That's the commitment you make as a teacher—not just to manage the classroom."[143] Discipline is also an important component in being teachable. Hebrews 12:4–11 confirms discipline is for instruction and correction. Kant writes, "A moral education [gives] the child more freedom through discipline."[144] Every child knows when he or she disobeys punishment ensues and privileges are taken away, but the reward of obedience is to live in freedom and liberty to do as one chooses within the confines of discipline or self control.

Meekness Is Willing to Do the Will of God[145]

When we display meekness in our life, we willingly surrender our will to the will of God. Meekness is the antithesis of *willful*ness. Meekness is *willing*ness, and God is seeking servants with willing hearts. Jesus characterizes this in the parable of the father and his two sons. The son whose heart is willing to obey his father (even though he does not) is the son whom Jesus commends for it is that son who aligns his own will with the will of his father (see Matthew 21:28–32). Romans chapter 2 declares of men, "The essential requirements of the Law are written in their hearts and are operating there; with which their conscience (sense of right and wrong) also bears witness; and their [moral] decisions (their arguments of reason, their condemning or approving thoughts) will accuse or perhaps defend and excuse [them]" (v. 15, AMP).

According to Immanuel Kant, "In man is found a sense of duty, the 'I ought,' or the moral law, which is logically prior to experience and which springs from man's innermost nature."[146] June Nichols concurs with Kant when she describes the voice of the Holy Spirit in our life as more often the *I oughts* than the *thou shalts.*[147] We must be willing to act according to our conscience which tells us to follow the will of God. What is helpful for us to realize today is that God is still in the business of using people. But not just anyone! God is looking for the man or woman whose heart is committed to doing God's will (2 Chron. 16:9). "That means that he/she has humbly committed themselves to considering God's will to be more important than their own. The famous missionary to South America, Jim Elliot, said it so well when he stated, 'Man has yet to see what God can do with a man (or woman) whose heart is completely committed to Him.'"[148]

Jesus displays the essence of meekness through His willing Spirit which He demonstrates in His life and in His death. Satan tempts Jesus in the wilderness with this challenge: "Cast yourself off this temple, for it is written that you have a legion of angels at your disposal to keep you from dashing your foot against the mountain." (See Luke 4:1–12; Matthew 4:1–11.) Yet Jesus yields all of His will—all of His power and authority—to the will of the Father. He continues to set this example throughout the Gospels, as in the Garden of Gethsemane when He declares, "Nevertheless, not My will, but Yours, be done." (Luke 22:42).

Meekness Is Open to the Voice of God

Young or old, when we demonstrate meekness in our life we open ourselves to hear God's voice, and through that we open ourselves to the vastness of opportunities that await us when we say *YES* to the Savior. Anthony and Benson write of such examples:

> Retired adults with years of wisdom and experience have all of the resources they need to teach young children overseas. Single adults who have a background in business, science, mathematics, or social ecology are invaluable assets

> on the mission field school campus… A little education can go a long way toward shaping and influencing a child (and a country) in the name of Jesus.[149]

However we must be open to the voice of God through the Holy Spirit and act upon it. Bill Wilson, shepherd of Metro Ministries of Brooklyn, New York, offers a good example of how God speaks to someone who in meekness listens to God's voice. Because of Wilson's openness to the voice of God, his "Sidewalk Sunday School" effectively ministers to more than twenty thousand children every Sunday, all over the world.[150] Walking in meekness makes it possible for us to hear the still small voice of the Holy Spirit when He gently speaks to our hearts, "This is the way, walk ye in it" (Isa. 30:21, KJV). Following is a list of examples of what God's voice sounds like in our life over and against that of the voice of Satan.

The Voice of God vs the Voice of Satan

- God's voice stills
- God speaks deep within my spirit
- Satan's voice rushes
- The devil speaks to my soul or mind
- God's voice leads
- God's voice is gentle and persuasive, free from pressure
- Satan's voice pushes
- Satan is loud and clamoring, always demanding an immediate response
- God's voice reassures
- God's voice produces peace and a sense that everything is under control
- Satan's voice frightens
- Satan's voice speaks of despair, you have missed it, all is lost
- God's voice enlightens
- God's voice is always clear and distinctive, giving us clear direction in which to go

- Satan's voice confuses
- The voice of Satan perplexes, causes confusion, loss of direction
- God's voice encourages
- God tends to speak when I am seeking and listening for Him
- Satan's voice discourages
- Satan breaks into our thoughts uninvited
- God's voice convicts
- God's Spirit convicts of specific sins, leaving no doubt what needs to be confessed
- Satan's voice condemns[151]
- Satan and self speak in generalities[152]

Meekness Is Obedience to God

To be meek is to obey God when He speaks; we can't separate meekness from obedience. It would be incongruent with meekness if God gives us a directive and we walk away from His instruction to us. The writer of the book of James declares, "Therefore, to him who knows to do good and does not do it, to him it is sin" (James 4:17). When we violate the good we know to do, we disobey God; we sin. Barclay writes, "We need to keep our priorities in line and view Scripture as absolute truth. Knowledge of the inerrant Word of God becomes the lens through which we develop our worldview and philosophical beliefs."[153] Without the scribes' strict adherence to the virtually flawless, tedious, and painstaking technique of transcribing the Hebrew writings and scrolls, the Truth of the Holy Scriptures would not be as error free as they exist today. In 1780 "God … stirred the heart of a man who was obedient to His calling, a common businessman by trade, but a willing heart was all that was required. Robert Raikes, although trained as a newspaper editor, became responsible for countless millions of souls being brought into the kingdom of Christ through the efforts of the Sunday school."[154]

Obedience is a requisite to walk and live in truth to the degree that we understand truth and thus enables us to discern truth from error. True obedience is one of the highest forms of worship we can offer to an all deserving Holy God—true obedience provides life-giving sustenance to our soul and our spirit. We live our faith through obedience to His marvelous Word. R. Paul Stevens, author of *The Other Six Days: Vocation, Work, and Ministry in Biblical Perspective*, defines obedience as "lived truth."[155]

Chapter 5

BENEFITS OF THE TRUTH: LIGHT, CLARITY, CLEAR VISION

> Ever since the Fall, the human race has been divided into two distinct groups—those who follow God and submit their minds to His truth, and those who set up an idol of some kind and then organize their thinking to rationalize their worship of that idol. Over time, as people's ultimate commitments shape the choices they make, their perspective is inevitably molded to support those choices. A false god leads to the formation of a false worldview.
>
> —Nancy Pearcey[156]

The Truth
Positive Effects in the Believer

Absolute truth is the standard that sets the behavior for the believer. When the believer has truth as the moral compass for life's decisions, the light of God's truth produces clarity for decisions, parameters are easily set, and vision becomes clear. Authors Anthony and Benson assert, "The Law set the standard of moral absolutes."[157] The two cite the writer of Galatians to support this assertion; "The law was our schoolmaster to bring us unto Christ, that we might be justified" (3:24).[158] The Jews demonstrate

God's own faithfulness to honor the faithfulness of His children to keep the Sabbath holy with a quote from *Gates of Prayer*: "As Israel has kept the Sabbath, so the Sabbath has kept Israel."[159]

The authors further qualify this truth with Exodus 20:10 and illustrate the reasoning behind the import of the Jews keeping the Sabbath, for example, with these words from C. L. Wirtschafter: "The Jewish people were commanded to remember that they were once enslaved in Egypt and God brought them deliverance from their suffering. They were released from the bondage of their work and are reminded to take this weekly opportunity to rest and reflect on God's Salvation."[160]

The Jews insist that to receive God's blessing it is not enough to obey the law, and to do right, and give to the poor. Although these are important virtues, the key to God's blessing is "to maintain a pure and unadulterated relationship with Jehovah."[161] God's interest is a matter of the heart and not the deed—for the deeds will follow the heart. God demonstrates this to a floundering people. Through His "character and nature as a patient and merciful Father … [He still] seeks to instill His commands, instructions, and guidelines to His people."[162]

It is God's desire that His children wholeheartedly seek Him and commit to do His will from the heart, and to occupy—do His business—until Christ's return to earth for His Bride (Luke 19:13). When God's children walk in His Truth and in honesty and truthfulness, obeying His Word, they grow physically and spiritually and emotionally. It is through strong secure men and women of God who walk in truth and know how to discern truth from error and say yes to Christ's Great Commission—to "go and make disciples of all nations, baptizing them in the name of the Father and of the Son and of the Holy Spirit, and teaching them to obey everything I have commanded you" (Matt. 28:19–20, NIV)—that ministries rise up and believers begin to grow in the grace and the knowledge and the Truth of Christ and thus learn themselves to discern truth from error.

To go into the world and preach the Good News—the free gift of salvation and healing through Christ alone—fills new believers who are hungry for Truth. Ray Anderson, author of *The Soul of Ministry: Forming Leaders for God's People*, depicts Moses as a type of Christ and the redemption process, and parallels his commission through the burning bush to redeem God's people alongside Jesus' commission through His baptism by John to "fulfill God's messianic promise."[163] It is through Jesus Christ—God incarnate—that God redeems man to his "intended health and wholeness."[164]

The primary ministry of a servant is to serve the master; the servant's secondary ministry is to serve others. Because Jesus' ministry is "grounded in Sonship,"[165] "his conscience was governed not by human need but by the Father's will and purpose."[166] This service is inescapable for Christians in the ministry of Christ. Jesus' humanity provides the basis for "a manifesto for Christian ministry"[167] where "Christians turn toward the world for the sake of Christ's ministry of healing and hope."[168]

Positive Effects in the Church

The Holy Bible is God's absolute Truth—complete, cohesive, comprehensive, lacking nothing—which engenders and provides *light*, *clarity*, and *clear vision* to His Church to discern truth from error. The writer of 1 John declares, "This is the message which we have heard from Him and declare to you, that God is light and in Him is no darkness at all" (1:5). Timothy affirms, "All Scripture is given by inspiration of God, and is profitable for doctrine, for reproof, for correction, for instruction in righteousness, that the man of God may be complete, thoroughly equipped for every good work" (2 Tim. 3:16–17). The Holy Bible is the God-inspired Truth that spans the annals of history and time immemorial and withstands the scrutiny of the most discerning scholars and historians of world renown. Larry Wilson writes:

> It's easy to tell that the Bible is a single, unified book. That's why it is so remarkable that this one book is an anthology of sixty-six different books, written by at least thirty-six different authors in three different languages (Hebrew, Aramaic, and Greek) over a period of about fifteen hundred years. These human authors didn't sit down as a committee and agree what to write. They

> were separated by time, space, and circumstances. But there's no contradiction or confusion. The agreement is amazing.[169]

The Bible tells one story that revolves around one person. The Old Testament points forward to the Savior to come; the New Testament tells of the Savior who came. Wilson qualifies his assertions with the following Scriptures (Wilson's emphasis):

- And beginning with Moses and all the Prophets, he interpreted to them *in all the Scriptures* the things *concerning himself* (Luke 24:27).
- All things must be fulfilled which were written in the Law of Moses and the Prophets and the Psalms *concerning Me* (Luke 24:44).
- You search the Scriptures because you think that in them you have eternal life; and it is they that bear witness *about me* (John 5:39).[170]

Anthony and Benson examine the radical departure of twentieth-century liberal theology from traditional evangelical theology and the difference between the two forms of theology. They enlist a quote from John Milburn Price who reflects on "the deadness of liberal theology and its lack of hope for man's condition."[171] The authors cite Eavey who writes that John Wycliffe "reached the conclusion that the pope is the Antichrist, since his deeds opposed those of Christ."[172] Yet incongruent with this position the authors assert that according to Eavey, "Wycliffe was unrelenting in his desire to see the Catholic Church become more relevant and meaningful to the masses."[173] Though this inconsistency poses potential to undermine the credibility of Wycliffe's other assertions, the remainder of his work is replete with indisputable evidences that prove otherwise.

Spiritual empowerment is necessary to effectively minister to persons and face the giants of everyday life. Anderson makes this declaration, "The Holy Spirit is thus the creative power and presence of Jesus Christ … or inner logic of God's purpose in creating the church as the missionary people of God sent into the world."[174] The Holy Spirit at Pentecost breaks with tradition and anoints male and female, Jew and Gentile for ministry and sets "the context for the new theological paradigm."[175] When it is truth we seek as a necessity in our daily life, His Truth will faithfully reveal truth and dispel error. Old Testament female prophets such as Huldah, Deborah, Miriam, and Noadiah are the Biblical antecedents of this new theological paradigm.[176] "The overall strategy of the church," Anderson asserts, "is conformity to Christ's coming to the world for the sake of its reconciliation with God." He adds, "This strategy must never be abandoned, else the world would be left to its own hopeless and fatal plunge into the abyss."[177] Stevens asserts obedience plays a major role in new theological paradigms. He explains,

> In 1949 Ian Fraser wrote a seminal article in the *Scottish Journal of Theology*, entitled "Theology and Action." In his article Fraser avers: "Obedience to the living God must always surge beyond present theological containing walls. When Abraham went out, he knew not whither he went. The business of theology is not to circumscribe such obedient action. It is to feed on it... Theology draws its very life from worship, and in that life draws its nourishment from obedience."[178]

An in-depth look at what apostles are and how they function is vital to understand how the Church is to function in Truth. Anderson explains, "The first apostle, Jesus is the cornerstone for the apostolic foundation." He writes that Peter refers to Jesus as "'the living cornerstone' and the members of the church as 'living stones.'"[179] He describes what he terms the "threefold apostolic ministry of Christ," which consists of (1) the humanity (*incarnational*) of Jesus, (2) the resurrection and proclamation (*kerygmatic*) of Christ, and (3) the soon-coming King (*eschatological*) (author's paraphrase).[180] He concludes, "To be apostolic the church must be a mission, not merely have a mission."[181] The Church as a mission must of necessity engender truth in Her followers that they may be able to know and recognize truth and thus recognize and reject the very appearance of deception.

Positive Effects in Education

Teaching truth with excellence comes at a premium, yet teaching others is inescapable for the Christian. It is intrinsic in the call of Christ on the lives of each of His followers. Jesus' Great Commission to His followers is to "'go therefore and make disciples of all the nations, baptizing them in the name of the Father and of the Son and of the Holy Spirit, teaching them to observe all things that I have commanded you; and lo, I am with you always, even to the end of the age.' Amen" (Matt. 28:19–20).[182]

Truth in education is an imperative, and the methodology the educator employs to communicate truth is crucial. Pullias and Cottle make this observation, "One of life's greatest truths: 'the journey is more important than the destination; the process is more significant than the end.'"[183] It is in that journey we encounter and discover what is true and what is false. For if the road map is not truthful but is in error, we will not reach our destination. Pullias and Cottle endorse the active/interactive learning methodology with their equation of education to an adventurous journey. This effective teaching-learning methodology incorporates the five senses and every learning style and thereby exponentially increases the retention level of learners helping them learn from experience over against oration. The essence of the teaching-learning or active/interactive learning style is: "Tell me and I'll forget it. Show me and I may remember. Involve me and I'll understand."[184] To help His followers learn truth from error, Jesus employs the active/interactive learning methodology throughout His ministry with lessons like the loaves and fishes, the fish and the coin, washing the feet of His disciples, and the Bread and the Wine.[185] This teaching-learning methodology is effectively amenable to teaching truth with excellence to avoid error.

To understand truth at its core is essential to teach truth with excellence. To recognize and know truth at its core is the springboard to recognize and avoid error. Pearcey contends, "Biblical truth takes hold of our inner being, and … God's Word becomes a light to *all* our paths, providing the foundational principles for bringing every part of our lives under the Lordship of Christ, to glorify Him and to cultivate His creation."[186] The overarching implications of truth in education is to "attract the serious and abort the superficial"[187] in an effort to cultivate the virtues of *integrity*, *humility*, and *meekness* to effect sound "timeless biblical truth"[188] in learners and the ability to discern and reject error. Although God holds all educators to a high standard of accountability, He holds Christian educators to a higher standard in educating learners in His Kingdom principles (see James 3:1).[189] The writer of the epistle of James admonishes those who desire to hold the position of teacher in Christian education:

> Not many [of you] should become teachers (self-constituted censors and reprovers of others), my brethren, for you know that we [teachers] will be judged by a higher standard *and* with greater severity [than other people; thus we assume the greater accountability and the more condemnation].
>
> —James 3:1, AMP

The cost to all who desire to teach truth with excellence is to walk in truth through the virtues of integrity, humility, and meekness before God and man. It requires the fear of God and not of man. It insists on resistance of pride, willfulness, and stubbornness toward change through godly reform and renewal. It necessitates trust in God and the promptings of His Holy Spirit. It requires walking in God's love and obeying His Word. It demands rejection of deception and the embrace of truth at every level of life.

Therefore Christian educators must sift through education methodologies to find the truth therein. Anthony and Benson write,

> Sunday school classrooms that employ discussion-oriented learning, activity-based instruction, problem-solving methods, and relevant Bible teaching with clear application to life demonstrate what is best about instrumentalism, progressivism, and pragmatism... The believer is called to analyze these educational philosophies critically... We must be cautious not to reject all of the outcomes as unacceptable.[190]

Like Jesus, the apostle Paul also models to Christian educators what it means to teach truth with excellence through example and involvement. Paul's list of credits in effectively educating believers include church planting, teaching and training leaders in the church, acting as spiritual father to new converts, manifold writings of instruction and admonition, and laying down his own life for the cause of Christ.[191]

The fourth chapter of Philippians is Paul's flagship curriculum. He admonishes,

> For the rest, brethren, whatever is true, whatever is worthy of reverence and is honorable and seemly, whatever is just, whatever is pure, whatever is lovely and lovable, whatever is kind and winsome and gracious, if there is any virtue and excellence, if there is anything worthy of praise, think on and weigh and take account of these things [fix your minds on them].
>
> —PHILIPPIANS 4:8, AMP

Paul endorses himself as an example to follow: "Practice what you have learned and received and heard and seen in me, and model your way of living on it, and the God of peace (of untroubled, undisturbed well-being) will be with you" (Phil. 4:9, AMP);[192] as does Timothy endorse himself: "And the things that you have heard from me among many witnesses, commit these to faithful men who will be able to teach others also" (2 Tim. 2:2).

Pazmino references 2 Timothy 2:2 as the source for his assertion that "all that Christians gain from their pursuit for truth and wisdom was to be passed on to others who in turn could teach." He explains, "Paul was clear about the source of this truth for it is in Christ Himself that 'are hidden all the treasures of wisdom and knowledge' (Col. 2:3), and the task before Christians is 'taking every thought captive to the obedience of Christ' (2 Cor. 10:5),"[193] and following His example of teaching truth with excellence.

The roots of Christian education are found in Hebrew, Greek, and Roman philosophy. The Hebrews, Greeks, and Romans had a significant influence on the education system of the Early Church, which creates a balance, and lays "the foundation for early Christian church education."[194] Significant aspects of the Hebrew education are the patriarchs, the Law, and "the priests, judges, and prophets."[195] These are the foundations of "God's original design for education,"[196] and greatly impact Christian education. The Greeks had no standard of curriculum. The common goal among Greek educators was to prevent societal "racism, bigotry, and intolerance."[197] The Athenians introduced philosophical thought into every branch of education through "Socrates, Aristotle, and Plato."[198] According to Anthony and Benson, "the Roman form of education, society, and governance laid the foundations for the birth of Christianity,"[199] which evolved from the Roman home school model to the contemporary model of "home, elementary, grammar, and rhetorical"[200] school, the premise of modern education.

Anthony and Benson assert that Roman education had the greatest contribution to modern education. The proof of this, according to the authors, is the Roman alphabet, which pervades life throughout most of the world to this day—thus the "contribution of the great Roman Empire to the beginnings of Christianity cannot be overstated."[201] Because the Roman education system placed great emphasis on learning family values and practical life skills, the Roman Empire had a significant effect on Christianity and gave evidence to Christ's birth during this era.[202]

The Middle Ages lacked discovery and inspiration, yet despite this lack the Church flourished. Monastery schools were the predominant educational institutions during this era. According to Anthony and Benson and educators Fredrick Eby and Charles F. Arrowood, "Theology was considered to be the lens through which education would be viewed."[203] The Renaissance marked "one of history's most significant transitional periods."[204] Artists, scientists, philosophers, and literary scholars offered new paradigms which dramatically affected society and education with "Renaissance humanism."[205] Yet Christian education abounded and rapidly adjusted to the advent of the printing press and to the establishing of early childhood educational structures. The printing press and the subsequent mass production of paper hallmark revolutionary feats in education, and the Bible—now in print—forever transformed Christian education.[206] Martin

Luther led the Reformation in the sixteenth century—the reverberations of which permeated and spilled over into twenty-first-century Christian education—when he nailed his "ninety-five theses to the door of the Catholic church at Wittenburg, Saxony,"[207] in 1517 and thus forever altered the Church as well as education in the Church. Luther's unyielding posture on truth and speaking truth and confronting error at all cost was reminiscent of Jesus' admonition to His followers, "But let your 'Yes' be 'Yes,' and your 'No,' 'No.' For whatever is more than these is from the evil one" (Matt. 5:37).

Both modern Christian education and Sunday school have roots in Europe. Amid child labor and the subsequent profound abuse of children, Robert Raikes of England (1736–1811) founded weekly Sunday school in private homes and with his personal financial capital he evangelized and cared for poor children, teaching them in the subjects of "reading, writing, morals, and manners."[208] German educator Friedrich Wilhelm August Froebel (Fröbel) (1782–1852)[209] established the first kindergarten—a vital part of education to this day.[210]

Christian education in the eighteenth, nineteenth, and twentieth centuries revealed that the diverse colonial educational systems were decidedly Christian. However, laws and academic structures created chasms between regional, class, and religious distinctions and reduced curriculum to "ethos, culture and tradition... What began as freedom of religion slowly evolved into a freedom from religion."[211] Yet amid this slippery slope toward secularism in the nineteenth century, the Second Great Awakening began the "Bible college movement [and] Christian higher education,"[212] which continued with such success that Anthony and Benson claim: "Christians are now influencing the agendas of secular institutions all over North America."[213]

In the twentieth century Christian education shifted from evangelism to social issues or the "social gospel." This "social gospel"[214] depicted "Jesus as the 'Supreme Educator' rather than ... 'the Redeemer.'"[215] Virtually all nineteenth- and twentieth-century theologians advocated some type of social gospel.[216] The adherents of the social gospel—the ethics of Jesus—are those "having a form of godliness, but denying its power" (2 Tim. 3:5). The writer of this passage in 2 Timothy warns, "From such people turn away!" Yet amid this socialization of the gospel, the Truth of the

Gospel message remained. John Westerhoff writes, "Christian education is the deliberate, systematic, and sustained efforts of the community of faith which enable persons and groups to evolve Christian life styles."[217] Gangel and Hendricks agree, "Teachers of Christian truth must do more than simply accumulate and dispense vast amounts of information about the Bible; they must help the disciples of Jesus grow in their relationships, morals, theology, and service."[218]

There are philosophical approaches to the foundational truths of Christian education and personal ministry. The philosophical position the Christian educator holds determines how the educator presents the Truth. Certain philosophies are dangerous, bordering on heresy.[219] Personal background, life experiences, and spiritual gifting make philosophy of ministry unique to each person. To realize and embrace personal values assists Christian educators in discovering their personal philosophy of ministry to become more effective communicators of truth.[220] Philosophical idealism does not acknowledge truth *per sé* but only as it exists in correct knowledge. An example of *philosophical idealism* is Dewey's approach to education where truth only exists within the constraints of proof of knowledge.[221] However, philosophical realism contends that real truth transcends and supersedes knowledge. An example of *philosophical realism* is Sir Isaac Newton's discovery of the law of gravity. Newton's knowledge of this law does not act upon the law of gravity one way or the other. Once separate from the limb, the apple falls to the ground *now*, as it did *before* Newton's discovery, with or without knowledge of the law of gravity.[222] Our knowledge or belief system has no bearing on what is true.

Positive Effects in Society

Experts agree educators have a profound effect on society, in that it is the responsibility of educators to teach truth with excellence if the effect is to be a positive one. Enlightenment philosopher Johann Heinrich Pestalozzi maintains, "The schoolmaster ... should be one of the most important persons in the community ... a person of strong emotional and ethical character and capable of loving children from every strata of society."[223] Dewey asserts that to help someone discover his or her propensities "enables a person not just to be good but to 'be good for something'—and that is the 'capacity to live as a social member so that what he gets from living with others balances with when he contributes.'"[224] This dangerous line of thinking pollutes truth and promotes error by placing greater value on those who contribute to society than our intrinsic value as God's creation. The truth is we are valuable because of who we are and not because of what we do. W. T. Jones writes, "The shepherd will have to bear the blame if the Master finds anything wrong with the flock."[225]

Rather than attempt to legislate right behavior from the outside in, truth engenders genuine holiness in us from the inside out. Jesus declares it is not what goes into the mouth that makes a person unclean, but rather what comes out of the mouth that makes a person unclean (Matt. 15:11). The Savior teaches what goes in the mouth comes out through natural functions. However what comes out of the mouth comes from within the heart (see Matthew 15:17–20). The truth is, we model in our behavior what we think and believe in our hearts and our behavior ultimately affects society.

The natural outcome of walking in truth and truthfulness is a life of holiness from inside out. When we walk in truth and truthfulness, we are better able to discern truth from error; and the result is we become more honest with ourselves, with others, and with God—for the very nature of truth necessarily holds us accountable to truth and truthfulness. The import of Truth and truthfulness in society is evident in Jesus' admonition to His followers in Matthew 5:37 taken from *The Expositor's Study Bible*:

> But let your communication be (verbal communication with others), Yes, yes; No, no: for whatsoever is more than these comes from evil (the followers of Christ must stand out by their truthfulness, honesty, and integrity; subterfuge and doubletalk are out).[226]

Jesus emphasizes the import to walk in the light of truth:

> The light of the body is the eye (a figure of speech; He is, in effect, saying that the light of the soul is the spirit):

> if therefore your eye be single (the spirit of man should have but one purpose, and that is to Glorify God), your whole body shall be full of Light (if the spirit of man is single in its devotion to God [meaning not divided] then all the soul will be full of light). But if your eye be evil, your whole body shall be full of darkness (if the spirit be evil the entirety of the soul will be full of darkness). If therefore the light that is in you be darkness (the light is not acted upon, but rather perverted), how great is that darkness (the latter state is worse than if there had been no light at all)! No man can serve two masters: for either he will hate the one, and love the other; or else he will hold to the one, and despise the other. You cannot serve God and mammon (this is flat out, stated as, an impossibility; it is total devotion to God, or ultimately it will be total devotion to the world; the word, "mammon" is derived from the Babylonian "Mimma," which means "anything at all") (Matt. 6:22–24).[227]

To that end let us walk in the truth as the Holy Spirit gives us light, let us honestly and truthfully deal with God and man, let us unambiguously serve the Creator and not the creation—and in discerning truth from error—let us choose truth at every turn.

Part III
FATHER OF LIES

The Red Thread
Discerning Truth from Error

There were difficult times during her daughters' teen years when they would want to listen to certain bands popular with their friends, or they would ask to wear certain styles of clothes their friends were wearing. Rita Frye would listen to the lyrics of these bands and determine they were inappropriate for any ears—much less the ears of teenage girls whose minds and habits are still being formed. And their father, Bill, would assess what their friends were wearing and explain to his daughters from a male's perspective what boys would think of their scantily clad friends and their outfits. It was difficult to get them to understand why they *could not* but their friends *could* listen to this music or wear these clothes, until one day Rita's sister came up with the perfect analogy using breakfast cereal. Rita used this analogy during their next tête-à-tête over music and clothes.

The girls loved sugar on their breakfast cereal. Rita told them that inside one year's time she could have them not using sugar on their cereal; and not only would they not miss the sugar, but they wouldn't even know when they stopped using it. Their curiosity piqued, the girls asked how their mother would accomplish such a feat. Rita explained she would simply eliminate a few grains of sugar from the teaspoon each day until finally, within a year's time, she would be putting no sugar on their cereal. Because the process of eliminating the sugar would be so gradual, they would not even miss it.

Rita explained to her captive audience this is how Satan works in our life. Rarely does he aggressively or overtly attack us. Rather, his favorite modus operandi is to come to us as he did with Eve, "Hath God said?" Just enough said to plant an idea or a seed of doubt in our hearts; and over time—a little here, a little there—our commitment to truth is eroded and our ability to discern truth from error is all but a thing of the past.[228]

Chapter 6

MAN REJECTS THE TRUTH: DISINGENUOUS LIFE AND PURPOSE

> For the time will come when they will not endure sound doctrine; but after their own lusts shall they heap to themselves teachers, having itching ears; And they shall turn away their ears from the truth, and shall be turned unto fables.
>
> —2 TIMOTHY 4:3–4, KJV

The Great Exchange

Humanity's propensity to seek out messengers and friends who would ease their conscience and agree with their right to do as they please—to the exclusion of the Truth—has never been more prevalent than it is in society today. In John 14:6 Jesus declares Himself to be "The Truth." The apostle Paul establishes the theological basis of the Truth and the Lie in his discourse in 2 Thessalonians 2:9–12, when he speaks of man's propensity to reject the Truth and embrace the Lie:

> And by unlimited seduction to evil and with all wicked deception for those who are perishing (going to perdition) because they did not welcome the Truth but refused to love it that they might be saved. Therefore God sends

> upon them a misleading influence, a working of error and a strong delusion to make them believe what is false, In order that all may be judged and condemned who did not believe—who refused to adhere to, trust in and rely on—the Truth, but [instead] took pleasure in unrighteousness.
>
> —2 THESSALONIANS 2:10–12, AMP

The exchange of the Truth for the Lie or the outright rejection of the Truth and the embrace of the Lie renders man vulnerable to "a working of error and a strong delusion" (2 Thess. 2:11, AMP). Paul admonishes in Romans that Christians are not immune to making this same mistake. Paul warns the Church, "Therefore God gave them up in the lusts of their [own] hearts ... [b]ecause they exchanged the truth of God for a lie and worshiped and served the creature rather than the Creator, Who is blessed forever! Amen" (Rom. 1:24–25, AMP). The writer of 1 Timothy issues a warning to believers, "Now the Spirit expressly says that in latter times some will depart from the faith, giving heed to deceiving spirits and doctrines of demons, speaking lies in hypocrisy, having their own conscience seared with a hot iron" (1 Tim. 4:1–2).[229] Paul issues yet another warning to Christians in 2 Timothy 4:3–4: "For the time will come when they will not endure sound doctrine; but after their own lusts shall they heap to themselves teachers, having itching ears; And they shall turn away their ears from the truth, and shall be turned unto fables" (KJV).

Man's fallen state and his propensity for deception and the subsequent implications of the redemption of Christ on the human condition is the result of man's rejection of truth. Anderson describes man's fallen state and bases his thesis on the human condition on the words we read in Ephesians 2:1–2, "You were dead in your trespasses and sins, in which you formerly walked according to the course of this world, according to the prince of the power of the air" (NAS). Anderson declares, "We live in a world which is under the authority of an evil ruler. Originally God created Adam and his family to rule over creation. But Adam forfeited his position of authority through sin, and Satan became the rebel holder of authority to whom Jesus referred as 'the ruler of this world' (John 12:31; 14:30; 16:11)." He explains:

> During Jesus' temptation, the devil offered Him "all the kingdoms of the world and their glory" (Matt. 4:8) in exchange for His worship. Satan's claim that the earth "has been handed over to me, and I give it to whomever I wish" (Luke 4:6) was no lie. He took authority when Adam abdicated the throne of rulership over God's creation at the fall. Satan ruled from Adam until the cross. The death, resurrection and ascension of Christ secured forever the final authority for Jesus Himself (Matt. 28:18). That authority was extended to all believers in the Great Commission so that we may continue His work of destroying the works of the devil (1 John 3:8).

He continues:

> All of us were born spiritually dead and subject to the ruler that Paul called 'the prince of the power of the air' (Eph. 2:2). But when we received Christ, God 'delivered us from the domain of darkness, and transferred us to the kingdom of His beloved Son' (Col. 1:13). Our citizenship was changed from earth to heaven (Phil. 3:20). Satan is the ruler of this world, but he is no longer *our* ruler, for Christ is our ruler.

Anderson concludes:

> But as long as we live on the earth, we are still on Satan's turf. He will try to rule our lives by deceiving us into believing that we still belong to him. As aliens in a foreign, hostile kingdom, we need protection from this evil, deceptive, hurtful tyrant. Christ has not only provided protection from and authority over Satan, but He has equipped us with the Spirit of truth, the indwelling Holy Spirit, to guide us into all truth and help us discern the evil one's schemes. (John 16:13).[230]

The Essence of the Lie

Subsequent to the Fall of Man in the Garden of Eden (Gen. 3:4–6) and ever since, man has knowledge of good and evil—the Truth and the Lie. From the beginning God's plan was that man should not know evil apart from having a loving relationship with Himself.[231] The knowledge of evil apart from God puts man in the precarious position of making decisions on his own; thus leaving him susceptible to in-authentic life and purpose. As a consequence of the Fall and man's subsequent knowledge of evil, to avoid evil it is now crucial that man understands what it means to lie or deceive.

New Age philosophies like *The Secret* promote Biblical principles and quote Scripture to endorse their claims, thereby deceiving unwary Christians; qualifying Paul's warning that "in latter times some will depart from the faith, giving heed to deceiving spirits and doctrines of demons, speaking lies in hypocrisy, having their own conscience seared with a hot iron" (1 Tim. 4:1–2). *The Secret* and its counterpart New Age philosophies are not new. James Walker examines Wallace Wattles' early 1900s work *The Science of Getting Rich* and exposes the similarities of its philosophy to *The Secret* along with a plethora of Mind Science religions like Christian Science, founder Mary Baker Eddy; The Church of Religious Science, founder Ernest Holmes; and The Unity School of Christianity or Unity, founders Charles and Merle Filmore.[232] Walker explains, "The New Age Movement professes a broad-minded openness to all religions, but its basic underlying philosophy represents a carefully calculated undermining of Judeo-Christian beliefs with various combinations of Gnosticism and occultism."[233] (Gnosticism is an ancient world-view stating that Divine essence is the only true or highest reality, and that the unconscious Self of man is actually this essence.)

In lockstep with many false religions and New Age philosophies, *The Secret* cites Scripture while it omits God altogether. As with other false teachings and doctrines of error, this philosophy counterfeits, perverts, and substitutes God's eternal principles with notions like, "The Universe emerges from thought. We are the creators not only of our own destiny but also of the Universe." And, "Now you know the Truth of Who You Really Are. You are the master of the Universe. You are the heir to the kingdom. You are the perfection of Life."[234]

Jesus declares that anyone who enters the heavenly places any other way than through Himself is a thief and a robber. He warns, "Most assuredly, I say to you, he who does not enter the sheepfold by the door, but climbs up some other way, the same is a thief and a robber" (John 10:1). Because God's eternal principles work for believers and unbelievers alike, *The Secret* employs God's universal Biblical principles for self-gratification and personal avarice. Yet, it is to God's praise and man's benefit that God declares His Word will not return void—that it will accomplish what He purposes it to accomplish. He says, "So shall My word be that goes forth from My mouth; It shall not return to Me void, But it shall accomplish what I please, And it shall prosper in the thing for which I sent it" (Isa. 55:11). Without this eternal truth or universal principle, we would have no guarantee that the universe would exist tomorrow. Yet, it is this marvelous eternal truth that also allows God's laws to work for believers and unbelievers alike. Jesus affirms this truth when He says, "That you may be sons of your Father in heaven; for He makes His sun rise on the evil and on the good, and sends rain on the just and on the unjust" (Matt. 5:45).[235] For this reason it is imperative that we humbly walk in truth and avoid the very appearance of error.

The Secret employs God's universal Biblical principles and trains the *naïve* and unsuspecting how to apply these principles for self-serving purposes. *The Secret counterfeits, perverts,* and *substitutes* many of God's universal principles by embedding them into its erroneous philosophy and esteeming an arbitrary universe—rather than God the Creator of the universe—as the benefactor of these principles. Consider these examples of Biblical principles *The Secret* violates (crucial elements of respective Scriptures that *The Secret* eliminates are noted in brackets):

- Bringing every thought into captivity [to the obedience of Christ] (2 Cor. 10:5b).
- In everything give thanks [for this is the will of God in Christ Jesus concerning you] (1 Thess. 5:18, KJV).

- Whatever things are [true, whatever things are noble, whatever things are just, whatever things are pure, …] lovely, whatever things are of good report, [if there is any virtue and if there is anything praiseworthy] meditate on these things (Phil. 4:8).
- [But seek first the kingdom of God and His righteousness, and] all these things shall be added to you (Matt. 6:33).
- As a man thinks in his heart, so is he. [As one who reckons he says to you, eat and drink, yet his heart is not with you] (Prov. 23:7, AMP).

Clearly the authors of these verses have something completely different in mind than *The Secret's* self-seeking, self-aggrandizing, self-serving perversion of God's truth. The writer of 2 Corinthians 10:5b calls us to bring our thoughts captive *to the obedience of Christ* as a prescription to effectively do spiritual warfare—not to coerce some ethereal universe into giving us the man or woman of our dreams. In 1 Thessalonians 5:18, the apostle Paul admonishes us to have a glad heart, and be thankful to God in all things *because this is God's will for our lives in Christ Jesus*—not because we want to manipulate the universe into giving us a new car. In Paul's epistle to the Philippians (4:8) he instructs us to keep our minds stayed on Him and His goodness *because it is through this that we experience God's peace of mind and heart*—not because positive thoughts will ultimately give us that big house on a hill. In Matthew 6:33 Jesus gives us the prescription for provision when He instructs us that He will sustain us and provide all our needs *because we seek God's Kingdom and all its righteousness first*—not because the universe will bring good things into our lives because we deserve them. Finally, when the writer of Proverbs 23:7 states that we are what we think, clearly *he is warning us against hypocrisy by speaking one thing and thinking the opposite*, and not giving us a recipe to amass material gain or garner honor and prestige to ourselves.

As is the case with many false religions and New Age philosophies, *The Secret*—and its illusory *Law of Attraction*—counterfeits, perverts, and substitutes Biblical truths to create a New Age philosophy that accommodates man's propensity to control his own life and destiny (indeed, to be god of his own life) seeking the creation rather than the Creator. How formidable that *The Secret* and its New Age counterparts would employ God's eternal principles—without Him as the Source—to advance personal gain and self-aggrandizement rather than to glorify God.

Great Folly

When we are not firmly rooted in the truth of God's Holy Word, we are ignorant of the truth and unable to discern truth from error. Thus Satan is able to gain entrance into our belief system with his lies, and what we believe ultimately controls our thoughts and actions. However, when we root ourselves in the Truth of God's Word, we believe Him when He instructs us, "Submit yourselves, then, to God. Resist the devil, and he will flee from you" (James 4:7, NIV); The outgrowth of our act of submission to God and our subsequent resistance of evil is freedom from the clutches of the evil one. Author and teacher Neil Anderson provides insight into how Satan leads man away from the truth and into the lie. He writes, "If people believe Satan's lies, those lies will control their lives. These people need to be freed from the shackles of Satan's lies by God's truth. Only truth can free us from deception. Jesus said: 'You shall know the truth, and the truth shall make you free'" (John 8:32).[236] Accordingly, it is vital that we *know* the truth of God's Word.

How effortless it is to walk away from truth and into error. All it requires is that we defer to the father of lies rather than "the Father of lights, with whom there is no variation or shadow of turning" (James 1:17). The writer of John identifies the father of lies: "He [the devil] was a murderer from the beginning, and does not stand in the truth, because there is no truth in him. When he speaks a lie, he speaks from his own resources [nature]; for he is a liar, and the father of lies" (John 8:44). To walk away from truth merely requires that we yield to the flesh rather than the Spirit, as is the case of Esau, Isaac's son, who encountered a test of integrity and walked away from truth when his flesh cried out for satiation. To satisfy his flesh for only moments in light of eternity, Esau relented and chose to sell his birthright for a mere bowl of beans (Gen. 25:29–34). Life is replete with incidents like Esau's where we have an opportunity to choose truth over deception. In a previous chapter Jessica wisely made her choice to walk in truth and honesty without hesitation because she counted the high price she would pay to walk in deception rather than truth—Esau was not so wise.

Biblical Models
The Pilate Model: Intellectualism and Unbelief

We've already noted Pilate's intellectual query to Jesus' declaration. "What is truth?" Pilate asks of Jesus (John 18:38a). Let's take a closer look at this exchange. Prior to Pilate's query, Jesus declared to Pilate, "You say rightly that I am a king. For this cause I was born, and for this cause I have come into the world, that I should bear witness to the truth. Everyone who is of the truth hears My voice" (v. 37). To this Pilate replied, "What is truth?" (v. 38a). Neil Anderson makes this observation, "Pilate sends Jesus to Herod and Herod sends Him back to Pilate (see Luke 23:1–11). Like Pilate, everyone must make a personal decision about what to do with Jesus."[237] As Pilate attempted to intellectualize the truth of Jesus' words, he revealed his own unbelief. In Pontius Pilate's interrogation of Jesus, he exposed the error of dependence on intellectual ability when he answered Jesus with his rhetorical question, "What is Truth?"(John 18:38a).[238] In this very brief exchange with the Savior, Pilate revealed his ignorance and inability to discern truth from error—for surely if he did not know truth, neither could he know the difference between truth and error.

Editor of *The Essays of Francis Bacon*, Clark Northup, concludes this of Bacon's characterization of Pilate's query of Jesus, "Having asked this question of Jesus, [Pilate] disregarded truth, and chose instead 'the wickedness of falsehood and breach of faith.'"[239] James Stevens cites Bacon's essay "Of Truth" and makes the observation of Bacon's emphatic belief in the import of Truth: Francis Bacon "paraphrases Lucretius: 'No pleasure is comparable to the standing upon the vantage ground of Truth.'"[240] To that end, great freedom and peace are our reward when we speak the truth, live the truth, and act upon the truth at all times and under all circumstances. We have freedom from fear and rejection, and we have peace in knowing our life is an open book—an epistle as Paul states—to be read of men.

The Nicodemus Model: Deception and Pride

"Are you *really* the Son of God?" appeared to be the overarching essence of Nicodemus' query when he approached Jesus in the dark of night, but pride and deception appeared to be his motivation (see John 3:1–21). Jesus responded to the covert inquisition of Nicodemus, "He who practices truth [who does what is right] comes out into the Light; so that his works may be plainly shown to be what they are—wrought with God [divinely prompted, done with God's help, in dependence upon Him]" (v. 21, AMP). With this answer Jesus directly addressed Nicodemus' deception and pride.

Indeed Nicodemus revealed his own heart of deception and pride when he sought the Savior in the darkness of night rather than the light of day. Nicodemus acknowledged that Jesus must be of God and that God must be with Him because of the miracles and signs surrounding Jesus' ministry. Yet his decision to approach Jesus after dark tells us he intentionally wanted to conceal his inner struggle about the deity of Christ from his peers. His cunning to keep his contemporaries and his colleagues unaware of his midnight mission revealed the deception of his heart—and we cannot ignore his fear of rejection by his peers. Because Nicodemus did not fear God, he was vulnerable to be snared by the fear of men. He would have done well to heed the psalmist's admonition, "Do not think like everyone else does. Do not be afraid that some plan conceived behind closed doors will be the end of you. Do not fear anything except the LORD Almighty. He alone is the Holy One. If you fear him, you need fear nothing else. He will keep you safe" (Isa. 8:11–14, NLT).

In his queries of Jesus, Nicodemus acknowledged he did not have all the answers. Yet Nicodemus exposed his pride in his response to Jesus' declaration that a person must be born again (John 3:3), saying, "How can a man be born when he is old? Can he enter a second time into his mother's womb and be born?" (v. 4). Although Nicodemus ultimately has a change of heart toward Jesus (19:38–40), at this juncture deception and pride constrain him from embracing the Truth.

Chapter 7

SATAN'S VERY NATURE: DECEPTION

> The quest for justice continues, and the weapons and the hatred pile up; but truth was an early casualty. The lies on behalf of which our wars have been fought and our peace treaties concluded! The lies of revolution… The lies of advertising, of news, of salesmanship, of politics! The lies of the priest in the pulpit, the professor at his podium, the journalist at his typewriter! The lie stuck like a fishbone in the throat of the microphone, the hand-held lies of the prowling cameraman! … It is truth that has died, not God.
>
> —Malcolm Muggeridge[241]

The Essence and Character of the Lie

The very essence and character of Satan is deception for he is the antithesis of Truth. Proving the authenticity of the Bible through the examination and scrutiny of Biblical scholars and Christian theologians like Saint Augustine (AD 354–430), as well as secular scholars and Jewish historians like Flavius Josephus (AD 37–101), qualifies the Bible as accurate and authoritative. And the Bible declares of Satan, "He was a murderer from the beginning, and does not stand in the truth, because there is no truth in him. When he speaks a lie, he speaks from his own resources, for he is a liar and the father of it" (John 8:44). Thus Satan's very nature is deception and malevolence in every sense.

As noted, on the surface *The Secret* appears to be congruent with a plethora of Biblical principles and—like Satan in the Garden when He quotes God's Holy Word to deceive Eve—*The Secret* even cites Scripture to support its doctrines. Moreover, this New Age philosophy employs Biblical virtues such as: love, faith, gratitude, positive confession, positive thinking, and living beyond the realm of sight to advance its appeal. Yet, just beneath the surface lies a malevolence that dissents from Biblical Truth and spawns false teachings and blasphemies. The roots of *The Secret*—like any false doctrine and false teaching—go back to the Garden of Eden and beyond, to the fall of Lucifer himself. The prophet Isaiah provides the account of Satan's recompense for his sin:

> How you are fallen from heaven, O Lucifer, son of the morning! How you are cut down to the ground, You who weakened the nations! For you have said in your heart: "I will ascend into heaven, I will exalt my throne above the stars of God; I will also sit on the mount of the congregation On the farthest sides of the north; I will ascend above the heights of the clouds, I will be like the Most High." Yet you shall be brought down to Sheol, To the lowest depths of the Pit.
>
> —Isaiah 14:12–15

God divulges the account of Lucifer's existence prior to and after his fall in Ezekiel 28:14–16:

> You were the anointed cherub who covers; I established you; You were on the holy mountain of God; You walked back and forth in the midst of fiery stones. You were perfect in your ways from the day you were created, Till iniquity was found in you. By the abundance of your trading You became filled with violence within, And you

> sinned; Therefore I cast you as a profane thing Out of the mountain of God; And I destroyed you, O covering cherub, From the midst of the fiery stones.

There are striking similarities between the account of Satan's fall and what *The Secret* engenders in its adherents. At the heart of Satan's sin is pride, rebellion, self-importance, haughtiness, aggression, lawlessness, and corruption—in a word, *SELF*, the very underlying doctrine of *The Secret.*

Moral Depravity

Molly Henderson[242] is a professing Christian. Her Christian upbringing has its roots in the Baptist denomination; and subsequent to her marriage to her husband of twenty-seven years, her denominational persuasion is now Lutheran. Molly believes *The Secret* is responsible for her accomplishing many goals including a deadline to arrive at the television studios of a prominent international figure just in time to audition as a contestant for an episode featuring a contest advancing "The Big Give,"[243] a New Age philosophy that seemingly promotes philanthropic deeds with no apparent remuneration other than the joy one derives from the act of giving. However, at the other end of this contest was a cash prize of $1,000,000 awaiting the winning contestant—nullifying any philanthropic motives. En route to the studios, Molly and her husband encountered inclement weather; but Molly convinced her husband to persevere, which subsequently placed them just beyond the bad weather. This extra push brought them to the studios in time for Molly to audition as a contestant for "The Big Give." Although Molly ultimately was not one of the contestants, she and her friend Joan—to whom Molly refers as her "life coach" of *The Secret*—attributed the success of Molly's business and her women's foundation to this audition.

There are two versions of *The Secret.* Molly insists she only adheres to first version. This version of *The Secret* incorporates The Law of Attraction, a New Age philosophy that has its roots in the occult and employs the channeling of demonic entities as a means to success in life.[244] Yet Molly believes this version of *The Secret* does not conflict with her Christian faith.

Moreover, she believes this version actually enhances her faith. Molly's story presents compelling evidence of how easily we can fall into false teachings and heretical philosophies if our roots are not in truth. Rather than first seek God and His counsel for her life's purpose and direction, Molly determined to take the fast track to success—the same fast track Satan tempted Adam and Eve with in the Garden: you can have all this without God. The same fast track he tempted Jesus with in the wilderness: all this is yours now if you worship me just once. God creates man to worship; and if man does not worship the God of Truth, he will worship someone (or something) else. The outcome of this fast track—Satan's Lie—is man ultimately worships the creature rather than the Creator and falls prey to every form of deception and depravity (Rom. 1:21–32).

Molly's belief system is the archetype of our unwitting incorporation of false teachings into our faith and the subsequent deception that follows. In his recent article "On Truth," Stanley Fleming offers this formula to ascertain "the state of truth"[245] in one's life: "If truth, according to the definition, is the real state of things, then something can be completely true, partially true, or not true. In the example of a formula we might assign complete truth to 'A.' If 'A' and only 'A' is completely true, then 'A+B' is partially true, and 'B+C' is not true at all." Fleming admits, "This is an oversimplification. Yet, my point is that what people believe and build their lives upon may be true, partially true, or not true at all. Ideas have consequences; hence, generations can possibly be influenced by 'A+B' and 'B+C' (partial or no truth)."[246] Applying Fleming's formula to Molly's belief system, "A+B" would represent Molly's Christian faith together with her faith in *The Secret*, and "B+C" would represent her faith in *The Secret*.

According to Fleming's system, the formula for Molly's belief system would be "A+B" and "B+C." According to this formula, Molly believes—and is building her life on—partial truth or no truth at all. However, this assessment and its formula are a misreading of truth, for King Solomon declares, "Dead flies putrefy the perfumer's ointment, and cause it to give off a foul odor; So does a little folly" (Eccl. 10:1). In reality there is no "partial truth." Truth is what it is—truth stands alone. The truth is that something either is true or it is not true; we cannot have it both ways. If we mix truth with untruth, the result is not "partial truth" but "no truth" at all or "total deception." The product of an illegal fabrication of a dollar bill is not legal tender with an alteration, rather it is a counterfeit of the authentic dollar bill; and as such, nullifies the monetary value of the dollar altogether. The bill is fake and thus holds no value or functionality other than to deceive the unwary. Therefore, if "A" is completely true, and "B" is partially true, then "A+B=C" is not true at all.

In the end Molly's belief system has no basis in truth; rather her belief system has its basis in deception at its very core. Indeed, when we choose to walk away from the Truth, we forfeit the ability to discern truth from error and are susceptible to every false doctrine that cunningly seduces us into the Lie.

Heretical Doctrine
The Tree of Knowledge of Good and Evil

The fruit of the Tree of Knowledge of Good and Evil is death (see Genesis 2:17) and is born through disobedience to God's Holy Word. When we choose to disobey God's Word, we give ourselves over to the flesh rather than the Spirit; and the apostle Paul warns, "The mind governed by the flesh is death" (Rom. 8:6, NIV). It is virtually impossible to walk in Truth and be governed by the flesh for the apostle Paul cautions us the flesh is God's constant enemy (see Galatians 5:16–21); thus we are left without defense against deceiving spirits and New Age philosophies like *The Secret*.

Heretical doctrines such as *The Secret* substitute the God of the universe with the universe itself. Satan's temptation of Jesus in the wilderness characterizes his temptation to all of humanity:

> To You I will give all this power and authority and their glory (all their magnificence, excellence, pre-eminence, dignity, and grace), for it has been turned over to me, and I give it to whom I will; Therefore if you will do homage to and worship me [just once], it shall all be Yours.
>
> —LUKE 4:6–7, AMP

To which Jesus replies, "Get behind Me, Satan! It is written, You shall do homage to and worship the Lord your God; and Him only shall you serve" (Luke 4: 8, AMP). Worship is due to God alone. (See Luke 8:28; 17:16; Psalm 72:11; Isaiah 45:14; 46:6; Matthew 2:11; Revelation 4:10; 5:8; 22:8.)[247] Yet, *The Secret* makes heretical claims, such as:

- Trust the Universe. Trust and believe and have faith.[248]
- All you require is You, and your ability to think things into being.[249]
- You are a spiritual being. You are energy, and energy cannot be created or destroyed—it just changes form. Therefore, the pure essence of you has always been and always will be.[250]
- Your mind is the creative power of all things.[251]
- So your purpose is what you say it is. Your mission is the mission you give yourself. Your life will be what you create it as, and no one will stand in judgment of it, now or ever.[252]

When we contrast *The Secret* to Biblical Truth, the most revealing heretical doctrines of *The Secret* are: "You are God in a physical body. You are Spirit in the flesh. You are Eternal Life expressing itself as you. You are a cosmic being. You are all power. You are all wisdom. You are all intelligence. You are perfection. You are magnificence. You are the creator, and you are creating the creation of You on this planet."[253]

There is nothing new about *The Secret* or its first version, *The Law of Attraction*. Its roots are in the occult, false religions, and New Age philosophies, including Channeling, Buddhism, Hinduism; and the Mind Science religions like Christian Science, The Unity Church, Scientology, Unitarianism, Universalism, and Transcendentalism. *The Secret* cites a man who purportedly put The Law of Attraction to the test when he imagined a feather in full detail and experienced the exact feather falling at his feet two days later. Of this man's newfound powers, it concluded, "He realized his amazing ability and power to attract something to himself through the power of his mind. With total faith, he has now moved onto creating much bigger things."[254] The man's exercise of mind control demonstrates the occult influence on *The Secret* or *The Law of Attraction*. The man placed his faith in his own power to create with his mind. This is exemplar of how *The Secret* substitutes the work of the Holy Spirit in its adherents.

The Law of Attraction: The Basics of the Teachings of Abraham, *Ask and It Shall Be Given*, *The Astonishing Power of Emotions*, and *The Amazing Power of Deliberate Intent* advocate channeling as a means to self-gratification and fulfillment in life. The biographical entry at the conclusion of *The Law of Attraction: The Basics of the Teachings of Abraham* reads, "Excited about the clarity and practicality of the translated word from the Beings who call themselves Abraham, (authors) Esther and Jerry Hicks began disclosing their amazing Abraham experience to a handful of close business associates in 1986."[255] The biographical entry continues,

> Abraham—a group of obviously evolved Non-Physical teachers—present their broader perspective through Esther Hicks. And as they [these Beings or Non-Physical entities] speak to our level of comprehension through a series of loving, allowing, brilliant, yet comprehensively simple essays in print and in sound—they guide us to a clear connection with our loving *Inner Being*, and to uplifting self-empowerment from our Total Self.[256]

SELF is at the philosophy's very core. The entities to which *The Law of Attraction* refer as "Abraham" speak in the collective form of "we." This New Age philosophy cites more heretical dogma from the entities, "We [the entities] are often accused of teaching selfishness, and we always agree that we certainly do teach selfishness, for you cannot perceive life from any perspective other than from that of yourself… Everyone is selfish. It is not possible to be otherwise."[257] This dangerous philosophy employs doctrines such as:

> All that you do pleases that which you seek to please. There is not a list of things that are right and a list of things that are wrong—there is only that which aligns with your true intent and purpose, and that which does not. You may trust your Guidance that comes forth from

> within you to help you know when you are in alignment with your state of natural Well-Being."[258]

The Secret and its dangerous counterpart *The Law of Attraction* are replete with occult content and heretical doctrines that supplant the ability to discern truth from error in the life of its adherents.

The Secret—like many heretical doctrines—is a garden variety of erroneous thoughts borrowed from false religions like Buddhism to formulate its own philosophy. It quotes Buddha (563–483 BCE), "All that we are is a result of what we have thought."[259] Expert on false religions, the occult, and New Age philosophies and author of *In Search of the True Light*, Mike Shreve, says this about Buddhism:

> The Sanskrit word *dharma* means, "that which is established." It refers to both doctrine and duty: the way of life a person embraces in order to achieve enlightenment. Buddhists are taught to take refuge in "the *dharma*:" the teachings of Buddha. Adherents of this religion believe that Buddha's instructions to his disciples "set the wheel of *dharma* in motion." The eight spokes [of the symbol of the wheel] represent the "Eightfold Path."[260]

The Secret bears striking resemblance to the tenets of Hinduism. Hinduism teaches chanting as a means of power to "access oneness with [what Hinduism terms] the Absolute, the Source of all things."[261] Shreve writes,

> Though a variety of beliefs exist in Hinduism concerning the soul's ultimate state, [one of] two main veins of thought seem to dominate. Sankara, an eighth-century teacher; believed that when souls (*atman* or *jiva*) are finally released from the cycle of rebirths (*samasara*) they do not retain their individual personality. Instead they are absorbed into God. They actually *become* God...

> Sankara's system of thought was based on the idea that God is impersonal.[262]

The Secret is an extension of this system of thought.

The Secret incorporates the teachings of one of the early founders of the New Thought Movement like Christian D. Larson (1866–1954), and cites *The Hidden Secret* on man's propensity to be the god of his own life, "That a man can change himself ... and master his own destiny is the conclusion of every mind who is wide-awake to the power of right thought."[263] Following are excerpts from chapter 1 of *The Hidden Secret*. The title of chapter 1 is, "With Faith All Things Are Possible," and the chapter opens with, "To him who has faith all things are possible."[264] *The Hidden Secret* offers perverse thoughts on faith by systematically eliminating God from the context of faith:

- Faith is that something in man that transcends every form of limitation and opens the mind to the limitless powers of the soul.
- It is faith that emancipates the person; it is faith that unfolds the unbounded greatness of the soul; it is faith that removes the veil of mystery and reveals to man that wonderful world, that limitless world, that divinely beautiful world that is within.
- Faith has been the hidden secret of the great souls in every age; faith has been the secret through which all miracles have been wrought; faith has been the secret through which the prophet gained his wisdom and his power; faith has been the secret through which the sons of glory gained their rare and wonderful genius; faith has been the secret through which everything high, everything worthy, and everything beautiful has been given to the world.
- It is faith that the awakened minds have eternally sought to find, though not always knowing that the hidden secret was faith, and faith alone; and it is faith that will change the world, as the world should be changed, when its inner sanctuary has been entered by the mind of man.

- Faith is the hidden secret to everything; the key that unlocks every door that may exist in the universe; faith is the perfect way to that inner world from which all things proceed; faith is the royal path to unbounded power, immeasurable wisdom, and limitless love; faith is the gates ajar to that kingdom which first must be sought if all other things are to be added; faith is the hidden secret to every desire and need of man.[265]

The truth is faith does indeed open us to limitless power, faith does free us, faith is the secret through which miracles are brought forth, faith can and will change the world, and faith is the gate to operating in the Kingdom. The writer of Hebrews declares, "Without faith it is impossible to please [God]" (11:6). The question is, *Faith in what or whom*? Is our faith in the Creator—the only Omnipotent, Omnipresent, Omniscient God of the universe and all that is in it—as the author of Hebrews heralds? Or is our faith in the creation—the universe itself which is lifeless without the Creator and holds no power of its own? Clearly, the New Thought Movement is a perversion of truth relegating its adherents to no ability to discern truth from error.

The Secret ascribes honor to Wallace D. Wattles, early twentieth-century author whose works are replete with Hinduism and New Thought philosophy. The preface of his 1910 work, *The Science of Getting Rich: Financial Success Through Creative Thought*, explains its thesis has its roots in Hinduism and the New Thought Movement and attributes Oriental philosophies as its philosophical foundations citing philosophers of world renown to lend credibility and authority to the erroneous philosophical theories. It asserts,

> The monistic theory of the universe—the theory that One is All, and that All is One; that one Substance manifests itself as the seeming many elements of the material world—is of Hindu origin, and has been gradually working its way into the thought of the Western world for two hundred years. It is the foundation of all the Oriental

> philosophies, and of those of Descartes, Spinoza, Leibnitz, Schopenhauer, Hegel, and Emerson.[266]

Throughout the pages of *The Science of Getting Rich*, it perverts the Word of God with the philosophy of the New Thought Movement. This philosophy warns its adherents with this mandate:

> You must lay aside all other concepts of the universe than this monistic one; and you must dwell upon this until it is fixed in your mind... If a doubt comes to you, cast it aside as a sin. Do not listen to arguments against this idea; do not go to church or lectures where a contrary concept of things is taught or preached. Do not read magazines or books which teach a different idea; if you get mixed up in your faith, all your efforts will be in vain.[267]

On whether the New Thought Movement is a perversion of Biblical Christianity, Shreve refers to a chart contrasting the two: "Just look at the following glaring differences ... about the Mind Sciences and New Thought Movement as contrasted over against Christianity":

New Thought vs Biblical Christianity

- New Thought: Sin is an illusion.
- Biblical Christianity: Sin is real and separates us from God (Rom. 3:23; Gal. 3:22; 1 John 1:8).
- New Thought: All people are sons and daughters of God.
- Biblical Christianity: Only those born again are sons and daughters of God (1 John 3:1).
- New Thought: God is within every human being.
- Biblical Christianity: Man is separate from God and must be restored to relationship (by grace through faith in Jesus Christ alone) (Eph 2:8).
- New Thought: All human beings have a divine essence.
- Biblical Christianity: Human beings (are created in the likeness and image of God but) are not divine in essence (Rom. 3:23).

- New Thought: Jesus was merely an example, a way-shower, not a Savior.
- Biblical Christianity: Jesus is the Savior of the world; according to his own words, He is God—One in essence and being with the Father and the Holy Spirit (John 10:30).
- New Thought: Jesus did not die on the cross for the sins of the world.
- Biblical Christianity: Jesus did die on the cross and shed His blood for the remission of our sins (1 Cor. 12:15–17).
- New Thought: Jesus did not rise from the dead.
- Biblical Christianity: The Son of God conquered death and arose victorious (1 Cor. 12:15–17).
- New Thought: Christ is a principle, a consciousness, accessible to everyone.
- Biblical Christianity: Christ is a person—God incarnate (Acts 8:37; Gal. 5; Mark 13:6).
- New Thought: Heaven and hell are states of mind.
- Biblical Christianity: Heaven and hell are actual spiritual locations (John 1:32; 6:33; Acts 1:2; Matt. 13; Mark 9; Luke 12; Matt. 25:41).
- New Thought: All human beings have eternal life.
- Biblical Christianity: Only those who are saved have eternal life (John 3:15; John 10:28; John 17:2; and numerous other texts).
- New Thought: We are not accountable to God or ever to be judged by Him.
- Biblical Christianity: We will all stand before the judgment seat of Christ (Heb. 9:27.)
- New Thought: The physical bodies of the dead will not be resurrected.
- Biblical Christianity: The saved will receive a resurrected, glorified form (1 Cor. 12:51–52).

Concerning the Faith Movement, Shreve explains, "There are similarities between the New Thought Movement and the Faith Movement within Christianity—however it is different. In the Faith Movement it is vitally important to confess God's Word, to declare what God has decreed, in order to see it manifested as reality."[268] He clarifies, "However, practitioners are not really creating their own reality; they are merely uniting with God's assessment of their situation, and expecting Him to watch over His Word (as it is confessed) to fulfill it. God is still in the superior role."[269] Bill Kline offers this concluding thought, "The key difference between New Thought and the Christian Faith Movement is the *Object* of your faith."[270]

Alongside *The Secret* is a contemporary substitute of Biblical Christianity attacking today's generation—*The Moses Code*. Christopher Larson deems "*The Moses Code* a dangerous occult technique, a preposterous claim and a New Age lie."[271] This philosophy is much like *The Secret* only its primary emphasis focuses on giving rather than receiving. This form of mind control asserts that all one needs to do is employ God's answer to Moses, when He declares of Himself, "I AM THAT I AM," as an incantation. For this incantation to invoke the promised power, practitioners must pause and breathe in and out—or insert a comma—between "that" and "I." The symbol for this occult practice is the "comma," which is representative of the cult-like breathing technique. When one inserts the comma, one alleges, "I am that," and confirms this allegation with, "I am" substituting the great "I AM" with oneself. "That" refers to whatever object one is contemplating at that particular moment. It could be a tree; it could be a trash can. This is pantheism, which claims that "God is everything, and everything is God."[272]

An example of a contemporary substitute of God's law of sowing and reaping that lines up with the false teachings of *The Secret* is found in the new earth philosophy *A New Earth: Awakening to Your Life's Purpose*. This philosophy is similar to *The Secret*, except—like *The Moses Code*—it emphasizes giving rather than receiving.[273]

The Secret pays "homage to the featured co-authors of *The Secret*"[274] for their "wisdom, love, and divinity"[275] and assigns the term "*avatar*"[276] to those whom it considers "master teachers from the past." The selection of the term *avatar* to identify these teachers speaks of *The Secret's* connection to Hinduism as *Avatar* is a Hindu term which refers to the incarnation of a higher being. To ascribe the term *Avatar* to the thinkers to whom the philosophy pays homage further demonstrates the roots of Hinduism behind this New Age philosophy. The list of master teachers include Robert Collier, Wallace Wattles, Charles Haanel, Joseph Campbell, Prentice Mulford, Genevieve Behrend, and Charles Fillmore—all whose teachings have their roots in the New Thought Movement. Indeed, the very essence of the depiction of Truth in *The Secret* is heresy. The description of Truth set forth in *The Secret* is this:

> There is a truth deep down inside of you that has been waiting for you to discover it, and that Truth is this: *you deserve all good things life has to offer.* You know that inherently, because you feel awful when you are experiencing the lack of good things. All good things are your birthright! You are the creator of you, and the law of attraction is your magnificent tool to create whatever you want in your life. Welcome to the magic of life, and the magnificence of You![277]

The Secret comports with the father of Lies in its appraisal of Truth that humanity deserves all good things life offers. Yet the apostle Paul declares in Romans 3:23 that "all have sinned and fall short of the glory of God," and that because of this sin, what man deserves is—not all good things but—death (Rom 6:23a). However what man receives from God in His mercy is the free gift of eternal life through His dear Son (v. 23b).

Two Scriptures cited often in *The Secret* are declarations from Jesus Himself, "Whatsoever ye shall ask in prayer, believing, ye shall receive" (Matt. 21:22, KJV) and, "What things soever ye desire, when ye pray, believe that ye receive them, and ye shall have them" (Mark 11:24, KJV).[278] This philosophy takes Jesus' words out of context and employs counterfeits, perversions, and substitutes of Biblical principles by eliminating God from His own eternal principles, twisting their meaning to suit its own heretical doctrines, and attributing the outcome to an arbitrary universe rather than to God—the Author and Creator of the universe. For Christians to attempt to walk in the Truth of God's Holy Word and implement heretical doctrines like *The Secret* is incongruent and thus counterintuitive to the Biblical principles themselves. Francis Beckwith illustrates:

> If someone offers to show you a square circle for the small charge of two dollars, save your money. Square circles cannot exist because the notion is contradictory. One need not explore the universe to know that such a claim is false. The error is self-evident: contradictory things cannot both be true. There are squares and there are circles, but there are no square circles.[279]

All of these false religions and New Age philosophies have their roots in Satan's original sin of his self-deifying pride and determination to be god, counterfeiting, perverting, and substituting God's eternal principles with the unsound doctrine of placing *SELF* on the throne rather than God. From man's first parents to the sinless Son of God—and every generation since, Satan's malevolent maneuver is to deceive man into believing the Lie that *you can have all this without God*. To recognize, discern, and reject the counterfeits, perversions, and substitutes of God's eternal principles with fallacious New Age philosophies and other doctrines of deception, we must walk in truth and truthfulness, exercising the same integrity, humility, and meekness the Son of God demonstrates in His life, in His death, and in His resurrection—for He is the paradigm of Truth and truthfulness.

Deceptions of the Lie
Counterfeits of Truth: "Satan … Masquerades as an Angel of Light"

As with Molly, our proclivity to be god of our own life renders us vulnerable to false teachings and counterfeits of truth. Therefore Satan approaches man in the guise of a messenger of God—masquerading himself as an angel of light (2 Cor. 11:14)—and counterfeits God's eternal laws of the universe and reveals how to implement God's laws without God. Jesus Christ is the Truth; His way is the way of the Cross; there are no shortcuts.

He will perfect His image in us—if we will permit. He will supply all that we need—if we will allow.

Counterfeits have their roots in deception. In her article "What Is Deception?" Reverend René Monette declares, "It is trickery, subtlety, cleverness, substituting the false for the true, and getting people to believe it. Deception has been around as long as the devil has. However, if Jesus warns us that deception would be a real problem in the church, then we would be wise to examine how we can overcome deception in the church."[280] *The Secret* and its kin are counterfeits of God's eternal law of Seedtime and Harvest or the Law of Reciprocity. Jesus sums up the Law of Reciprocity with this, "Therefore, whatever you want men to do to you, do also to them, for this is the Law and the Prophets" (Matt. 7:12).

The Secret invokes the principles of God's Law of Reciprocity of asking, believing, and receiving to promote selfish ambition and garner personal gain and cites a personal empowerment advocate[281] to define three *all-important* steps to implement this counterfeit of God's Biblical principles:

- The first step is to ask. Make a command to the Universe. Let the Universe know what you want. The Universe responds to your thoughts."[282]
- Step two is believe. Believe that it's already yours. Have what I love to call unwavering faith. Believing in the unseen."[283]
- Step three, and the final step in the process, is to receive. Begin to feel wonderful about it. Feel the way you will feel once it arrives. Feel it now."[284]

This *ask of the Universe, receive from the Universe, believe in the Universe* formula to fame or fortune, asserts: the universe is your genie; your wish is the universe's command.

Clearly *The Secret* counterfeits the Biblical principles of having faith and hope in the God of Truth. The author of Hebrews announces, "Now faith is the substance of things hoped for, the evidence of things not seen" (Heb. 11:1). *Matthew Henry's Concise Commentary* expounds on

Hebrews 11:1–3 and makes the distinction of the right of the believer to exercise these virtues over against the lack of privilege of the unbeliever: "Faith always has been the mark of God's servants, from the beginning of the world. Where the principle is planted by the regenerating Spirit of God, it will cause the truth to be received, concerning justification by the sufferings and merits of Christ. And the same things that are the object of our hope, are the object of our faith."[285] The Commentary explains, "It is a firm persuasion and expectation, that God will perform all he has promised to us in Christ. This persuasion gives the soul to enjoy those things now; it gives them a subsistence or reality in the soul, by the first-fruits and foretastes of them." The conclusion:

> Faith proves to the mind, the reality of things that cannot be seen by the bodily eye. It is a full approval of all God has revealed, as holy, just, and good. This view of faith is explained by many examples of persons in former times, who obtained a good report, or an honorable character in the word of God. Faith was the principle of their holy obedience, remarkable services, and patient sufferings. The Bible gives the most true and exact account of the origin of all things, and we are to believe it, and not to wrest the Scripture account of the creation, because it does not suit with the differing fancies of men. All that we see of the works of creation, were brought into being by the command of God.[286]

Matthew Henry's Concise Commentary makes clear that Biblical principles of faith and hope belong to the Christian who walks in the truth of God's Word "by the regenerating and transforming power of the Spirit of God."[287]

Perversions of Truth: "Hath God Said?"

God's Word is Truth, and from the beginning Satan's goal is to pervert Truth. Perversion of truth has never been more prevalent than it is today, and it has never been more imperative that we walk in absolute truth to discern truth from error. Editor of *New Horizons Magazine*, Larry Wilson, observes that "the first recorded words of the devil constitute a challenge to God's word, 'Yea, hath God said …?' (Gen. 3:1)." Satan's methodology is to draw the Truth of God's Word into question and cast doubt in the hearts and minds of man. Yet God's Truth continues to prove to be Truth. According to Wilson, John Wesley presents a compelling argument for the Truth of God's Word:

> The Bible must be the invention either of good men or angels, bad men or devils, or of God. It could not be the invention of good men or angels, for they neither would nor could make a book and tell lies all the time they were writing it, saying "Thus saith the Lord" when it was their own invention. It could not be the invention of bad men or devils, for they could not make a book that commands all duty, forbids all sin, and condemns their souls to Hell for all eternity. Therefore, the Bible must be given by Divine inspiration.[288]

Bill Kline qualifies Wesley's argument with this verse, "The Bible itself warns 'they fall when they disbelieve the Word'" (1 Pet. 2:8).[289]

Perversion bends and twists the Truth of God to create doubt and confusion in the mind of the unwary. God's Word identifies Satan as the author of confusion (2 Cor. 4:4). Phil Enlow of *Midnight Cry Ministries* explains, "The truth of God confronts the desperate condition of man without compromise. It offers nothing but the absolute sentence of death to the old nature while it gives newness of life and everlasting hope to the repentant sinner" (Rom. 6:3–4).[290] Enlow continues:

> Satan, on the other hand, accommodates human nature, allowing it to live and flourish. It is the same as if a supposed doctor were to treat a terrible disease by feeding and encouraging the disease while covering up some of the more obvious symptoms (Jer. 6:13–14). Mankind is "infected" with sin, a self-willed, self-pleasing rebellion against divine

> authority. This rebellion is especially manifest when that authority is expressed through men.[291]

Enlow concludes:

- What religion does is to clean up the outward man and make him appear to be righteous while leaving the inward man unchanged and, in time, unchangeable (Matt. 23:2–39). There comes a time when God ceases to deal with those who receive not "the love of the truth." The result is not simply delusion but strong delusion (2 Thess. 2:10–12).
- Strong delusion is being absolutely sure you are right, but you are wrong.[292]

Perversion takes an existing truth and twists it to mean something entirely different from its original meaning. Perversion creates doubt and confusion in the mind of its victims. *The Secret* asserts that there is no judgment in life or in death. It advocates feelings as the gauge to determine success. Exemplars of these perverse claims are apparent in the following quotes from *The Secret*:

- Your life will be what you create it as, and no one will stand in judgment of it, now or ever.[293]
- The only thing you need to do is feel good now.[294]
- All power is from within and therefore under our control.[295]
- You are energy, and energy cannot be created or destroyed. The pure essence of you has always been and always will be.[296]

The writer of 2 Corinthians illumines the import to walk in obedience to Christ, "[Inasmuch as we] refute arguments and theories and reasonings and every proud and lofty thing that sets itself up against the [true] knowledge of God; and we lead every thought and purpose away captive into the obedience of Christ (the Messiah, the Anointed One)" (10:5, AMP). In his work "Taking Every Thought Captive," Neil Anderson offers a case study of how we unwittingly are led away from truth and into error. He warns:

> Satan's perpetual aim is to infiltrate your thoughts with his thoughts and to promote his lie in the face of God's truth. If Satan can control your thoughts, he can control your behavior. He can introduce his thoughts, tempting you to act independently of God, as if they were your own thoughts or even God's thoughts, as he did with David (1 Chronicles 21:1), Judas (John 13:2) and Ananias (Acts 5:3).[297]

Anderson illustrates this truth with a personal encounter with one of his students:

> One of my students exemplified how deceptive Satan's thoughts can be. Jay came into my office one day and said, "Dr. Anderson, I'm in trouble. When I sit down to study, I get prickly sensations all over my body, my arms involuntarily raise, my vision gets blurry and I can't concentrate."
>
> "Tell me about your walk with God," I probed.
>
> "I have a very close walk with God. When I leave school at noon each day, I ask God where He wants me to go for lunch. If I hear a thought that says Burger King, I go to Burger King. Then I ask Him what He wants me to eat. If the thought comes to order a Whopper, I order a Whopper."
>
> "What about your church attendance?" I continued.
>
> "I go every Sunday wherever God tells me to go."
>
> For the last three Sundays "God" told him to go to a Mormon church![298]

Anderson explains that "Jay sincerely wanted to do what God wanted him to do. But he was passively paying attention to a deceiving spirit (1

Tim. 4:1) instead of 'taking every thought captive to the obedience of Christ;' (2 Cor. 10:5). In so doing he had opened himself up to Satan's activity in his life, resulting in the sabotage of his theological studies."[299] *The Secret* advocates opening the mind; yet Anderson's case study cautions of the dangers of such practices. "We must assume our responsibility for choosing the truth. We can't always tell whether the thought comes from the TV set, our memory bank, our imagination or a deceiving spirit. Regardless of where a thought originates, examine it in the light of God's Word and choose the truth."[300]

Scenarios like Jay's happen with regularity. We naïvely embrace every wind of doctrine and with itching ears pursue control of or, as in case studies like Jay, abdicate control of our own lives to deceiving spirits. This is the essence of *The Secret's* perversion of God's Truth. The writer of Acts pens, "Casting down arguments and every high thing that exalts itself against the knowledge of God, bringing every thought into captivity to the obedience of Christ" (2 Cor. 10:5). We are to cast down every vain imagining that exalts itself against the knowledge of God. The author of "The Knowledge of God" writes, "Our battle is to break down every deceptive argument and every imposing defense that men erect against the true knowledge of God."[301]

Substitutes of Truth: "All These Things I Will Give You if You Will Fall Down and Worship Me"

From the beginning Satan's goal was to trick humanity to worship him rather than the God of the universe. Satan allures us today with the same temptation he used to tempt Christ in the wilderness, "All these things I will give to you if you will fall down and worship me" (Matt. 4:9). Satan substitutes the Truth with the Lie—in this instance *The Secret*—and attempts to deceive us to believe this lie: if we just take the shortcut he presents to us, then we can be god of our own destiny and decide for ourselves what is right and wrong, good and evil (see Genesis 3:5b). The truth is that man cannot genuinely know good or evil without God.[302]

The roots of *The Secret's* heretical doctrine are found in the Garden of Eden where Satan essentially tells Adam and Eve they can have everything they desire without God—that they can know good and evil apart from God. In like manner Satan offers Jesus all the kingdoms of the world if He will just bow down and worship him. To wit Satan attempts to deceive Jesus to believe He can fulfill His divine purpose without God. He can save the world without going to the Cross—taking no thought of whose will He performs—His own will or God's will. In Romans 1:24ff and 2 Thessalonians 2:9ff, Paul refers to this temptation as the Lie. Shreve clarifies, "*The Secret* is not about getting what you want in life, it is about being god of your own life." He continues, "This temptation is as old as time itself. However, Joshua says we cannot have it both ways—we must choose—we *Will* either serve God, or we *Will* serve the flesh. Joshua challenges us with these words, 'Choose this day whom you will serve.'" Shreve cites Joshua 24:15 to reveal Joshua's personal choice, "As for me and my household, we *Will* serve the Lord" (author's emphasis).[303]

What does *The Secret* or *The Law of Attraction* really propagate? Walker writes, "The law of attraction … goes way beyond positive thinking. It begins to ascribe supernatural god-like characteristics and attributes to the human mind—to the person. So it's not just that you're positive; at the end of the book—you are actually God. That's not healthy positive thinking, in my opinion."[304] He reveals the real truth behind *The Secret*:

> What is the secret? Most readers of *The Secret* would probably say, "[T]houghts become things," or "Our minds are like powerful television transmitters," or perhaps "The Law of Attraction." You may be surprised to learn that every one of those answers is wrong. While Rhonda Byrne does share these secrets in her book, they are not *the* Secret. So what is the *real secret*? The casual reader will probably not catch it. Very few reviews of *The Secret* make mention of it. Most miss the main point.
>
> The most powerful secret in the book is not the Law of Attraction. It has nothing to do with attracting necklaces or visualizing new sports cars. The main secret is not about quantum mechanical theories or curing cancer. The most

> significant secret is not even about creating world peace... The lesser, minor secrets—the Law of Attraction, thoughts become things, thought transmission and vibration—may be found in the first few pages of *The Secret.* Like a good author, Rhonda Byrne saves the BIG SECRET, the most important secret, for the closing sections of her book. The real secret is not about things, it is about YOU. It is about your true nature. It is the sacred secret.[305]

Walker concludes his reply to "What is the secret?" with *The Secret's* own declaration: "You are God in a physical body. You are Spirit in the flesh. You are Eternal Life expressing itself as You... You are perfection. You are magnificence. You are the creator and you are creating the creation of You on this planet."[306] The sum of *The Secret's* thesis is, "You are God manifested in human form."[307]

The Secret clearly substitutes man for God and substitutes what *The Secret* proffers in lieu of God's Word as it weaves deceptions throughout. The naïve, the unsuspecting, and the rebellious who do not walk in truth and truthfulness are led away from the truth by the subtle lies of Satan in their various forms and rendering them defenseless against deception and error.

The writer of 2 Timothy warns believers against those who are "lovers of pleasure rather than lovers of God, having a form of godliness but denying its power. And from such people turn away! For of this sort are those who creep into households and make captives of gullible women loaded down with sins, led away by various lusts, always learning and never able to come to the knowledge of the truth" (2 Tim. 3:4–7). He continues, "For the time will come when they will not endure sound doctrine, but according to their own desires, because they have itching ears, they will heap up for themselves teachers; and they will turn their ears away from the truth, and be turned aside to fables" (4:3–4). The writer concludes with this admonition, "But you be watchful in all things, endure afflictions, do the work of an evangelist, fulfill your ministry" (v. 5).

The writer of 2 Corinthians encourages us to live our lives before one another as examples of the life of Christ. He pens, "You are our epistle written in our hearts, known and read by all men; clearly you are an epistle of Christ, ministered by us, written not with ink but by the Spirit of the living God, not on tablets of stone but on tablets of flesh, that is, of the heart" (3:2–3). Let truth and honesty be our mantle, let discerning truth from error be our safeguard, and let this be the living testimony that others read of our lives. Let His truth reign supreme in us and through us for all to see.

Chapter 8

DETRIMENTS OF THE LIE: DARKNESS, CONFUSION, CLOUDY VISION

> It is now a tacit assumption that the hallmark of modern education is skepticism, harking back more to the seventeenth-century model of Rene Descartes, whose quest for certainty began with the certainty of doubt. However, tragically, unlike Descartes, there is no god postulated to guard us against deception, and where Descartes began the modern skeptic has ended.
>
> —Ravi Zacharias[308]

The Lie
Negative Effects in the Believer

Absolute truth is the moral compass that sets the behavior of the believer. Where there is no absolute truth, there is no moral compass. The result is to turn to social ethics where societal behavior sets the standard. Author Larry John sums up the difference between morals and ethics.

> Morals: Conforming to a standard of right behavior
> Ethics: Choosing principles of conduct as a guiding philosophy[309]

When a believer allows social ethics to set the standard of behavior, the believer's behavior conforms to the world rather than God's eternal Truth. When we yield to political correctness rather than eternal truth and conform to secular humanism rather than Kingdom principles to order our lives, we lose our ability to see clearly to discern truth from error and thereby make wise, godly, sound-minded decisions and choices. Jesus admonishes: "The eye is the lamp of the body. So, if your eye is sound, your entire body will be full of light; But if your eye is unsound, your whole body will be full of darkness. If then the very light in you [your conscience] is darkened, how dense is that darkness!" (Matt. 6:22–23, AMP). Luke records Jesus' warning: "Make sure that the light you think you have is not actually darkness" (Luke 11:35, NLT). He declares the Truth of God's eternal Word: "Heaven and earth shall pass away, but my words shall not pass away" (24:35, KJV). The writers of Hebrews and Malachi confirm the unchanging God with these words: "Jesus Christ is the same yesterday, today, and forever" (Heb. 13:8), and "I am LORD, I change not" (Mal. 3:6). The apostle Paul admonishes:

> Do not be conformed to this world (this age), [fashioned after and adapted to its external, superficial customs], but be transformed (changed) by the [entire] renewal of your mind [by its new ideals and its new attitude], so that you may prove [for yourselves] what is the good and acceptable and perfect will of God, even the thing which is good and acceptable and perfect [in His sight for you].
>
> —ROMANS 12:2

Without absolute truth as the standard of behavior, the believer has no moorings and is like the Israelites when "there was no king in Israel, but every man did that which was right in his own eyes" (Judg. 17:6, KJV). Sandy Simpson pens:

> The state of Christianity today has returned to the same condition that Israel was in during the time of the judges. This statement in Judges 17:6 and 21:25 is not a positive

> statement about Israel, but a negative one. This sin of "doing that which was right in (their) own eyes" was what accounted for the sin of Micah in continuing in idol worship. There were no judges in the land to point out this sin or restrain the people from it. The law of God had been forsaken and replaced with subjectivism. This is exactly what we are seeing today in our postmodern, relativist culture. It is to be expected that the world will act like this, but this attitude has also entered and almost overwhelmed Christendom as we know it. Christianity is being remade in the image of imaginations of men (Rom. 1:21). The rules are being set by false teachers, and the Christian masses are quick to follow. Only those who listen to the judges of today, those with Holy Spirit and biblical discernment, will be saved in this age of apostasy.[310]

The psalmist declares, "Your Word is a lamp to my feet And a light to my path" (Ps. 119:105). Yet in the absence of truth, believers flounder. Imagine trying to drive a curvy mountain pass at midnight with no headlights and no moon to light the way. Destruction would be imminent, and its effects lasting. Jesus is the light of the world (John 8:12). Light dispels darkness; darkness is forever the servant to light. Jesus is the truth (14:6); He is the Word made flesh (1:14). Thus God's Word is Truth. There is safety in truth. Jesus prays on behalf of His followers, "Sanctify them [purify, consecrate, separate them for Yourself, make them holy] by the Truth; Your Word is Truth" (17:17, AMP). When the believer ceases to walk in God's Truth, there is only darkness, confusion, and cloudy vision. According to E. W. Bullinger there is only one Truth, and that is God's Truth:

> Only One Word is employed to denote a certain thing, though that word may be used and occur many times.
>
> The Hebrew noun for *Truth* is a remarkable illustration of this. Many are the words used for deceit and lies, but

> there is *only one word for truth.* God's truth is one! Man's lies are almost infinite! The [Hebrew] word (*Emeth*) means *firmness* and *stability, perpetuity, security.* This is what God is. This is exactly what man is not! Man is altogether vanity. "All men are liars" (Ps. cxvi. 11). His Mouth is full of cursing, deceit (Heb. pl., *deceits*), and fraud; under his tongue is ungodliness and vanity" (Ps. x. 7). "They speak vanity every one with his neighbour: with flattering lips and a double heart do they speak" (Ps. xii. 2).
>
> *Truth* is found only in the Word of God, in Christ, who says of Himself, the living Word, "I am the truth" (John xiv. 6) …
>
> Truth is heard only in the Word of God.[311]

Negative Effects in the Church

The negative effects of error in the Church are staggering. An article in *The Washington Times* by Julia Duin cites a recent George Barna report on truth among clergy in America. The article "Statistics: Moral Values, America a Christian Nation, and More" reflects alarming numbers.

> Only 51 percent of all senior Protestant pastors have what Mr. Barna called 'a Biblical worldview,' based on several criteria: believing that God is all knowing and all-powerful; that Jesus Christ never sinned; that Satan is real; that salvation only comes through faith in Christ and not by good deeds; that the Bible is accurate; that absolute moral truth exists and is described in the Bible; and that Christians should share their faith with nonbelievers.[312]

Charles E. Sellier released two television specials on *The Secret* to broadcast on national television following his 2007 national poll, which revealed 56 percent of consumers would purchase a DVD on *The Secret.* The research results:

- This concept tests at 56% on a five point scale. 56% would "Go Out of Their Way to Purchase" the DVD (the fifth choice).
- The gatekeepers/buyers at the big retail stores (Wal-Mart, Target, and others were sampled) like the concept. They rate it a 7 out of 10.
- The gatekeepers at the big 4 networks don't like it.
- The gatekeepers at the networks that GAP currently does business with do like it. (These television networks are *i*on Network, Trinity Broadcasting Network, Total Living Network, and others.)[313]

The Secret and its corresponding *Law of Attraction* are nothing more than God's Law of Reciprocity or Seedtime and Harvest, without God in the equation. Following is a short list of counterfeits of God's Biblical principles embedded in the New Age philosophy *The Secret*:

1. Bring every thought into captivity.
2. In everything give thanks.
3. Whatsoever is good, pure, loveable, lovely … think on these things.
4. All these things shall be added to you.
5. Whatsoever a man thinks in his heart, so is he.
6. Speak what is not as though it were.

As discussed in another chapter, Jesus *does not* say that one cannot access the heavenly places any other way than through Himself. What He *does* say is that anyone who accesses the heavenly places any other way than Himself is the same as a thief and a robber. In Christ's own words He elucidates, "Verily, verily, I say unto you, He who enters not by the door into the sheepfold (proclaims to us that there is a 'door,' and, in fact, only one 'door!'), but climbs up some other way, the same is a thief and a robber (using a 'way' other than Christ; He Alone as the Door)" (1 John 10:1, *The Expositor's Study Bible*).[314] The essence of *The Secret* is to access the heavenly places through means other than Christ. This clearly violates God's Holy Word and His divine principles.

R. Paul Stevens contends laypersons formulate their own theology when they give voice to personal opinions on a particular subject. He warns having one's own theology can be dangerous. Jesus' thought provoking warning gives us reason for pause:

> Not everyone who says to me, "Lord, Lord," will enter the kingdom of heaven, but only he who does the will of my Father who is in heaven. Many will say to me on that day, "Lord, Lord, do we not prophesy in your name, and in your name drive out demons and perform many miracles?" Then I will tell them plainly, "I never knew you. Away from me you evildoers!" Therefore everyone who hears these words of mine and puts them into practice is like a wise man who built his house on the rock. The rains came down, the streams rose, and the winds blew and beat against that house; yet it did not fall, because it had its foundation on the rock.
>
> —MATTHEW 7:21–25, NIV[315]

These sobering words demonstrate the import to walk in truth and obedience to God's Holy Word in thought and deed, of thinking God's thoughts after Him and following the promptings of His Holy Spirit—to have the mind of Christ on every issue.

Negative Effects in Education

The lack of truth in education places every individual and every segment of society in jeopardy. The lack of truth defeats the purpose of education, which is to communicate knowledge and truth to the learner. Without truth knowledge is ineffective, and without knowledge truth is ineffective. You can have a recipe for soufflé, but without the correct ingredients and the exact measurements and accurate baking instructions, your recipe will not yield soufflé. Nelson Mandela acknowledged the power education holds over the populace—for good or for evil—when he said, "Education is the most powerful weapon which you can use to change the world."[316] According to Pearcey, "The Christian worldview challenges the secular worldview at its core and eclipses the secular worldview through the discovery of DNA, thereby proving Intelligent Design."[317]

Exemplar of how the Christian worldview challenges the secular worldview (in regards to education and truth) is the hotly contested *evolution vs. creation* debate. Pearcey contends that "up to the advent of Charles Darwin's theory of evolution, science and Christianity support one another. Early scientists like Newton and Galileo acknowledge God's call to reveal His wisdom and design, and praise God through their scientific discoveries."[318] Yet she explains, "Ever since Darwin, evolutionists choose philosophy over against fact. Although, Darwin's theory of gradualism evolution and punctuated equilibrium are debunked as not viable theories most biologists continue to present Darwinism as fact."[319] The fact is most evolutionists refuse to entertain any hypothesis that does not support naturalism[320] over creationism.[321] Pearcey exposes the truth with this, "S. C. Todd admits, 'Even if all the data point to an intelligent designer, such an hypothesis is excluded from science because it is not naturalistic.'"[322]

John Elias warns against the lack of truth in Christian education, and is "highly critical of the established church"[323] that embraces the Enlightenment *philosophes* and propose "a new worldview totally devoid of God," and the *scientific method* which pervades Christian education today.[324] Dawkins admits that "genetics has become a branch of information technology. The genetic code is truly digital... This is not some vague analogy, it is the literal truth."[325] Mandela's words warn that the abuse of education can shape or reshape the values and the mindset of entire societies.[326] Editors Goodlad and McMannon believe the public purpose of education is socialization and unification of a societal mindset, and that its primary purpose is "not to teach that which is peculiar to any one of the professions; but to lay the foundation which is common to them all."[327] This is a dangerous proposition. Like Goodlad and McMannon, many educators believe the democratic approach to public education helps people determine personal talents, and that "schools ... may have little to do with the education of the soul or character, and, hence, little to do with the substantive development of democracy."[328] While Goodlad and McMannon argue the reality of the disintegration of "public morality ... and the disintegration of a national identity of all Americans,"[329] they acknowledge that as public life disintegrates so do the "norms, standards, values, and rules"[330] in public education. This leads to "bitter divisions over race, language, religion, and moral values"[331]—a vicious cycle which educational policymakers exploit to advance their personal agendas. Authors David Berliner and Bruce Biddle evidence the narcissistic trend maligning the public schools in America, contending that those in positions of power

> are pursuing a political agenda designed to weaken the nation's public schools, redistribute support for those schools so that privileged students are favored over needy students, or even abolish those schools altogether. To this end, they have been prepared to tell lies, suppress evidence, scapegoat educators, and sow endless confusion.[332]

In an effort to create competition through options in the education system to provide sound curriculum to better educate their children, many parents agree with vouchers. Goodlad and McMannon argue that rather than provide vouchers for private schools, public schools must draw parents back through incentives and help effect change in public education;[333] yet curriculum remains of paramount import to parents. Don Ernst of the Association for Supervision and Curriculum Development explains among those who create standards for "School-to-Work," there is "absolutely no language ... about education for moral and democratic purposes... People with lots of power—governors and others—are pushing school reform agendas without any sense of how schools might address the moral and political dimensions involved in educating our young citizens."[334] Ted Sizer pays tribute to parents who take a stand for sound curriculum with this sentiment, "Folks ... are saying, 'We're not gonna take this anymore... We can't wait around for the polity to argue this out. We're just gonna do it. And if you don't like it, do something about it.'"[335] He affirms, "Grassroots-level initiative on behalf of children is democracy in its purest form."[336]

Although the editors of *The Public Purpose of Education and Schooling* advocate that "personal well-being requires a civil society ... part of which is schooling that balances private and public purpose,"[337] Goodlad and McMannon relegate a preponderance of its substance to the common growth and common good of society rather than the personal growth and personal good of individuals. However, healthy individuals make healthy societies. Therefore, the greater emphasis of education is incumbent upon the latter while the former exposes the overarching ungodly mindset and approach of public education that shapes America's children.

To examine the state of decline of public education today, we need look no further than a daily local newspaper, which provides a snapshot of how deception impacts students in the public education system. Consider the headline and byline from the *Reporter-Herald*, December 2, 2008, Loveland, Colorado, which reads, "1 in 5 young adults has personality disorder: Mental illness on campus sometimes leads to violence."[338] The article reveals there are "numerous disorders with more than 5,000 young people ages 19 to 25,"[339] and continues, "Study co-author Dr. Mark Olfson of Columbia University and New York State Psychiatric Institute called the widespread lack of treatment particularly worrisome, [and] it should alert not only 'students and parents, but also deans and people who run college mental health services about the need to extend access to treatment.'"[340] Rather than explore how the lack of a sound moral compass and self-discipline may contribute to these alarming statistics, experts relegate culpability to pressures of "the pursuit of greater educational opportunities and employment prospects, development of personal relationships, and for some, parenthood."[341]

Negative Effects in Society

Trends and statistics reveal the decline of Truth and truthfulness in the Church, which has a subsequent negative effect on society. In his dissertation, "The Efficacy of Ministerial Training: An Assessment of Accredited and Non-accredited Theological Education from a Pastoral

Perspective," Arley S. Enloe sheds light on the deceptions that millions of Christians in America walk in today and provides statistics from the Barna Research Group which reveal nearly half of American protestant pastors have a secular worldview on absolute truth. These statistics reveal that 49 percent of protestant pastors in America do not believe "the accuracy of biblical teaching, the sinless nature of Jesus, the literal existence of Satan, the omnipotence and omniscience of God, salvation by grace alone, and the personal responsibility to evangelize."[342] Dietrich Bonhoeffer identifies a "cheap grace"[343] that asserts the lie that the Church can do whatever She chooses with impunity. In a recent poll among America's teens, the Josephson Institute exposes alarming statistics on the new morality among secular and Christian youth in America. The study reveals that teens who attend Christian schools are more likely to lie and cheat than teens who attend public schools. These alarming numbers translate into impending disaster on society as the teens of today become society's leaders tomorrow. Author Mike Wilson concludes from the study:

- If you want to see the future of a country, just look at the present generation of youth. The Josephson Institute, a California-based organization promoting character and ethics, did just that and the results were alarming. The good news is that not all American teens lie, cheat and steal, just the vast and overwhelming majority of them. The bad news is that teens attending private and religious schools are among the worst of them. The Institute's biannual survey of nearly 30,000 high schools indicated that 83 percent of students confessed to lying to a parent about something significant, but religious and private school students were some two percent more likely to lie to parents than those attending public schools.
- Moreover, 26 percent confessed to lying on at least one or two questions on the survey. But lying wasn't the only problem. The Institute reports, "Students attending non-religious independent schools reported the lowest cheating rate (47 percent) while 63 percent of students from religious schools cheated." Those attending religious schools were less likely to steal. The theft rate among all schools was 30 percent and some 19 percent of those who attend

religious schools admitted to stealing something from a store in the past year. Honor students, students involved in youth activities and student leaders were less likely to steal, but even among those, more than 20 percent stole something in the last year.

- The Josephson Institute says these results are alarming because someday soon these teens will be America's politicians, corporate executives, police, teachers, journalists, generals and parents. What's alarming to me is that the survey found that those who are attending religious private schools are overall slightly more likely to lie and cheat than those attending public schools. If this is true—well, maybe the public school kids are better liars on the survey than the Christian kids—we as Christians are doing a very poor job transferring Christian values and morals to our children and grandchildren.
- The Bible has a lot of good advice for raising children. Often quoted is Proverbs 22:6: "Train up a child in the way that he should go: and when he is old, he will not depart from it." Teaching a child right from wrong and the discipline to live a righteous life seems to be an ingredient missing in much of Christianity. Drifting away from the Bible and its instruction and relying on man's interpretations, curricula, or even the imbalance of showing grace and mercy without consequences are all recipes for disaster. Another Proverb, 13:34, says, "He that spares the rod, hates his son: but he that loves him chastens him quickly." We must do a better job teaching love, truth, honor, justice and responsibility.[344]

New faith trends reveal the decline of Truth in the Church and its subsequent negative impact on society—the effects are reaching "Any Town, U.S.A." according to the *Reporter-Herald*. This article reveals that pluralism in the world of religions is on the rise even among Christians in small towns across America. A third-page article features a picture of a young woman wearing a gold chain around her neck, and hanging from the gold chain are three religious icons. The center icon is the Cross of Christ, which represents the death and resurrection of the Savior of the world. To the left of the Cross is the Star of David representing the Jewish faith, and to the right of the Cross is the Crescent and Star representing the Islam faith. Beneath this photo reads, "Three women from New York City—Ranya Idliby, a Muslim; Suzanne Oliver, a Christian; and Priscilla Warner, a Jew—will speak in Fort Collins on Tuesday about their interfaith dialogue and the book that resulted, 'The Faith Club.'"[345] The caption across the photo reads, "Spiritual journey shared by Muslim, Christian and Jew inspire local women to do the same—Faithful Friends."[346] The article summarizes, "They [the three friends] share a common ancestor, Abraham, and they worship the same God."[347] Martha Conant, a resident of Fort Collins, Colorado, and professing Christian says, "We Christians understand our impact, our world is very Christian-oriented, but that doesn't mean that Christianity is the right answer for everybody."[348]

This article is representative of manifold Christians who walk in such deception through the lack of truth—at the very least—in their belief system. Without truth at the core of our belief system, we have no safeguard to discern truth from error.

The profound impact of the Lie on society is not new. Although the three major monotheistic world religions—Judaism, Islam, and Christianity—have ties to one another, the associations are *not* that of which the above article alludes. The account of a father and his two sons four thousand years ago ultimately engages the entire world. Abraham and his sons: Ishmael—his first son born to him of his wife's handmaid, an Egyptian woman bearing the name of Hagar (Gen. 16:3), and Isaac—his first son born to him of his wife, Sarah, and his son of promise, and the enmity between the siblings and its profound worldwide implications echo throughout the history of mankind and is incumbent upon society to this day.[349] Rabbi Shlomo Riskin states:

> The Jews and the Arabs are cousins... The founder of the Jewish people, Abraham, had two sons. One was Isaac, and the other was Ishmael—Isaac, who continued the Jewish line, Ishmael who began the Arab line... God promised Abraham that ... the land stretching from the

> Sinai Desert north and east to the Euphrates River would belong to his descendants.[350]

Today the world knows this region as the Holy Land, and the two brothers, or cousins born of the two brothers, the world knows as the nation of Israel and the Arab nations.[351]

God pronounces a blessing on Abraham's son Ishmael, and makes a covenant with his son Isaac:

> Then God said: "... Sarah your wife shall bear you a son, and you shall call his name Isaac; I will establish My covenant with him for an everlasting covenant, and with his descendants after him. And as for Ishmael, I have heard you. Behold, I have blessed him, and will make him fruitful, and will multiply him exceedingly. He shall beget twelve princes, and I will make him a great nation. But My covenant I will establish with Isaac, whom Sarah shall bear to you at this set time next year."
>
> —Genesis 17:19–21

Thus God blesses Abraham's son Ishmael with great wealth and power, apparent in the vast wealth and the world power Ishmael's descendants possess from the oil in some twenty-two Arab nations. Moreover God makes a covenant with Abraham's son Isaac, the son born of Abraham's wife, Sarah, for the land of Canaan, the land of promise, a covenant with Isaac and all his descendants—of whom Christ Jesus and His followers are descendants—as an everlasting possession to Isaac and all his descendants. The covenant relationship between the God of the Bible and Abraham's son Isaac rests on all the descendants of Isaac.

While *it is true* the three major world religions are direct descendants of Abraham; *it is not true* that the three share the same God as the article erroneously suggests. The truth is Jews and Christians, the descendants of Isaac, worship 'Adonay, while Muslims, the descendants of Ishmael, worship Allah; *and*—of a certainty—'Adonay and Allah *are not* one-and-the-same.

> The truth of the matter is that over the past thirty years, the American mind has been transformed dramatically. One of the most telling examples is our view of truth. In the 1960s, 65 percent of Americans said they believed the Bible is true; today that figure has dropped to 32 percent. Even more dramatically, today 67 percent of all Americans deny that there's any such thing as truth. Seventy percent say there are no moral absolutes. This confusion over truth is the fundamental crisis of our age.
>
> —Charles Colson[352]

Staggering Statistics
In the Believer

Many believers continue to wallow in what Dietrich Bonhoeffer identifies as "cheap grace," swallowing the lie that they can do whatever they choose; after all, their salvation is secure through the grace of God and the saving work of Calvary. Bonhoeffer warns, "It is the preaching of forgiveness without requiring repentance, baptism without church discipline, Communion without confession, absolution without personal confession. Cheap grace is grace without discipleship, grace without the cross, grace without Jesus Christ, living and incarnate."[353] *Naïveté* in the Church leaves us vulnerable to all forms of deception and every wind of doctrine which would lead us away from God's eternal Truth and into the cunning and the deceptiveness of Satan's perpetual Lie that "we can be like God" if we would but fall down and worship at his throne of *SELF.* Dr. Stanley warns, "Truthfulness is an essential character quality for believers. When it's lacking, both individuals and nations begin to crumble internally. Because Jethro understood this, he advised Moses, his son-in-law, to only appoint men who feared God and hated dishonest gain to positions of leadership (Exod. 18:21). But the truth is we all influence others, so we must be people who know and speak truth."[354]

In the Church

The Church leaders must take the initiative to counter the downward trend in the Body of Christ to compromise truth and truthfulness—moral character. They can do this through the integration and implementation of effective training of the Truth of God's eternal Word and of truth and truthfulness in the form of moral character into the programs in the local churches, in the schools, and in society. The alarming statistics we read from the late Chuck Colson that reveal that less than one-third of all Americans believe the Bible is true are indicative of the profound decline in the Church's view of truth. With staggering numbers such as these, if the Church is to help its parishioners safeguard against deception and error, its leadership must of necessity initiate teaching to effectively train and encourage its members that their daily walk must include God's eternal Truth, truth, truthfulness, honesty, integrity, humility, meekness, and all the manifold virtues Christ models to His Church in Scripture.

In Education

The absence—or undermining—of absolute and authentic truth in education and in the world at large through the humanist secularization of the education system, whether sacred or secular, is staggering. Because of this, rather than Christians leading the way in education with light, clarity, and clear vision to establish the necessity to walk in Truth and truthfulness to help discern truth from error, there is a propensity for Christians—leaders and lay persons alike—to flounder in darkness, confusion, and cloudy vision on the subject of Truth. The disturbing numbers in Mr. Colson's statistics reveal 67 percent of all Americans—including professing Christians—do not believe there is such a thing as truth in any form; and this is being taught in our educational institutions to our next generation of leaders. These numbers are indeed staggering by any paradigm and demonstrate that an inordinate number of Christian leaders and lay persons display darkness, confusion, and cloudy vision on the subject of Truth.

In Society

According to Mr. Colson an astonishing 70 percent of American society today does not believe there is such a thing as moral absolutes. These numbers reveal an incredible lack of understanding on the part of the Church of the necessity to walk in Truth and truthfulness in every area of life. If the Church is to be the salt and light God intends, It must emerge on the world scene and light the path for all to see and follow. While society wants to set its own standards of behavior, it still looks to the Church as the proverbial "beacon on a hill" to provide light, and clarity, and clear vision to a lost and dying world. Charles Stanley cautions, "Though the world is reluctant to hear the answer, Jesus tells us He is the truth and that He has given His Church the Spirit of truth so they can know and understand His Word. However, becoming people of truth won't happen automatically. We must be willing to accept and speak it, even when it causes us discomfort or pain (Gal. 4:16)."[355]

Therefore it behooves us as Christians to make changes surfeit to our daily walk with Christ "that He might present to Himself the church in all her glory, having no spot or wrinkle or any such thing; but that she would be holy and blameless" (Eph. 5:27, NAS). Indeed, until truth and truthfulness are in full operation in the individual lives of the followers of Christ providing light and clarity and clear vision to discern truth from error, the Church without spot or wrinkle is an elusive platitude to which She aspires in vain.

Part IV
THE GOSPEL TRUTH

The Red Thread
Discerning Truth from Error

Carol Roberts loved God and served Him faithfully in her daily walk, her prayer life, her church attendance, and serving in the Women's Ministry at her local church. At a certain point she thought she could stand to lose a few pounds. Although Carol knew the dangers of dabbling in the occult, she did not equate a certain popular exercise program that employed deep muscle control in its technique with the occult; therefore, she saw no danger in using this exercise technique. To shed those unwanted pounds, she joined the local exercise program with a friend who initially had suggested this particular program. Carol was faithful to her new exercise routine and was almost immediately rewarded with shedding some of those unwanted pounds; and—as a bonus—her energy levels were off the charts.

Carol was both amazed and pleased with such positive results so early-on in her new venture and decided she would increase her efforts to twice a week. Soon she increased to three and four times a week; all the while her physical and mental and emotional wellbeing seemed to increase exponentially—until. One day as Carol walked back up the steep hill from her mailbox at the bottom of her 500 foot driveway, she felt tired from her little trek to the mailbox and back. She realized she should have been a bit winded from her walk; but rather than breathing heavier from her exertion, she was not breathing at all. Then she heard that still small voice of the Holy Spirit warning her that she had learned to take such control of her muscles—both voluntary and involuntary—that she was losing her ability to breathe unless she was making a conscious effort to do so. How dangerous it can be when we decide to take control of our lives rather than yield that control to God.[356]

While Carol's case may be the exception rather than the rule, how many of us would acknowledge that once we start down that slippery slope of *compromise over conviction*, at what point do we dive in and throw caution to the wind, only to find ourselves at the foot of the Cross, our life in a shambles because we decided at some point to be god of our own life, deciding for ourselves what is right or wrong—good or bad? It is just like in the Garden when the serpent deceived Eve into believing she could be god of her own life by knowing good and evil for herself.

Chapter 9

BUT, I WOULD NEVER DO THAT: THE TRUTH ABOUT THE TRUTH

Then Y'shua said to them, "You all will be caused to sin this night because of Me, for it is written: 'I will strike the Shepherd, and the sheep of the flock will be scattered' (Zech. 13:7). But after My resurrection, I will meet you in Galilee." And Peter said to Him, "If all will be caused to sin because of You, I shall never be caused to sin." Y'shua said to him, "Truly I say to you that on this night before a cock crows you will deny Me three times." Peter said to Him, "Even if it would be necessary *for* me to die with You I will **not** deny You." And all the disciples said likewise.

And Peter was sitting outside in the courtyard: and one maid came to him saying, "And you were with Y'shua of Galilee." But he was denying *it* before all saying, "I do not know what you are saying." Then went he went out into the gateway another *maid* saw him, and said to those there, "This one was with Y'shua of Nazareth." And again he denied with an oath "I don't know the Man." And after a little while, as those who were standing *around* approached, they said to Peter, "Truly then you are *one* of them, for even your dialect gives you away." Then he

> began to curse and to swear, "I don't know the Man!" And immediately a cock crowed. Then Peter remembered the remark Y'shua had spoken that "Before a cock crows, you will deny Me three times." Then going outside he wept bitterly.
>
> —MATTHEW 26:31–35; 69–75,
> ONE NEW MAN TRANSLATION

Conviction or Compromise[357]
I Don't Know the Man!

Margaret Thatcher made this wise observation concerning compromise over conviction, "If you set out to be liked, you would be prepared to compromise on anything at any time, and you would achieve nothing."[358] When we face circumstances that challenge our convictions and friends and colleagues advise us to compromise, or when fear of monumental proportions grips us, will we stand by our convictions as Moses did? In response to Pharaoh's offer that would leave the children of Israel with no means to worship their God with sacrifice, he replies, "Our livestock also shall go with us; *there shall not a hoof be left behind*; for of them must we take to serve the Lord our God, and we know not with what we must serve the Lord until we arrive there" (Exod. 10:26, AMP, author's emphasis). Will our conviction and resolve be that of Moses: "Not one hoof"?[359] Or, will we compromise as with Peter, when, after his declaration to Jesus of his undying faithfulness to the Savior, he lied and flatly denied even knowing Jesus—not once, but three times: "I don't know the man!" (Matt. 26:72, 74, NIV; see also v. 70).

I Am Not!

It is apparent Peter loved God with all his heart. We see Peter had right motives and a sincere heart toward God as we read Jesus' commendation of his profound response to Jesus' query, "'But who do you say that I am?' Simon Peter answered and said, 'You are the Christ, the Son of the living God.' Jesus answered and said to him, '*Blessed are you, Simon Bar-Jonah, for flesh and blood has not revealed this to you, but My Father who is in heaven*'" (Matt. 16:15–17, author's emphasis). Yet shortly after this account Jesus rebuked Satan in Peter after Peter took Jesus aside and reproved Him for yielding to the cross (vv. 22–23). Given this, how is it Peter could not perceive his own capacity to deceive himself? If we are honest with ourselves, we will confess there is a bit of Peter in each of us. Let's look at ourselves in the mirror as we examine Peter's life more closely.

Peter trusted God enough to get out of the boat, but he began to sink when he shifted his focus from Jesus to the circumstances (Matt. 14:28–30). In his discomfort in the presence of the Glory of God, he decided he must do something, so he suggested building tents for Jesus, Elijah, and Moses (Luke 9:32–33). When Jesus prepared to wash the feet of His disciples, Peter refused to allow Jesus to perform such an act of humility on him until Jesus told him if he disallowed Jesus to wash his feet, he would have no part in Him. Upon hearing this, Peter then impetuously replies, "Then wash my whole body and head as well" (see John 13:9). Once again, we see Peter's flesh rising when he cuts off the ear of the centurion arresting Jesus (John 18:10). And, we can't forget Peter's argument with Jesus over whether he would deny Him, and we know how that turns out! "You are not also one of the disciples of this Man, are you? He said, I Am Not!" (v. 17, AMP).

This pattern continued in Peter's life when during breakfast by the seaside while Jesus was restoring Peter, rather than considering his own condition, his mind was on the status of another. He queries Jesus, "But Lord what about this man?" (John 21:21) to which Jesus replies, "If I will that he remain till I come, what is that to you? You follow Me" (v. 22). (See John 21:14–22.) After Jesus' resurrection and ascension, Peter had a marvelous epiphany and—with conviction rather than compromise—he preached to the masses with 3,000 coming to repentance in one day (Acts 2:41); and he wrote his letters where he warned us to be aware of the value of truth. Yet, even after such success, it took God three attempts at telling Peter that he was to minister to the Jews as well as the Gentiles, before Peter finally yielded to God's command (see Acts 10:9–16). Paul rebuked Peter for his "When in Rome, do as the Romans" attitude (see Galatians

2:11–21). How many of us would be honest enough to acknowledge we identify with Peter in every one of his weaknesses?

"Ah," but you say, "While I may identify with Peter's impetuousness and double-mindedness, I would never compromise my convictions. I may tell an occasional lie and—even then—only to spare the feelings of a friend or protect my family from harm or guard myself against fear or embarrassment, but I would never compromise my convictions."

Yes, That Was the Price!

Ananias and Sapphira were a part of the first Church, and—being of "one heart and one soul" (Acts 4:32ff)—all the members were to sell their property and bring the proceeds into a common storehouse for all to use. Apparently the couple worked hard to make a good living and to set aside a little for their retirement. Possibly they knew they had twice as much in savings as the others and thus justified holding back a portion for themselves—which would have been all right if the story ended there. But the two not only decided together they would keep a portion of the money for themselves, they colluded to lie and tell Peter that what they were bringing was the entire amount of the sale of their land. Acts chapter 5 records:

> But a certain man named Ananias, with Sapphira his wife, sold a possession. And he kept back part of the proceeds, his wife also being aware of it, and brought a certain part and laid it at the apostles' feet. But Peter said, 'Ananias, why has Satan filled your heart to lie to the Holy Spirit and keep back part of the price of the land for yourself? … Why have you conceived this thing in your heart? You have not lied to men but to God.' Then Ananias, hearing these words, fell down and breathed his last.
>
> —Acts 5:1–5

When Sapphira came in several hours later, Peter queried her, and her answer was the same as that of Ananias: "'Yes,' she replied, 'that was the price'" (Acts 5:8, NLT). "Then Peter said to her, 'How is it that you have agreed together to test the Spirit of the Lord?'" (v. 9). An attempt to deceive the Holy Spirit is one of the gravest offenses against God—particularly when we *conspire with another* to test the Spirit of the Lord—and Sapphira's end was the same as her husband's (Acts 5:10). As Ananias and Sapphira corroborated one another's lie in an attempt to deceive the Holy Spirit, they sealed their fate and both died on the spot.

I Didn't Laugh!

Sarah was no stranger to deception. Angels of God appeared to her husband, Abraham, and announced to him that in one year's time his wife, Sarah, would bear him a son. Now, at this stage of their life, Sarah was well into her nineties and Abraham was approaching 100 years. As she quietly listened from inside the tent to the conversation between Abraham and the Angels outside, and she contemplated what she had overheard and considered the physical likelihood of it coming to pass, Sarah laughed to herself. She realized the Angels of the Lord had heard her laughter when she heard the Lord ask Abraham why his wife was laughing. In great fear and awe, she lied. She replies, "'I did not laugh;' for she was afraid. And He said, 'No, but you did laugh!'" (Gen. 18:15, AMP). As was the case with Sarah, the Holy Spirit is faithful to gently yet clearly convict us when we sin. It is up to us to be quick to acknowledge our sin, confess it to God, and repent of it as the Holy Spirit sheds His spotlight of Truth on our misdeed. This requires an open and intimate relationship with God.

I Am He!

Conversely, we see Jesus speak the truth at all times—no matter the cost. In the Garden of Gethsemane the night before His crucifixion—knowing full well what was about to happen—rather than wait until the soldiers and guards of the high priests and Pharisees approached Him, Jesus walked toward His accuser and His captors and began to query them. "Who are you looking for?" (John 18:4, NLT). They reply, "Jesus the Nazarene" (v. 5, NLT). Jesus responds in all Truth, "I AM He" (v. 5, NLT). The magnitude and power of the Truth behind His declaration of His identity caused those who had come to seize Him to fall backwards to the ground (v. 6).

Apparently a cloud of confusion beset the soldiers and guards; and as they came out of their stupor and raised themselves to their feet, Jesus reminded them of their mission when He queries again, "Who are you looking for?" (John 18:7, NLT). Yet in the midst of all this, His concern was for the safety of His followers as He tells the guards and soldiers, "'I told you that I AM HE… And since I am the one you want, let these others go.' He did this to fulfill his own statement: 'I did not lose a single one of those you have given me'" (vv. 8–9, NLT). Because of His utter truth at all times, He never loses sight of who He is and His purpose for coming to earth.

You Say I Am a King!

Again, Jesus refused to compromise His conviction to walk in truth at all times when Pontius Pilate confronted Jesus concerning whether He was a King. Ignoring the inevitable consequences, He tells Pilate, "You say I am a king" (John 18:37, NLT). He continues,

> [You speak correctly!] For I am a King. [Certainly I am a King!] This is why I was born, and for this I have come into the world, to bear witness to the Truth. Everyone who is of the Truth [who is a friend of the Truth, who belongs to the Truth] hears and listens to My voice.
>
> —JOHN 18:37, AMP

Jack Hayford warns that we think we can dabble with the serpent—charm the snake, so to speak. But the day will come when that serpent will strike and deal its deadly blow when we are already trapped in a set of circumstances that are unmanageable and completely out of control.[360] James admonished us to submit ourselves to God, and resist the devil and he will flee from us (James 4:7). The writer of Ephesians warned us to leave no foothold for the devil and to make no provision for evil (4:27). Second Corinthians instructed us to bring every thought into captivity to the obedience of Christ, rather than open our minds to every fleeting thought that would distract us away from His purpose for our lives (10:5).

As these Scriptural accounts posit the import to walk in the Truth as well as walk in truth and honesty in every aspect of our life, I think we can agree God does not take lightly compromise over conviction—regardless of the motivation. Moreover, in light of all the evidence this book presents, we can agree that Truth—at every level in our life—is of the utmost import to the Father and to that end must be of paramount import to us.

Jesus is our example, for He understands we cannot walk in truth *and* deception—the end results are devastating. We must make a choice: either we choose to walk in truth, or we choose to not walk in truth—which leads to deception. The two are mutually exclusive; thus we cannot have it both ways. Truth brings life; deception brings death—physically or spiritually. In Matthew chapter 6 Jesus admonishes us, "No one can serve two masters; for either he will hate the one and love the other, or he will stand by and be devoted to the one and despise and be against the other. You cannot serve God and mammon (deceitful riches, money, possessions, or whatever is trusted in)" (v. 24, AMP).

God sets before us this choice:

> Today I have given you the choice between life and death, between blessings and curses. Now I call on heaven and earth to witness the choice you make. Oh, that you would choose life, so that you and your descendants might live! You can make this choice by loving the LORD your God, obeying him, and committing yourself firmly to him. This is the key to your life. And if you love and obey the LORD, you will live long in the land the LORD swore to give your ancestors Abraham, Isaac, and Jacob..
>
> —DEUTERONOMY 30:19–20, NLT

To that end, let us resolve—from this day forward—to walk in the Truth of God's Word, to walk in truth and honesty in our daily life, and to reject all deceit and dishonesty, compromise and duplicity; submitting ourselves to God and resisting the devil and all his craftiness and slyness (see James 4:7); and seeking the One who is Truth at all times and in every circumstance, for He declares that if we know the Truth, then the Truth *shall* set us free! (see John 8:32). Amen, and amen!

Chapter 10

IMPLEMENTING TRUTH IN DAILY LIFE: BEGINNING AT THE BEGINNING

> In the beginning was the Word, and the Word was with God, and the Word was God ... And the Word became flesh and dwelt among us, and we beheld His glory, the glory as of the only begotten of the Father, full of grace and truth.
>
> —John 1:1; 14–15

The Question Is *The Who*

Some of you may say you were born into the Christian faith—the faith of your father or mother. Others of you may say you became a Christian when you were baptized into the faith as a child. Still others may say you became a Christian when you completed Catechism or when you were confirmed as a Christian by your particular denomination.

I was born into a mainstream Christian denomination where I was baptized at three years of age, attended Sunday school and vacation Bible as a child, and was confirmed at twelve years old. I could recite the major Bible stories like Joseph and his coat of many colors, Peter walking on the water, and Jesus and the loaves and fishes. I said my prayers every night, wondering if that might be the night Jesus would return. But I had this notion that if I were to die having even one sin on my soul, I would not go to heaven. Though I knew Jesus was the Savior of the world, if someone were to ask me if I knew Jesus personally, I would have to say, "No." I knew Jesus in the same way I know the President of the United States—I could point Him out in a crowd or in a picture, but I had never had a personal encounter or conversation with Him.

❖

> Jesus answered, "Most assuredly, I say to you, unless one is born of water and the Spirit, he cannot enter the kingdom of God. That which is born of the flesh is flesh, and that which is born of the Spirit is spirit. Do not marvel that I said to you, 'You must be born again.'"
>
> —John 3:5–7

The What

I finally met Jesus personally on Easter Sunday in 1966 at a church in North Hollywood, California, when He was introduced to me for the first time as my personal Savior. I walked the aisle to the altar that morning and asked forgiveness for my sins and invited Jesus into my heart to become my personal Lord and Savior. The writer of the book of Romans explains that "if you confess with your mouth the Lord Jesus and believe in your heart that God has raised Him from the dead, you will be saved. For with the heart one believes unto righteousness, and with the mouth confession is made unto salvation" (Rom. 10:9–10). At the very moment I invited Jesus into my heart, I was saved, I was born again—born of the Spirit, and my life would never be the same.

❖

> For He says: "In an acceptable time I have heard you, And in the day of salvation I have helped you." Behold, now is the accepted time; behold, now is the day of salvation.
>
> —2 CORINTHIANS 6:2

The When

While tradition is good and can help us live a good, clean life, tradition cannot save us; it is no substitute for what Jesus terms being "born of the Spirit." Religion is man's pursuit of God; salvation through Christ is God's pursuit of man "for the Son of Man has come to seek and to save that which was lost" (Luke 19:10). Jesus explains, "That which is born of the flesh is flesh, and that which is born of the Spirit is spirit" (John 3:6). No matter how good we are, we can never be good enough. Scripture declares "all our righteousnesses are like filthy rags" (Isa. 64:6). Sin separates us from God, but Jesus reconciles us to Him. Scripture tells us "all have sinned and fall short of the glory of God" (Rom. 3:23) and "the wages of sin is death" (Rom. 6:23a). But it also says, "The gift of God is eternal life" (v. 23b). John 3:16 tells us, "For God SO LOVED the world that He gave His one and only Son, that WHOEVER believes in Him shall not perish but have eternal life" (NIV, author's emphasis).

If your story is similar to mine—if you cannot say with absolute certainty where you would spend eternity if you were to die at this moment, then for you today is the day to be born of the Spirit. *Knowing if you are born of the Spirit is like knowing if you are married—you're either married, or you're not—there's no confusion.*[361] If you cannot say with certainty you have been born of the Spirit and that your final destination is heaven, then pray this prayer with me:

> *God, I believe no matter how good I am, and no matter how well I obey the Commandments, I am still a sinner and cannot earn my way to heaven. Please forgive my sins and come into my heart. Thank You that I am now born of the Spirit, I am now a child of God, and I am now heaven-bound. My eternal destination is heaven where I will live*

with You for all eternity. For it is in the mighty name of Jesus, I pray, Amen.

> For those who live according to the flesh set their minds on the things of the flesh, but those who live according to the Spirit, the things of the Spirit. For to be carnally minded *is* death, but to be spiritually minded *is* life and peace.
>
> —ROMANS 8:5–6

The Why

Satan's strategy to lead us astray is three-fold and is as old as time. He simply and effectively appeals to the lust of our flesh, the lust of our eyes, and the pride of life (1 John 2:16). In the Garden he appeals to: (1) Eve's flesh, "the tree was good for food," (2) her eyes, "it was pleasant to the eyes," and (3) her pride of life, "desirable to make one wise" (Gen. 3:6). Eve made a deadly mistake when she engaged in dialogue with the enemy of her soul and consequently succumbed to temptation and satisfied the lust of the flesh, the lust of the eyes, and the pride of life, setting the stage for all of mankind throughout the ages (see Genesis 3:1–5).

Yet Jesus—the Second Adam—understood man's weakness; for He also was tempted in all manner of sin, yet He sinned not: "For we do not have a high priest who is unable to sympathize with our weaknesses, but we have one who has been tempted in every way, just as we are—yet he did not sin" (Heb. 4:15, NIV). How did He do this? Through total submission to the will of the Father; Jesus only did what He saw the Father doing (John 5:19).

Jesus set the example of how to walk in truth in daily life. He led the path with integrity in His wilderness experience when Satan came to Him three times to tempt Him to relent to the lust of the flesh, the lust of the eyes, and the pride of life. Yet Jesus did not engage in dialogue with Satan, rather He rebuked him and used the Word of God as a weapon against the Lies of the enemy (see Luke 4:1–14). In a spirit of true humility, He said,

> I am able to do nothing from Myself [independently, of My own accord—but only as I am taught by God and as I get His orders]. Even as I hear, I judge [I decide as I am bidden to decide. As the voice comes to Me, so I give a decision], and My judgment is right (just, righteous), because I do not seek or consult My own will [I have no desire to do what is pleasing to Myself, My own aim, My own purpose] but only the will and pleasure of the Father Who sent Me.
>
> —John 5:30, AMP

In a genuine spirit of meekness, He submitted to the will of the Father "saying, Father, if You are willing, remove this cup from Me; yet not My will, but [always] Yours be done" (Luke 22:42, AMP).

> Study to show yourself approved to God, a workman that needs not to be ashamed, rightly dividing the word of truth.
>
> —2 Timothy 2:15, AKJV

The How

Paul exhorts us to put off the old nature of corruption and put on the new nature of truth (see Ephesians 4:22–24). Experts say it takes twenty-one days to break old habits and make new habits. Read Bible passages on Truth, honesty, and selflessness morning and night, and pray for God's help to apply His Word to daily life for the next twenty-one days. In so doing, break old habits of exaggeration or dishonesty, and selfishness and form new habits of being truthful in every circumstance, loving others enough to be completely honest with them at all times, and caring about others more than self under all conditions. According to Dr. Donald Colbert, "It takes twenty-one days to form a habit, and forty days to form a mindset."[362] The following pages contain a three-part lesson plan to follow daily for twenty-one days to form new habits or forty days to form a new mindset. This, alongside our cooperation with the Holy Spirit to work in us to make God's Word come alive in us, will help us make the changes we desire—and that God desires in us.

The apostle Paul reminds us it is "not that we are sufficient of ourselves to think of anything as being from ourselves, but our sufficiency *is* from God … for the letter kills, but the Spirit gives life" (2 Cor. 3:5–6b). As we confess it is God who works in us, as we acknowledge our own lack and God's sufficiency, and as we submit ourselves to His Lordship in every area of our lives, He is able to accomplish that which pleases Him in us and through us. As you follow the Twenty-One Days to Truth plan in chapter 11, ask the Father to make His Truth come alive in you by the power of His Holy Spirit. Do this and watch Him work the miracle of Truth in your life and in the lives of those closest to you.

But, first, retake the Exercise in Truth test on the following page and compare your new answers with your answers in the test you took at the beginning of the book.

An Exercise in Truth
The Dress; The Credit; The Windfall: DoubleTake

Answer these questions according to what you would do in each scenario.

The Dress

A friend asks how you like her new dress. In your opinion, her new dress is unflattering to her, but you don't want to hurt her feelings by telling her so. What would you do?

____

____.

The Credit

Your boss credits you for the success of a recent project. No one except you knows the credit for the success of this project belongs to a co-worker and not you. What would you do?

____

____.

The Windfall

The bank teller inadvertently forgets to post your $2000 withdrawal, and you notice on your next bank statement the $2000 is still in your account. What would you do?

____

____.

If your answers are different from the answers you gave in the test at the beginning of the book, why do you think this is so?

____

____.

If your answers are not different, why do you think this is so?

____

____.

Part V
A CLOSER LOOK

The Red Thread
Discerning Truth from Error

The temptation ever before us is to go along with the crowd—even if it means to walk in deceit rather than truth. Thus we compromise truth and set our standard of behavior by the current standard popular among our friends and acceptable by society. George Orwell contends, "During times of universal deceit, telling the truth becomes a revolutionary act."[363] He concludes, "The further a society drifts from the truth the more it will hate those who speak it."[364]

Yet amid the decline in truth and the rise of deception around the globe, there is a glimmer of hope among our young people today. A recent article in the *Washington Times* defies the universal deceit to which Orwell refers, and epitomizes what it means to walk in truth and honesty despite their decline in societal trends.

The article titled "Good Samaritans: Teens return bag with 85K inside" reads:

Talk about good Samaritans. Two teens riding aboard a Norwegian train had their truth and honesty meter put to full test this week, as they found a bag of cash left on a nearby seat.

"When I opened the bag, the first thing I saw were these wads and wads of bills," said one of the teens, 16, in a report from *Agence France-Presse*.

His first reaction? Not to keep it—but "to call the police," he said.

They delved deeper into the bag—which contained $81,500, all in cash—and found the owner's passport, AFP said. The owner, an elderly man in his 70s, was called to retrieve the cash at police headquarters, AFP said.

The train had been making a run between Oslo and a small southeastern Norway town, AFP said. Police cited in the report said they don't suspect the owner of the cash committed any crime.[365]

Indeed, our modern-day "Shadrach, Meshach, and Abednego" teens would not bow to the idol of universal deceit. When faced with their Exercise in Truth, our two young heroes walked away from their test with far more than the booty in the bag—they walked away with their reputation intact, their integrity secure, their conscience clear, and—without doubt—their ability to discern truth from error alive and fully functioning!

Chapter 11

TWENTY-ONE DAYS TO TRUTH: READ, PRAY, LIVE

> Teach me your way, O Lord, and I will walk in your truth; give me an undivided heart, that I may fear your name.
>
> —Psalm 86:11, NIV

How to Walk in Truth
Wax On – Wax Off

In the 1984 film *The Karate Kid* the life coach of the main character, Danny Larusso, promises to solve Danny's seeming insurmountable problem with an unlikely solution. To prepare Danny to defend himself against his arch enemies, the coach has him wax a car—carefully instructing him how to apply and remove the wax—"wax on wax off"—is how he instructs the teen. Little does Danny know the "wax on wax off"[366] exercise would build the precise muscles in him required to defeat his enemies. In the same way, the Twenty-One Days to Truth is an exercise designed to build character in its participants to a point where truth and truthfulness would become second-nature to those trained by it.

This exercise is designed to soften our heart toward God and toward others to a point where we become sensitive to God's voice and quick to obey as He bids, "I will give you a new heart and put a new spirit within you; I will take the heart of stone out of your flesh and give you a heart of flesh. I will put My Spirit within you and cause you to walk in My statutes, and you will keep My judgments and do *them*" (Eze. 36:26–27).

Three Steps to Truth in Twenty-One Days

As we pursue a life committed to walking in Truth always and in every way, there are three time-tested basics that will help us on our journey of truth: (1) Read—Scripture Reading, (2) Pray—Communication with God, and (3) Live—Life Application: Read, Pray, Live. As we embark on our pursuit of Truth and truthfulness in our daily life, let us be mindful of the five requisites to put off our old nature and put on our new nature: (1) be honest with God and man; (2) trust God and not self; (3) fear God and not man; (4) walk in God's love; and (5) obey God.

Read

There are Scriptures specific to the goals of this plan listed for both morning and evening reading in the companion Workbook to *Truth War*. It is suggested that you read Scriptures on Truth and truthfulness in addition to your normal Bible reading and daily devotions, for it is within the Scriptures that we find the verification of Truth. The writer of Acts tells us that when the Bereans were taught by the disciples, "they received the word with all readiness," but they also "searched the Scriptures daily to find out whether these things were so" (Acts 17:11). He who is the Truth declares, "You search the Scriptures ... and these are they which testify of Me" (John 5:9).

Pray

In the sixth chapter of the Gospel of Matthew, Jesus provided the perfect example of how to pray in what has become known as The Lord's Prayer. He instructs:

> Pray, therefore, like this: Our Father Who is in heaven, hallowed (kept holy) be Your name. Your kingdom come,

> Your will be done on earth as it is in heaven. Give us this day our daily bread. And forgive us our debts, as we also have forgiven (left, remitted, and let go of the debts, and have given up resentment against) our debtors. And lead (bring) us not into temptation, but deliver us from the evil one. For Yours is the kingdom and the power and the glory forever. Amen.
>
> —Matthew 6:9–13, amp

Among the many Bible scholars and theologians who break down The Lord's Prayer as a model for how to pray, Dr. Jack Hayford provides a straightforward, beneficial structure for how to effectively pray. Following is a simple adaptation of Hayford's formula to pray from The Lord's Prayer: (1) worship; (2) ask; (3) forgive; and (4) praise.[367] We will follow this structure for our daily prayer time. As the Holy Spirit reveals areas of need; repent, renounce, and replace[368] that negative behavior with God's Truth.

Live

It is not enough to merely read about, pray about, or even learn about Truth. For it to become a part of your character, you have to live it or apply it. It takes twenty-one days to make or break a habit (forty days to change a mindset), so be consistent. As the Holy Spirit reveals an area that needs to be dealt with, ask Him to help you make this change by gently reminding you as often as necessary to effect real and lasting change in your life, your daily habits, and your thinking.

Truth War: Discerning Truth from Error has a companion workbook, *Truth War: Discerning Truth from Error Workbook*, available with a list of activities suggested for you to follow each day in which you will watch for opportunities to walk in Truth in the form of integrity, humility, and meekness.

For an expanded version of the twenty-one day lesson plan for personal study, group study, or course study, the companion *Truth War: Discerning Truth From Error Workbook* contains a Study Guide. Also, a Journey of Truth Journal is included in the workbook to log your struggles and successes along your journey of truth. The journal contains forty-two pages; enough for those who desire to take the forty-day challenge to form a new mindset of truth and truthfulness in their daily life. For information on how to acquire this valuable tool to further assist you on your journey of truth, see Other Books and DVDs Available below or visit www.paracletepro.com. *Truth War: Discerning Truth from Error* and its companion *Truth War: Discerning Truth from Error Workbook* are also available through amazon.com, most Christian distributors, and your local Christian bookstore.

Other Books and DVDs Available

Other titles available through ParacleteProTruth:

Truth War: Discerning Truth from Error Workbook with Study Guide and Journey of Truth Journal

The Theology of Truth – Syllabus for 10-Hour Course on Truth

Change the Heart Change the World: A Totally New Perspective on the Israeli/Palestinian-Arab Conflict - DVD

Change the Heart Change the World: A Totally New Perspective on the Israeli/Palestinian-Arab Conflict - DVD 4-week Curriculum Package

For more information on pricing and how you can acquire these titles and others:

Call: 1-970-669-9443, or toll free at 1-877-669-9443
Email: marsha.rano@comcast.net
marsha.rano@gmail.com, or
marsha.rano@paracletepro.com
Visit: www.paracletepro.com

APPENDIX 1
OTHER SOURCES

Although the following list of sources are not cited in the body of this work *per sé*, each work in this list is an important contributor to the contents of this work in that each provides significant insights and offers valuable contributions to the thesis of this work. The works in this appendix that specifically lecture to the subject of the Israeli/Arab Conflict are particularly helpful to recognize the truth about the ownership of the land of Israel and offer a unique perspective on the import of truth and the profound ramifications of truth—or its lack—on a worldwide scale.

Anderson, Neil T. "We Are Butterflies." *Neil Anderson's Daily In Christ, Freedom In Christ Ministries*: 1–2. http://www.crosswalkmail.com (accessed October 30, 2008).

______. "Reprogramming the Mind." *Neil Anderson's Daily In Christ, Freedom In Christ Ministries:* 1–2. www.crosswalkmail.com (accessed August 11, 2008).

Anthony, Michael J., ed. *The Evangelical Dictionary of Christian Education.* Grand Rapids, MI: Baker Books, 2001, s.v. "Synagogue Schools." Quoted in Michael J. Anthony and Warren S. Benson, *Exploring the History and Philosophy of Christian Education: Principles for the 21st Century,* Grand Rapids, MI: Kregel Publications, 2003.

Ashton-Warner, Sylvia. *Teacher.* 1964. Quoted in Earl V. Pullias, with Ronald E. Cottle, *A Teacher: Models of Excellence,* Columbus, GA: TEC Publications, 2005.

Balfour, Arthur James. "Balfour Declaration 1917." *The Avalon Project at Yale Law* (November 1917). http://www.yale.edu/lawweb/avalon/mideast/balfour.htm (accessed October 13, 2007).

Barna, George. *The Second Coming of the Church.* Nashville, TN: Word Publishing, 2001. Quoted in John Jackson, *PastorPreneur: Pastors and Entrepreneurs Answer the Call*, Friendswood, TX: Baxter Press, 2003.

Berlin, Adele, and Marc Zvi Brettler, eds. *The Jewish Study Bible.* New York, NY: Oxford University Press, 2004.

Bloch-Smith, Elizabeth. "Life in Judah from the perspective of the dead." *Near Eastern Archaeology* 64, no. 2 (June 2002). http://newfirstsearch.oclc.org/ (accessed October 11, 2007).

Blomberg, Craig L. Interview of "Biblical Authors—Who Actually Wrote the Bible?" (ca. 2002). Ancient Secrets of the Bible Collection II. Grizzly Adams Productions Library, Baker City, OR.

Bronson, Rachel. "The Reluctant Mediator." *Washington Quarterly* 25, no. 4 (Autumn 2002).

Burge, Gary M. *Whose Land: Whose Promise? What Christians Are Not Being Told about Israel and the Palestinians.* Cleveland, OH: The Pilgrim Press, 2003.

_______. *Who Are God's People in the Middle East? What Christians are not being told about Israel and the Palestinians.* Grand Rapids, MI: Zondervan Publishing House Academic and Professional Books, 1993.

Canfield, Jack. Interview of "The Secret—The Secret Has Traveled Through Centuries … To Reach You." Fitzroy, Victoria, Australia: Prime Time Productions, (ca. 2005).

Darling-Hammond, Linda, and Jacqueline Ancess. "Democracy and Access to Knowledge." In Roger Soder, ed., *Democracy, Education, and the Schools*, San Francisco, CA: Jossey-Bass, 1996. Quoted in John L. Goodlad, and Timothy J. McMannon, eds., *The Public Purpose of Education and Schooling*, San Francisco, CA: Jossey-Bass, 1997.

Dawood, N. J., trans. with notes. *The Koran with a Parallel Arabic Text.* New York, NY: The Penguin Group, 2000.

DuBois, W.E.B. "The Freedom to Learn." In Philip S. Foner, ed., *W.E.B. DuBois Speaks*, New York, NY: Pathfinder, 1970. Quoted in John L. Goodlad, and Timothy J. McMannon, eds., *The Public Purpose of Education and Schooling*, San Francisco, CA: Jossey-Bass, 1997.

Dyer, Charles H., and Gregory A. Hatteberg. *The New Christian Traveler's Guide to the Holy Land.* Chicago, IL: Moody Publishers, 2006.

Edman, Irwin, ed. *The Works of Plato.* 1928. Quoted in Earl V. Pullias, with Ronald E. Cottle, *A Teacher: Models of Excellence*, Columbus, GA: 2005.

Edwards, Laurence. "No Rest(s) for the Wicked." *Sabbat* 5, no. 37 (July 7, 2001). http://urj.org/Articles/index.cfm?id=2819 (accessed March 1, 2008).

Elass, Mateen. *Understanding the Koran: A Quick Christian Guide to the Muslim Holy Book.* Grand Rapids, MI: Zondervan Publishing House, 2004.

Ellison, Stanley A. *The Arabic-Israeli Conflict: Who Owns the Land?* Portland, OR: Multnomah Press, 1991.

Ellison, Stanley A., and Charles H. Dyer. *Who Owns the Land? The Arabic-Israeli Conflict.* Wheaton, IL: Tyndale House Publishers, 2003.

Epp, Frank H. *Whose Land Is Palestine? The Middle East Problem in Historical Perspective.* Grand Rapids, MI: William B. Eerdmans Publishing Company, 1970.

Feith, Douglas, J. "A Strategy for Israel." *Commentary* 104, S (1997). http://newfirstsearch.oclc.org/images/WSPL/wsppdfl/HTML/03809/LU8UD/YSH.HTM (accessed October 10, 2007).

Fleming, Stanley F. *Gate Breakers: Answering Cults with Prayer, Love and Witnessing*, Book One. Columbus, GA: TEC Publications, 2000.

______. *Gate Breakers: Answering World Religions and the Occult with Prayer, Love, and Witnessing*, Book Two. Columbus, GA: TEC Publications, 2000.

Fredrichs, Jonathan. "Whose Land Is It? Apartheid in Israel/Palestine." *Christian Century* 119, no. 15 (July 30, 2002). http://newfirstsearch.oclc.org/images/WSPL/wsppdfl/HTML/03891/1EX1H/7FX.HTM (accessed October 11, 2007).

Gamzu, Yossi. "Isaac and Ishmael Write About Each Other." *Judaism* 3, no. 35 (Summer 1986). http://search.ebscohost.com/ehost/login.aspx?direct=true&db=rlh&AN=4881137&site=ehost-live (accessed October 12, 2007).

Garlow, James L., and Rick Marschall. *The Secret Revealed: Exposing the Truth About the Law of Attraction*. New York, NY: FaithWords, 2007.

Gay, Peter. *Age of Enlightenment*. New York, NY: Time, 1996. Quoted in Michael J. Anthony, and Warren S. Benson, *Exploring the History and Philosophy of Christian Education: Principles for the 21st Century*, Grand Rapids, MI: Kregel Publications, 2003.

Glaubach, Eliezer. "The Struggle for Freedom of Religion in the Holy Land: Solutions in Relation to the Middle East Crisis." *Dialogue & Alliance* 16, no. 2 (Fall–Winter 2002–2003). http://newfirstsearch.oclc.org/ (accessed October 10, 2007).

Goldmann, Eva, and Zeev Goldmann. *The Jewish People and Their Promised Land*. Thames, London: Thames and Hudson Ltd., 1968.

Hayford, Jack W. *E Quake: A New Approach to Understanding the End Time Mysteries in the Book of Revelation*. Nashville, TN: Thomas Nelson, 1999.

______. *The Key to Everything*. Lake Mary, FL: Charisma House, 1993.

Hess, Richard S. Interview of "Biblical Authors—Who Actually Wrote the Bible?" (ca. 2002). Ancient Secrets of the Bible

Collection II. Grizzly Adams Productions Library, Baker City, OR.

Hicks, Esther, and Jerry Hicks. *Ask and It Is Given: Learning to Manifest Your Desires*. Carlsbad, CA: Hay House, Inc., 2004.

_______. *The Astonishing Power of Emotions: Let Your Feelings Be Your Guide*. Carlsbad, CA: Hay House, Inc., 2007.

Highet, Gilbert. *The Art of Teaching*. Vol. 5. Nevitt Sanford. The American College. Quoted in Earl V. Pullias, with Ronald E. Cottle, *A Teacher: Models of Excellence*, Columbus, GA: 2005.

Hocking, William Ernest. *The Coming World Civilization*. (1956). Quoted in Earl V. Pullias, with Ronald E. Cottle, *A Teacher: Models of Excellence*, Columbus, GA: TEC Publications, 2005.

Jarbawl, Ali, and Yusuf Talal DeLorenzo, trans. "The Position of Palestinian Islamists on the Palestine-Israel Accord." *Muslim World* 84 (January–April 1994). http://newfirstsearch.oclc.org/ (accessed October 11, 2007).

Jeffrey, Grant R. Interview of "Ancient Prophets—Could the Ancients See the Future?" (ca. 2007). Ancient Secrets of the Bible Collection II. Grizzly Adams Productions Library, Baker City, OR.

Jersild, Arthur. *When Teachers Face Themselves*. New York, NY: Teacher's College Press, 1955. Quoted in Earl V. Pullias with Ronald E. Cottle, *A Teacher: Models of Excellence*, Columbus, GA: TEC Publications, 2005.

Krey, Peter. "You Are the Christ, the Son of the Living God." *Pentecost* 15, no. 24 (August 2008). http://peterkrey.wordpress.com/2008/08/24/you-are-the-christ-the-son-of-the-living-god-pentecost-xv-august-24-2008-alameda/ (accessed September 9, 2008).

Lemke, Steve W. "Truth for a Postmodern Era." *New Orleans Baptist Theological Seminary*, n.d.

Lewis, Bernard, ed. *Islam and the Arab World: Faith, People, Culture.* New York, NY: This is a Borzoi Book published by Alfred A. Knoph in association with American Heritage Publishing Co., Inc., 1976.

Maoz, Zeev. "Pacifism and Fightaholism in International Politics: A Structural History of National and Dyadic Conflict, 1816–1922." *International Studies Review* 6 (2004). http://psfaculty.ucdavis.edu/zmaoz/recentarticles.htm (accessed October 5, 2007).

Muncaster, Ralph. Interview of "Ancient Prophets—Could the Ancients See the Future?" (ca. 2007). Ancient Secrets of the Bible Collection II. Grizzly Adams Productions Library, Baker City, OR.

Peteet, Julie. "Words as Interventions: Naming in the Palestine—Israel conflict." *Third World Quarterly* 26, no. 1 (February 2005).

Preminger, Alex, and Edward L. Greenstein, eds. *The Hebrew Bible in Literary Criticism.* New York, NY: The Ungar Publishing Company, 1986.

Pullias, Earl V. "The Education of the Whole Man." *A Search for Understanding* (1965). Quoted in Earl V. Pullias with Ronald E. Cottle, *A Teacher: Models of Excellence*, Columbus, GA: TEC Publication, 2005.

Pusey, Nathan. *The Age of the Scholar.* 1963. Quoted in Pullias with Cottle, *A Teacher: Models of Excellence*, Columbus, GA: TEC Publications, 2005.

Roeper, Richard. *Debunked! Conspiracy Theories, Urban Legends, and Evil Plots of the 21st Century.* Chicago, IL: Chicago Review Press, 2008.

Spiro, Ken. "Jerusalem: Jewish and Moslem Claims to the Holy City." *aish.com* (2007). http://www.aish.com/jewishisssues/jerusalem/Jerusalem_Jewish_and_Moslem_Claims_to_the_Holy_City.asp (accessed October 9, 2007).

Sherwood, Yvonne. "Binding—Unbinding: Divided Responses of Judaism, Christianity, and Islam to the 'Sacrifice' of

Abraham's Beloved Son." *Journal of American Academy of Religion* 72, no. 4 (December 2004). http://newfirstsearch.oclc.org/ (accessed October 10, 2007).

Stafford, Tim. "The Pentecostal Gold Standard." *Christianity Today* (July 2005): 1–2. http://proquest.umicom/pqdweb?did=860351831&Fmt=2&clientld=40935&RQT=309&VName=PQD (accessed July 30, 2007).

Stern, Ephraim. "Israel at the Close of the Period of the Monarchy: An Archaeological Survey." *The Biblical Archaeologist* 38, no. 2 (May 1975). http://links.jstor.org/sici?sici=0006-0895(197505)38%3A2%3C26%3AIATCOT%3E2.0.CO%3B2-V (accessed October 14, 2007).

Synan, Vinson. *The Century of the Holy Spirit: 100 Years of Pentecostal and Charismatic Renewal.* Nashville, TN: Thomas Nelson, 2001.

Theologische Fragen und Antworten (1957). Quoted in R. J. Erler and R. Marquard, eds. Translated by G. W. Bromiley, *A Karl Barth Reader*, Grand Rapids, MI: Eerdmans, 1986. Quoted in R. Paul Stevens, *The Other Six Days: Vocations, Work, and Ministry in Biblical Perspective*, Grand Rapids, MI: Wm. B. Eerdmans Publishing Co., 2000.

Trever, John. Interview of "The Enigma of the Dead Sea Scrolls." (ca. 2003). Ancient Secrets of the Bible Collection II. Grizzly Adams Productions Library, Baker City, OR.

Whitehead, A. N. *The Aims of Education.* Quoted in Earl V. Pullias with Ronald E. Cottle, *A Teacher: Models of Excellence*, Columbus, GA: TEC Publications, 2005.

Whitney, Donald S. "A Review of *The Secret* by Rhonda Byrne." *Articles by Don Whitney* (2007). www.biblicalspirituality.org (accessed April 2, 2008).

Williams, George. *Some of My Best Friends Are Professors.* New York, NY: Abelard –Schuman, 1958.

Zacharias, Ravi. *The End of Reason: A Response to the New Atheists.* Grand Rapids, MI: Zondervan Publishers, 2008.

Zodhiates, Spiros, ed. *The Complete Word Study New Testament: Bringing the Original Text to Life*. Word Study Series. 2nd ed. Chattanooga, TN: AMG Publishers, 1992.

______. *The Complete Word Study Old Testament: Bringing the Original Text to Life*. Word Study Series. Chattanooga, TN: AMG Publishers, 1994.

______. *Hebrew-Greek Key Word Study Bible*. Chattanooga, TN: AMG Publishers, 1996.

APPENDIX 2
KEY FOR HOMONYMS AND UPPERCASE/LOWERCASE WORDS

Absolute Truth. When referring to the Truth of God and anything pertaining to Him.

Absolute truth. When referring to absolute truth in general.

Almighty. When referring to God as the All-in-All.

Biblical. When referring to the contents of God's Holy Word.

Body. When referring to the Body of Christ.

body. When referring to one's personal body.

Church. When referring to the body of Christ.

church. When referring to a building.

Creator. When referring to God as Creator.

creator. When referring to man or woman as creator.

devil. When referring to Satan's position.

Father. When referring to God's position to humanity.

father. When referring to man's position to his earthly children.

Garden. When referring to the Garden of Eden.

Holy. When referring to God or those things pertaining to Him as holy.

holy. When referring humanity as holy.

Law. When referring to God's Law.

law. When referring to man's law.

The Law of Attraction. When referring to the philosophy.

The Law of Attraction. When referring to Esther and Jerry Hicks' book.

Lie. When referring to the Lie Satan propagated in the garden.

lie. When referring to being untruthful and dishonest.
Omnipotent. When referring to God as All-powerful.
Omnipresent. When referring to God as Everywhere-present.
Omniscient. When referring to God as All-knowing.
Pronouns referring to God the Father, God the Son, and God the Holy Spirit are capitalized.
Scripture. When referring to God's Holy Word.
The Secret. When referring to the philosophy.
The Secret. When referring to Rhonda Byrne's book.
Son. When referring to Jesus' position to His heavenly Father.
son. When referring to a son's position to his earthly father.
Spirit. When referring to the Spirit of God.
spirit. When referring to the spirit of man or woman.
Truth. When referring to God's eternal Truth.
truth. When referring to being truthful and honest.
Satan. When referring him by his proper name.
Word. When referring to God's eternal Word.
word. When referring to the spoken word.

GLOSSARY

Chrislam. "Chrislam is an attempt to syncretize Christianity with Islam. While it began in Nigeria in the 1980s, Chrislamic ideas have spread throughout much of the world. The essential concept of Chrislam is that Christianity and Islam are compatible, that one can be a Christian and a Muslim at the same time. Chrislam is not an actual religion of its own, but a blurring of the differences and distinctions between Christianity and Islam."[369]

Christianity. William L. Thrasher, associate editor of Moody Press, identifies the foundational truths of Christianity as: "God; The Trinity; Names and Attributes of God; The Lord Jesus Christ; The Holy Spirit; The Bible; Doctrine; The Fall; Sin; The Incarnation; The Crucifixion; The Resurrection; The Gospel; and The New Birth."[370]

Counterfeit. 1: made in imitation of something else with intent to deceive: forged<counterfeit money>. 2a: insincere, feigned<counterfeit sympathy> 2b: imitation<counterfeit Georgian houses>.[371]

Darkness. A-1: Adjective, (4652, *skoteinos*), "full of darkness, or covered with darkness," is translated "dark" in Luke 11:36; "full of darkness," in Matt. 6:23 and Luke 11:34, where the physical condition is figurative of the moral. The group of *skot*-words is derived from a root *ska*—, meaning "to cover." The same root is to be found in *skēnē*, "a tent". *Note*: Contrast *phōteinos*, "full of light," e.g., Matt. 6:22. B-3: Noun (4655, *skotos*), a neuter noun, frequent in the Spet., is used in the NT as the equivalent of No. 1: (*a*) of "physical darkness," Matt. 24:45; 2 Cor. 4:6; (*b*) of "intellectual darkness," Rom. 2:19 (cf. C, No. 1); (*c*) of "blindness," Acts 13:11; (*d*) by metonymy, of the "place of punishment," e.g., Matt. 8:12; 2 Pet. 2:17; Jude 13; (*e*) metaphorically, of "moral and spiritual darkness," e.g., Matt. 6:23; Juke 1:79; 11:35; John 3:19; Acts 26:18; 2 Cor. 6:14; Eph. 6:12; Col. 1:13; 1 Thess. 5:4–5; 1 Pet. 2:9; 1 John 1:6; (*f*) by metonymy, of "those who are in moral or spiritual darkness," Eph. 5:8; (*g*) "evil works," Rom. 13:12; Eph. 5:11; (*h*) of the "evil powers that dominate the world," Luke 22:53; (*i*) "of secrecy" [as in No. 1, (*b*)]...[372]

Deceitfulness. A-1: Noun, (539, *apatē*), "deceit or deceitfulness" (akin to *apataō*, "to cheat, deceive, beguile"), that which gives a false impression, whether by appearance, statement or influence, is said of riches, Matt. 13:22; Mark 4:19; of sin, Heb. 3:13. The phrase in Eph. 4:22, "deceitful lusts," KJV, "lusts of deceit," RV, signifies lusts excited by "deceit," of which "deceit" is the source of strength, not lusts "deceitful" in themselves. In 2 Thess. 2:10, "all deceit of unrighteousness," RV, signifies all manner of unscrupulous words and deeds designed to "deceive" (see Rev. 13:13–15). In Col. 2:8, "vain deceit" suggests that "deceit" is void of anything profitable.... *Notes*: (1) *Planē*, rendered "deceit" in 1 Thess. 2:3, KJV, signifies wandering (cf. Eng., "planet"), hence, "error" (RV), i.e., a wandering from the right path; in Eph. 4:14, "wiles of error," KJV, "to deceive."[373]

Deceive. B-3: Verb, (5422, *phrenapataō*), lit., "to deceive in one's mind" (*phrēn*, "the mind," and No. 1), "to deceive by fancies" (Lightfoot), is used in Gal. 6:3, with reference to self-conceit, which is "self-deceit," a sin against common sense. Cf. Jas. 1:26 (above). *Note*: Cf. *phrenapataō*, No. 2, under DECEIVE.[374]

Foundational truths of Christianity. William Thrasher lists the following among the foundational truths of Christianity: "God; The Trinity; Names and Attributes of God; The Lord Jesus Christ; The Holy Spirit; The Bible; Doctrine; The Fall; Sin; The Incarnation; The Crucifixion; The Resurrection; The Gospel; and The New Birth."[375]

Humility. A-1: Adjective, (G5011, *tapeinos*) primarily signifies "low-lying." It is used always in a good sense in the NT, metaphorically, to denote (a) "of low degree, brought low," ... (b) humble in spirit.... A-2: Adjective, (G5424, *tapeinophron*) "humble-minded" (*phren*, "the mind").... B-1: Verb, (G5012, *tapeinoo*) akin to A, signifies "to make low," (a) literally, "of mountains and hills," Luke 3:5 (Passive Voice); (b) metaphorically, in the Active Voice ... 2 Corinthians 11:7 ("abasing") [KJV].[376]

Integrity. 1: firm adherence to a code of especially moral or artistic values: *incorruptibility*. 2: an unimpaired condition: *soundness*. 3: the quality or state of being complete or undivided: *completeness*.[377]

The Lie (of Satan). A-1: Noun, (5579, *pseudos*), "a falsehood, lie" (see also under LIAR), is translated "lie" in John 8:44 (lit., "the lie"); Rom. 1:25, where it stands by metonymy for an idol, as, e.g., in Isa. 44:20; Jer. 10:14; 13:25; Amos 2:4 (plural); 2 Thess. 2:11, with special reference to the lie of v. 4, that man is God (cf. Gen. 3:5); 1 John 2:21, 27; Rev. 21:27; 22:15; in Eph. 4:25, KJV "lying," RV, "falsehood," the practice; in Rev. 14:5, RV, "lie." (some mss. have *dolos*, "guile," KJV); 2 Thess. 2:9, where "lying wonders" is, lit., "wonders of falsehood," i.e., wonders calculated to deceive (cf. Rev. 13:13–15), the purpose being to deceive people into the acknowledgment of the spurious claim to deity on the part of the Man of Sin. *Note*: In Rom. 1:25 the "lie" or idol is the outcome of pagan religion; in 1 John 2:21, 22 the "lie" is the denial that Jesus is the Christ; in 2 Thess. 2:11 the "lie" is the claim of the Man of Sin.[378]

Lie. C: Verb, (5574, *pseudō*), "to deceive by lies," (always in the middle voice in the NT), is used (*a*) absolutely, in Matt. 5:11, "falsely," lit., "lying" (KJV, marg.); Rom. 9:1; 2 Cor. 11:31; Gal. 1:20; Col. 3:9 (where the verb is followed by the preposition *eis*, "to"); 1 Tim. 2:7; Heb. 6:18; Jas. 3:14 (where it is followed by the preposition *kata*, "against"); 1 John 1:6; Rev. 3:9; (*b*) transitively, with a direct object (without a preposition following), Acts 5:3 (with the accusative case), "to lie to (the Holy Spirit)," RV marg., "deceive"; v. 4 (with the dative case) "thou hast (not) lied (unto men, but unto God)."[379]

Light. A-1: Noun, (5457, *phos*), akin to *phaō*, "to give light" (from roots *pha*— and *phan*—, expressing "light as seen by the eye," and, metaphorically, as "reaching the mind," whence *phainō*, "to make to appear," *phaneros*, "evident," etc.); cf. Eng., "phosphorus" (lit., "light-bearing"). "Primarily light is a luminous emanation, probably of force, from certain bodies, which enables the eye to discern form and color. Light requires an organ adapted for its reception (Matt. 6:22). Where the eye is absent, or where it has become impaired from any cause, light is useless. … "Apart from natural phenomena, light is used in Scripture of (*a*) the glory of God's dwellingplace, 1 Tim. 6:16; (*b*) the nature of God, 1 John 1:5; (*c*) the impartiality of God, Jas. 1:17; (*d*) the favor of God, Ps. 4:6; of the King, Prov. 16:15; of an influential man, Job 29:24; (*e*) God, as the illuminator of His people, Isa. 60:19, 20; (*f*) the Lord Jesus as the illuminator of men, John 1:4, 5, 9; 3:19; 8:12; 9:5; 12:35, 36, 46; Acts 13:47; (*g*) the illuminating power of the Scriptures, Ps. 119:105; and of the judgments and commandments of God, Isa. 51:4; Prov. 6:23, cf. Ps. 43:3; (*h*) the guidance of God, Job 29:3; Ps. 112:4; Isa. 58:10; and, ironically, of the guidance of man, Rom. 2:19; (*i*) salvation, 1 Pet. 2:9; (*j*) righteousness, Rom. 13:12; 2 Cor. 11:14, 15; 1 John 2:9, 10; (*k*) witness for God,

Matt. 5:14, 16; John 5:35; (*l*) prosperity and general well-being, Esth. 8:16; Job 18:18; Isa. 58:8–10." (From *Notes on Thessalonians*, by Hogg and Vine, pp. 159, 160).[380]

Meekness. B-1: Noun, (4240, *prautes* / *praotes*) an earlier form, denotes "meekness." In its use in Scripture, in which it has a fuller, deeper significance than in nonscriptural Greek writings, it consists not in a person's "outward behaviour only; nor yet in his relations to his fellow-men; as little in his mere natural disposition. Rather it is an inwrought grace of the soul; and the exercises of it are first and chiefly towards God. It is that temper of spirit in which we accept His dealings with us as good, and therefore without disputing or resisting; it is closely linked with the word *tapeinophrosune* (humility), and follows directly upon it, Ephesians 4:2; Colossians 3:12; cp. the adjectives in the Sept. of Zephaniah 3:12, "meek and lowly;" … it is only the humble heart which is also the meek, and which, as such, does not fight against God and more or less struggle and contend with Him. This meekness, however, being first of all a meekness before God, is also such in the face of men, even of evil men, out of a sense that these, with the insults and injuries which they may inflict, are permitted and employed by Him for the chastening and purifying of His elect" (Trench, Syn. xlii). In Galatians 5:23 it is associated with *enkrateia*, "self-control." B-2: Noun, (G4236, *praupathia*) "a meek disposition, meekness" (*praus*, "meek," *pascho*, "to suffer"), is found in the best texts in 1 Timothy 6:11.[381]

New Age Movement: New Age or Old Occult? "The New Age Movement is a modern revival of very old ancient, divergent, religious traditions and practices. The actual original root is squarely centered in Genesis 3:1–5, and reverberates throughout the movement's continued historical expressions. In the original lie, Satan questions God's word, His authority and benevolent rule (v. 1), disputes that death results from disobedience (v. 4), and claims that through the acquisition of the secret or Gnostic wisdom man can be enlightened and can be 'like God' (v. 5)."[382]

Perversion. 1: the action of perverting: the condition of being perverted. 2: a perverted form; especially: an aberrant sexual practice or interest especially when habitual. Merriam-Webster Online Dictionary, s.v. "perversion," http://www.merriam-webster.com/dictionary/perversion (accessed March 3, 2012).[383]

Perverse, Pervert. 1: (G654, *apostrepho*) "to turn away" (*apo*, "from," *strepho*, "to turn"), is used metaphorically in the sense of "perverting" in Luke 23:14.... 2: (G1294, *diastrepho*) "to distort, twist" (*dia*, "through," and *strepho*), is translated "to pervert" in Luke 23:2.... 3: (G3344, *metastrepho*) "to transform into something of an opposite character" (*meta*, signifying "a change," and *strepho*,) as the Judaizers sought to "pervert the gospel of Christ," Galatians 1:7.... 4: (G1612, *ekstrepho*) "to turn inside out" (*ek*, "out"), "to change entirely," is used metaphorically in Titus 3:11.[384]

Substitute. A person or thing that takes the place or function of another.[385]

The Truth. A-2: Adjective, (228, *alēthinos*) akin to No. 1, denotes "true" in the sense of real, ideal, genuine, it is used (*a*) of God, John 7:28; (cf. No. 1 in 7:18 above); 17:3; 1 Thess. 1:9; Rev. 6:10; these declare that God fulfills the meaning of His Name; He is "very God," in distinction from all other gods, false gods (*alethes*, see John 3:33 in No. 1, signifies that He is veracious, "true" to His utterances, He cannot lie); (*b*) of Christ, John 1:9; 6:32; 15:1; 1 John 2:8; 5:20 (thrice); Rev. 3:7, 14; 19:11; His judgment, John 8:16 (in the best texts, instead of No. 1); (*c*) God's words, John 4:37; Rev. 19:9; 21:5; 22:6; the last three are equivalent to No. 1; (*d*) His ways, Rev. 15:3; (*e*) His judgments, Rev. 16:7; 19:2; (*f*) His riches, Luke 16:11; (*g*) His worshipers, John 4:23; (*h*) their hearts, Heb. 10:22; (*i*) the spiritual, antitypical tabernacle, Heb. 8:2; 9:24, not that the wilderness tabernacle was false, but that is was a weak and earthly copy of the heavenly.[386]

The truth and the lie. Zacharias defines the truth and the lie in simple terms: "Truth is stating what is. Falsehood is stating something to be so, when it is not."[382] The truth in this context B: (G226, *alētheuō*) denotes "speaking the truth."[383] The lie in this context B-1: (G5573, *pseudologos*) denotes "speaking falsely" ... and is applied to "demons," the actual utterances being by their human agents."[387]

Truth. B: Verb, (226, *alētheuō*), signifies "to deal faithfully or truly with anyone" (cf. Gen 42:16, Sept., "whether ye deal truly or no"), Eph. 4:15, "speaking the truth"; Gal. 3:16, "I tell (you) the truth," where probably the apostle is referring to the contents of his epistle.[388]

Truth. B: Noun, (530, *'ĕmûnāh*), "firmness; faithfulness; truth; honesty; official obligation." In Exod. 17:12 (the first biblical occurrence), the word means "to remain in one place": "And his [Moses'] hands were steady until the going down of the sun." Closely related to this use is that in Isa. 33:6: "And wisdom and knowledge shall be the stability of thy times.... " Quite often this word means "truthfulness," as when it is contrasted to false swearing, lining and so on. ... *'ĕmûnāh* means "true"—the personal sense, which identifies a subject as honest, trustworthy, faithful, truthful (Prov. 12:22); and the factual sense, which identifies a subject as being factually true (cf. Prov. 12:27), as opposed to that which is false.... one can both practice (Gen. 47:29) and speak the "truth" (Sam. 7:28)....[389]

Truthful. A-1: Adjective, (227, *alēthēs*), primarily, "unconcealed, manifest" ... hence, actual 'true to fact,' is used (*a*) of persons, 'truthful,' Matt. 22.16; Mark 12:14; John 3:33; 7:18; 8:26; Rom. 3:4; 2 Cor. 7:8 ... denotes the reality of the thing."[390] "But he who practices truth—who does what is right—comes out into the light; so that his works may be plainly shown to be what they are, wrought with God—divinely prompted, done with God's help, in dependence upon Him" (John 3:21).

The Truth of God. B: Noun, (225, *alētheia*), "truth," is used (*a*) objectively, signifying "the reality lying at the basis of an appearance; the manifested, veritable essence of a matter (Cremer), e.g., Rom. 9:1; 2 Cor. 11:10; especially of Christian doctrine, e.g., Gal. 2:5, where "the truth of the Gospel" denotes the "true" teaching of the Gospel, in contrast to perversions of it; Rom. 1:25, where "the truth of God" may be "the truth concerning God" or "God whose existence is a verity"; but in Rom. 15:8 "the truth of God" is indicative of His faithfulness in the fulfillment of His promises as exhibited in Christ ... not merely ethical "truth," but "truth" in all its fullness and scope, as embodied in Him.[391] "Sanctify them [purify, consecrate, separate them for Yourself, make them holy] by the Truth. Your Word is Truth" (John 17:17, AMP).

The Truth of God. B: Noun, (571, *'ĕmet*), "truth; right; faithful." This word appears 127 times in the Bible. The Septuagint translates it in 100 occurrences as "truth" (*aletheia*) or some form using this basic root. In Zech. 8:3, Jerusalem is called "a city of truth." Elsewhere, *'ĕmet* is rendered as the word "right" (*dikaios*)...[392]

SELECTED BIBLIOGRAPHY

"Activity-Centered Teaching-Learning." A term used to describe John Dewey's active teaching-learning methodology. This methodology incorporates all the senses in the learning experience, thereby increasing the retention level of the learner. This learning methodology is employed in the workshop curriculum as part of the research for this book.

Agno, John. "The Law of Reciprocity." *CoachThee.com—International Coach Federation.* http://home.att.net/~coachthee/Archives/reciprocity.html (accessed September 9, 2008).

Allen, Sharon Lubkemann. "Dispossessed Sons and Displaced Meaning in Faulkner's Modern Cosmos." *Mississippi Quarterly* 50, no. 3 (Summer 1997): 1. http://wf21a2.webfeat.org/ (accessed September 21, 2007).

Anderson, Neil T. "According to the Spirit." *Neil Anderson's Daily In Christ, Freedom In Christ Ministries*: 1–2. http://www.crosswalkmail.com (accessed October 2, 2008).

______. "Christ, Our Ruler." *Neil Anderson's Daily In Christ, Freedom In Christ Ministries*: 1–2. http://www.crosswalkmail.com (accessed October 13, 2008).

______. "The Father of Lies." *Neil Anderson's Daily In Christ, Freedom In Christ Ministries*: 1–2. http://www.crosswalkmail.com (accessed October 1, 2008).

______. "Highlights in Today's Reading, Luke 23–24." *Bible*

Pathways Devotional: 1–2. http://www.crosswalk.com (accessed October 31, 2008).

______. "Taking Every Thought Captive." *Neil Anderson's Daily In Christ, Freedom In Christ Ministries*: 1–2. http://www.crosswalkmail.com (accessed November 2, 2008).

Anderson, Ray S. *The Soul of Ministry: Forming Leaders for God's People.* 1st ed. Louisville, KY: Westminster John Knox Press, 1997.

Anthony, Michael J. "Synagogue Schools." In Michael J. Anthony, ed., *The Evangelical Dictionary of Christian Education*, Grand Rapids, MI: Baker Books, 2001.

Anthony, Michael J., and Warren S. Benson. *Exploring the History and Philosophy of Christian Education: Principles for the 21st Century.* Grand Rapids, MI: Kregel Publications, 2003.

Augustine. "Saint Augustine Quotes and Biography." *QuoteDB*: 1. http://www.quotedb.com/authors/saint-augustine (accessed November 10, 2008).

______. Cited in Henry Chadwick, *Augustine: A Very Short Introduction*, Oxford, England: Oxford University Press, 2001. Quoted in Nancy R. Pearcey, *Total Truth: Liberating Christianity from Its Cultural Captivity*, Study Guide edition, Wheaton, IL: Crossway Books, 2005.

"Avatar." *Merriam-Webster Online Dictionary.* s.v. "Avatar." http://www.merriam-webster.com/dictionary/avatar (accessed February 26, 2009).

Bacon, Francis. "The Essays." *Oregon State University* (1601). oregonstate.edu/instruct/phl302/texts/bacon/bacon_essays.html (accessed August 12, 2008).

Baker, Amber. "Faithful Friends." *Loveland Reporter-Herald.* November 8, 2008. This article discusses current negative trends regarding truth in Christianity over against other world religions.

Barclay, William. *Educational Ideals in the Ancient World.* Grand Rapids, MI: Baker, 1959. Quoted in Anthony, Michael J., and Warren S. Benson, *Exploring the History and*

Philosophy of Christian Education: Principles for the 21st Century, Grand Rapids, MI: Kregel Publications, 124.

Barna, George. *Growing True Disciples: New Strategies for Producing Genuine Followers of Christ*. Colorado Springs, CO: WaterBrook Press, 2001. Quoted in John Jackson, *PastorPreneur: Pastors and Entrepreneurs Answer the Call*, Friendswood, TX: Baxter Press, 2003.

______. "Only Half of Protestant Pastors Have a Biblical Worldview." *Barna Update* (January 12, 2004). http://www.barna.org/FlexPage.aspx?Page=BarnaUpdate&BarnaUpdateID=156 (accessed May 7, 2006). Quoted in Arley S. Enloe, "The Efficacy of Ministerial Training: an Assessment of Accredited and Non-accredited Theological Education from a Pastoral Perspective," DMin diss., Beacon University, 2008.

Bauer, Scott G. *The New Church on the Way: Reaching with God's Love and Power!* Van Nuys, CA: The Church on the Way, 2002.

Beahm, Anol W. "High Tech in Christian Education: Cure or Curse?" *Christian Education Journal* 6, no. 2 (1985): 20. Quoted in Kenneth O. Gangel, and Howard G. Hendricks, eds., *The Christian Handbook on Teaching: A Comprehensive Resource on the Distinctiveness of True Christian Teaching*, Grand Rapids, MI: Baker Books, 1998.

Beckwith, Francis J., and Gregory Koukl. *Relativism: Feet Firmly Planted in Mid-Air*. Grand Rapids, MI: Baker Books, 2006.

Berliner, David C., and Bruce J. Biddle. *The Manufactured Crisis: Myths, Fraud, and the Attack on America's Public Schools*. Reading, MA: Addison-Wesley, 1995.

Bonhoeffer, Dietrich. *The Cost of Discipleship*. Rev. ed. Translated by R. H. Fuller. New York, NY: Macmillan, 1960.

Bounds, E. M. "Prayer and Importunity." *The Necessity of Prayer*. www.jesus-is-savior.com/Books,%20Tracts%20&%20

Preaching/Printed%20Books/NOP/nop-chap_06.htm (accessed March 21, 2008).

Bowyer, Carlton H. *Philosophical Perspectives for Education*. Glenview, IL: Scott, Foresman and Company, 1970. Quoted in M. Halsey Thomas, *John Dewey: A Centennial Bibliography*, Chicago, IL: University of Chicago Press, 1962.

Boys, Mary C. *Educating in Faith*. San Francisco, CA: Harper and Row, 1989.

Bradley, Frances Herbert. (1846–1924). British philosopher.

Bradley, Ray. "Is Everything Relative, Including Truth?" *Philosophy of Science*. http://www.sfu.ca/philosophy/bradley/bradley.htm (accessed October 30, 2008).

Bucknell, Paul J. "Developing a Fear of God, Joshua 1:10." *Biblical Foundations for Freedom*. http://www.foundationsforfreedom.net/Topics/FearGodMan/FearGod019.html (accessed March 5, 2009).

Bullinger, E. W. *Number in Scripture*. New York, NY: Cosimo Classics, 2005. Originally published by Eyre and Spottiswoode in 1894.

Butts, R. Freeman. *A Cultural History of Education*. New York, NY: McGraw Hill, 1947. Quoted in Michael J. Anthony and Warren S. Benson, *Exploring the History and Philosophy of Christian Education: Principles for the 21st Century*, Grand Rapids, MI: Kregel Publications, 2003.

Byrne, Rhonda. *The Secret*. Hillsboro, OR: ATRIA Books/Beyond Words Publishing, 2006.

Cairns, Earle E. *Christianity Through the Centuries*. Grand Rapids, MI: Zondervan, 1996. Quoted in Michael J. Anthony and Warren S. Benson, *Exploring the History and Philosophy of Christian Education: Principles for the 21st Century*, Grand Rapids, MI: Kregel Publications, 2003.

Carlson, E. Leslie, Lowell Coolidge, Earl L. Core, Huber L. Drumwright, and Virtus E. Gideon. *The Expositor's Study*

Bible. N.d. Reprint, Baton Rouge, LA: Jimmy Swaggart Ministries, 2005.

Chicago (AP). "Mental illness on campus sometimes leads to violence." *Loveland Reporter-Herald*. December 2, 2008. This article discusses current emotional maladies and severe psychological disorders among a vast number of students enrolled in the public school system.

Chitwood, Oliver P. *History of Colonial America*. New York, NY: Harper and Row, 1961. Quoted in Michael J. Anthony, and Warren S. Benson, *Exploring the History and Philosophy of Christian Education: Principles for the 21st Century*, Grand Rapids, MI: Kregel Publications, 2003.

Churchill, Winston. "Quotes on Truth." *What Is Truth?*: 1–10. http://www.whatistruth.org.uk/quotesontruth.php (accessed August 12, 2008).

______. "Winston Churchill quotes." *TruthExist.com Quotations*: 1. http://thinkexist.com/quotation/the_truth_is_incontrovertible-malice_may_attack/220093.html (accessed March 19, 2013).

Colbert, Donald. Interview, *getv.org* (January 18, 2013). John Hagee Ministries, San Antonio, TX. Don Colbert, MD, one of the country's foremost authorities on the integration of natural and conventional health care, brings a twenty-first-century approach to a timeless message of healthy lifestyle habits. Dr. Colbert conducts comprehensive seminars in churches … and is a board-certified family practice physician, a best-selling author, and a dynamic public speaker. Over the past twenty years, he has treated more than 25,000 patients, integrating body, mind, and spirit into each of his health care strategies.

Colson, Charles. Quoted in Ravi Zacharias, *Can Man Live Without God*, Nashville, TN: W Publishing Group, 1994.

"Counterfeit." *Merriam-Webster Online Dictionary*, s.v. "Counterfeit." http://www.merriam-webster.com/dictionary/counterfeit (accessed March 3, 2012).

Craig, Marsha, Debra Lester, Connie Henderson, and Mary Granderson. "Discovering Gravity: What Goes Up Must Come Down." *Illinois Institute of Technology, Smile Program Chemistry Index, Basic Tools and Principles.* http://www.iit.edu/~smile/cheminde.html (accessed October 28, 2008).

"Creationism." *Encarta Dictionary*, s.v. "Creationism:" The belief that God created the universe.

Cubberley, Elwood P. *The History of Education.* Boston, MA: Houghton Mifflin, 1948. Quoted in Michael J. Anthony, and Warren S. Benson, *Exploring the History and Philosophy of Christian Education: Principles for the 21st Century*, Grand Rapids, MI: Kregel Publications, 2003.

"David Friedrich Hollaz," *Studium Exitar: The Journal of Confessional Language Studies at MLC* (2002, 2006), http://www.studiumexcitare.com/content/67 (accessed November 8, 2008). "The history of Lutheranism ascribes Hollaz, pastor and theologian, the title of the last great dogmatician of the period of Lutheran orthodoxy, a designation which modern students of Lutheran dogmatics recognize." However, "Pastor Hollaz, God's humble servant … unceasingly preached Christ crucified."

Dawkins, Richard. "Genetics: Why Prince Charles Is So Wrong." *Checkbiotech.org* (January 28, 2003). http://www.checkbiotech.org/root/index.cfm?fuseaction=news&doc_id=4575&start=1&control173&page_nr=101&pg=1. Quoted in Nancy R. Pearcey, *Total Truth: Liberating Christianity from Its Cultural Captivity*, Study Guide edition, Wheaton, IL: Crossway Books, 2005.

Delaney, W. Guy. "Obedience is Better Than Sacrifice." *Sermon Teaser.com* (2011): 1–2. http://www.sermonteaser.com/obedience-is-better-than-sacrifice/ (accessed March 11, 2013).

DeMoss, Mark. *The Little Red Book of Wisdom.* Nashville, TN: Thomas Nelson, 2007. Mark DeMoss is president of The

DeMoss Group, a public relations firm he founded in 1991 to serve Christian organizations and causes. A number of the largest non-profit organizations in America are counted among The DeMoss Group's clients. Mark has spent his life around wise people and has worked closely with some of the most prominent religious leaders of the past several decades. Mark and his wife April live in Atlanta, Georgia, with their three teenagers.

Dewey, John. *Democracy and Education*. 1916. Reprint, New York, NY: Free Press, 1966. Quoted in John I. Goodlad and Timothy J. McMannon, eds., *The Public Purpose of Education and Schooling*, San Francisco, CA: Jossey-Bass, 1997.

Dowden, Bradley, and Norman Swartz. "Truth." *The Internet Encyclopedia of Philosophy* (2006). http://www.iep.utm.edu/t/truth.htm (accessed October 30, 2008).

Duim, Lana. "Dr. Jack W. Hayford Biography." Los Angeles, CA: International Church of the Foursquare Gospel, 2007. Among Hayford's many honors and awards are, "Alumnus of the Year, Azusa Pacific University (1997); Gold Medallion (from Evangelical Publishers Association, for Spirit-Filled Study Guides); and Winner of Billy Graham Association's Decision Magazine Hymn Writer's Competition, 'We Lift Our Voice Rejoicing,' being selected from more than 900 int'l entries."

Duin, Julia. "Statistics: Moral Values, America a Christian Nation, and More." *The Washington Times*. December 31, 2004. http://www.ucmpage.org/news/barna_report1.html (accessed September 24, 2008).

Dumbrell, W. J. *Covenant and Creation: An Old Testament Covenantal Theology*. Nashville, TN: Thomas Nelson Publishers, 1984. Quoted in R. Paul Stevens, *The Other Six Days: Vocation, Work and Ministry in Biblical Perspective*, Grand Rapids, MI: Wm. B. Eerdmans Publishing Co., 2000.

Dunkel, Wilbur Dwight. "The Meek Shall Inherit the Earth: A Study In Shakespearean Tragedy." *Theology Today* 15, no. 3 (October 1958): 359–365. http://www.theologytoday.ptsem.edu.oct1958/v15-3-article7.htm (accessed February 21, 2008).

Easton, M. G. *Illustrated Bible Dictionary*, 3rd ed. Washington, DC: Thomas Nelson, 1897.

Eavey, Charles B. *History of Christian Education*. Chicago, IL: Moody, 1964. Quoted in Michael J. Anthony, and Warren S. Benson, *Exploring the History and Philosophy of Christian Education: Principles for the 21st Century*, Grand Rapids, MI: Kregel Publications, 2003.

Eby, Fredrick, and Charles F. Arrowood. *The History and Philosophy of Education: Ancient and Medieval*. Englewood Cliffs, NJ: Prentice-Hall, 1940. Quoted in Michael J. Anthony and Warren S. Benson, *Exploring the History and Philosophy of Christian Education: Principles for the 21st Century*, Grand Rapids, MI: Kregel Publications, 2003.

"Education quotes." *ThinkExist.com*. http://thinkexist.com/quotations/education/ (accessed March 27, 2008).

Elias, John L. *A History of Christian Education: Protestant, Catholic, and Orthodox Perspectives*. Malabar, FL: Krieger, 2002. Quoted in Michael J. Anthony and Warren S. Benson, *Exploring the History and Philosophy of Christian Education: Principles for the 21st Century*, Grand Rapids, MI: Kregel Publications, 2003.

Elliot, Jim. Quoted in Michael J. Anthony, and Warren S. Benson, *Exploring the History and Philosophy of Christian Education: Principles for the 21st Century*, Grand Rapids, MI: Kregel Publications, 2003.

Emerson, Ralph Waldo. "Quotes on Truth." *What Is Truth?*: 1–10. http://www.whatistruth.org.uk/quotesontruth.php (accessed August 12, 2008).

Enloe, Arley S. "The Efficacy of Ministerial Training: An Assessment of Accredited and Non-accredited Theological

Education from a Pastoral Perspective." DMin diss., Beacon University, 2008.

Enlow, Phil. "How Do You Know You Are Right?" *Midnight Cry Ministries*. http://midnightcry.org/howknow2.htm (accessed December 14, 2008).

Evans, Tony. Quoted in James Robison, "We Have a Choice: Humility or Humiliation," *Dallas Morning News*, October 24, 2006, http://www.wehaveachoice.org/ (accessed March 1, 2008).

Faith in Action. "Pilate: What is Truth? *The Passion of the Christ*." *Our Faith in Action* (February 2004). http://www.catholiceducation.org/articles/lesson_plans/lp0089.html (accessed August 12, 2008).

Finto, Don. *Your People Shall Be My People How Israel, The Jews and The Christian Church Will Come Together In The Last Days*. Ventura, CA: Regal Books, 2001.

Fleming, Stanley F. "On Truth." *Gate Breakers Ministries*: 1. www.gatebreakers.com (accessed November 3, 2008).

"Francis Schaeffer Library." *The Pulpit Page, Visionary Gallery*: 1–12. http://www.tillwehavefaces.net/the%20pulpit%20page.html (December 18, 2008).

Fraser, I. M. "Theology and Action." *Scottish Journal of Theology* 2, no. 4 (December 1949): 414–415; 411–423. Quoted in R. Paul Stevens, *The Other Six Days: Vocation, Work, and Ministry in Biblical Perspective*, Grand Rapids, MI: Wm. B. Eerdmans Publishing Co., 1999.

Frost, Severe F. *Historical and Philosophical Foundations of Western Education*. Columbus, OH: Charles E. Merrill, 1966.

Gamzu, Yossi. "Isaac and Ishmael Write About Each Other." *Judaism* 35, no. 3 (Summer 1986): 306–316. http://search3.webfeat.org/ (accessed September 21, 2007).

Gangel, Kenneth O., and Howard G. Hendricks, eds. *The Christian Handbook on Teaching: A Comprehensive Resource on the Distinctiveness of True Christian Teaching*. Grand Rapids, MI: Baker Books, 1998.

Gates of Prayer. New York, NY: Central Conference of American Rabbis, 1955. Quoted in Michael J. Anthony and Warren S. Benson, *Exploring the History and Philosophy of Christian Education: Principles for the 21st Century*, Grand Rapids, MI: Kregel Publications, 2003.

Gladdon, Gloria Jean. "An Assessment of the Hebrew Heritage of African Americans: Exploring the Lost Legacy, Renewal, and Revival of Their Faith." DMin diss., Beacon University, 2007.

Goodlad, John I., and Timothy J. McMannon, eds. *The Public Purpose of Education and Schooling*. San Francisco, CA: Jossey-Bass, 1997.

Gough, David. "Johann Heinrich Pestalozzi." Quoted in Anthony, ed., *The Evangelical Dictionary of Christian Education*, Grand Rapids, MI: Baker Books, 2001.

Groothuis, Douglas R. "New Age Movement: New Age or Old Occult?" *Biblical Discernment Ministries* (Revised November 2001): 1–16. http://www.rapidnet.com/~jbeard/bdm/Cults/newage.htm (accessed February 25, 2009). "The New Age Movement is a modern revival of very ancient, divergent, religious traditions and practices. The actual original root is squarely centered in Genesis 3:1–5, and reverberates throughout the movement's continued historical expressions. In the original lie, Satan questions God's word, His authority and benevolent rule (v. 1), disputes that death results from disobedience (v. 4, and claims that through the acquisition of secret or Gnostic wisdom man can be enlightened and can be 'like God' (v. 5)."

Grudem, Wayne. *Systematic Theology: An Introduction to Biblical Doctrine*. Grand Rapids, MI: Zondervan Publishers, 1994.

Grudem, Wayne, and Jeff Purshwell, eds. *Bible Doctrine: Essential Teachings of the Christian Faith*. Grand Rapids, MI: Zondervan Publishing House, 1999.

Gungor, Ed. *There Is More to the Secret: An Examination of Rhonda Byrne's Bestselling Book the Secret.* Nashville, TN: Thomas Nelson Publishers, 2007.

_______. Interview of "There Is More to The Secret." (2008). Grizzly Adams® Productions Library, Baker City, OR.

Habermas, Ronald T. "Catechism." In *The Evangelical Dictionary of Christian Education.* Grand Rapids, MI: Baker Books, 2001.

Hackett, Paul. "Not one hoof." ca. 1980s.

Halfon, Mark. "Integrity." *Stanford Encyclopedia of Philosophy* (April 9, 2001 revision May 26, 2005): 1–27. (1976): 54. http://plato.stanford.edu/entries/integrity/#6 (accessed February 21, 2008).

_______. "Integrity." *Stanford Encyclopedia of Philosophy* (April 9, 2001 revision May 26, 2005): 1–27. (1989): 37. http://plato.stanford.edu/entries/integrity/#4 (accessed February 21, 2008).

Hayford, Jack W. *The Church on the Way: Learning to Live in the Promise of Biblical Congregational Life.* Old Tappan, NJ: Chosen Books, 1983.

_______. Adapted from Jack W. Hayford's formula for praying from The Lord's Prayer. Matthew 6:9–13. (Lecture. Calvary Temple, Denver, CO. ca. 1986).

_______. "Integrity of Heart." *Jack Hayford Ministries*: 1–2. http://www.jackhayford.org/teaching/articles/integrity-of-heart/ (accessed February 8, 2013).

_______. *Pastors of Promise: A Practical and Passionate Call for Faithful Shepherds.* Ventura, CA: Gospel Light Publications, 1997.

_______. Quoted in Tim Stafford. "The Pentecostal Gold Standard." *Christianity Today* (July 2005): 1. http://search.ebscohost.com/login.aspx?direct=true&db=15h&AN=1741581&site=ehost-live (accessed July 30, 2007).

_______. *Prayer Is Invading the Impossible.* Gainesville, FL: Bridge-Logos, 2002. Hayford was president of the International

Church of the Foursquare Gospel from 2004–2008; chancellor and founder of King's College, 1987; founder of the Jack W. Hayford School of Pastoral Nurture, 1997; and founder and director of The King's Seminary, 1999. Author, composer, educator, and "a 'pastor to pastors,' Dr. Hayford continues to touch millions, who resonate with his passionate, balanced, biblical teaching via Living Way Ministries' radio, TV, and Internet broadcasts."

"Hebrews 11:1." *Matthew Henry's Concise Commentary, God's Word to the Nations* (Copyright 1995). http://bible.cc/hebrews/11-1.htm (accessed December 14, 2008). GOD'S WORD® is a copyrighted work of God's Word to the Nations. Quotations are used by permission. All rights reserved. God's Word to the Nations.

Henderson, Tom. "Newton's Third Law of Motion." *The Physics Classroom Tutorial* (1996–2007). http://www.glenbrook.k12.il.us/GBSSCI/PHYS/CLASS/newtlaws/u2l4a.html (accessed October 28, 2008).

Hendrickson, Mark. "High Tech: Its Progress, Problems, and Potential for Use in the Local Church." *Christian Education Journal* 6, no. 2 (1985): 9. Quoted in Kenneth O. Gangel, and Howard G. Hendricks, eds., *The Christian Handbook on Teaching: A Comprehensive Resource on the Distinctiveness of True Christian Teaching*, Grand Rapids, MI: Baker Books, 1998.

Hicks, Esther, and Jerry Hicks. *The Law of Attraction: The Basics of the Teachings of Abraham*. Carlsbad, CA: Hay House Publishers, 2006.

Hollander, Paul Jonathan. Quoted in Norman Swartz, "The Myth of the Flat Earth," Department of Philosophy, *Simon Fraser University* (August 8, 1995). http://www.sfu.ca/philosophy/swartz/flat_earth.htm (accessed December 27, 2008).

Hollaz, David Friedrich. In Thomasius, *Christi Person und Werk*, 1:137. Quoted in Augustus Hopkins Strong, *Systematic*

Theology, N.d. Reprint, Valley Forge, PA: Judson Press, 1985.

Holmes, Oliver Wendell Jr. "Law in Science and Science in Law." *Harvard Law Review* 12, no. 443 (1899). In *The Essential Holmes*, edited with an introduction by Richard A. Posner, Chicago, IL: University of Chicago Press, 1996, 188–190. See also E. Donald Elliott, "The Evolutionary Tradition in Jurisprudence," *Columbia Law Review* 85, no. 38 (1985): 52–53. This article provides a good overview of legal theories that draw explicit metaphors to evolution. Quoted in Nancy R. Pearcey, *Total Truth: Liberating Christianity from Its Cultural Captivity*, Study Guide edition, Wheaton, IL: Crossway Books, 2005.

Horowitz, Wayne, Takayoshi Oshima, and Seth Sanders. "A Bibliographical List of Cureiform Inscriptions from Canaan, Palestine; Philistia, and the Land of Israel." *Journal of the American Oriental Society* 122, no. 4 (October–December 2002). http://newfirstsearch.oclc.org/ (accessed October 10, 2007).

"Integrity." *Merriam-Webster Online Dictionary*. s.v. "Integrity." http://www.merriam-webster.com/dictionary/integrity (accessed February 27, 2009).

"Ishmael and Isaac." *Christian Science Monitor* 229, no. 92 (2007): 469–470. http://wf21a2.webfeat.org/sRoYI125/url=http://web.ebscohost.com/ehost/detail?vid=2&hid.htm (accessed September 21, 2007).

Jackson, John. *PastorPreneur: Pastors and Entrepreneurs Answer the Call*. Friendswood, TX: Baxter Press, 2003.

Jefferson, Thomas. *The Jefferson Bible: The Life and Morals of Jesus of Nazareth*. 1819. Reprint, Boston, MA: Beacon Press, 1989.

Jeremiah, David. Turning Point Ministries. July 9, 2011. Trinity Broadcasting Network, Channel 235.

"1 John 4:18." *Jamieson-Fausset-Brown Bible Commentary*. http://bible.cc/1_john/4-18.htm (accessed March 5, 2009).

John, Larry. "Morals vs Ethics—According to the Pragmatic Thinker." *Enzine Articles* (October 26, 2007): 1–2. http://EnzineArticles.com/?Morals-vs-Ethics-According-to-the-Pragmatic-Thinker&id=802720 (accessed December 6, 2010).

Jones, W. T., and Robert J. Fogelin. *A History of Western Philosophy: The Medieval Mind.* 2nd ed. New York, NY: Harcourt Brace Hovanovich, 1969.

Kant, Immanuel. Quoted in Michael J. Anthony and Harold S. Benson, *Exploring the History and Philosophy of Christian Education: Principles for the 21st Century*, Grand Rapids, MI: Kregel Publications, 2003.

______. In Harold H. Titus, *Living Issues in Philosophy*, New York, NY: Van Nostrand Reinhold, 1970. Quoted in Michael J. Anthony and Benson, *Exploring the History and Philosophy of Christian Education: Principles for the 21st Century*, Grand Rapids, MI: Kregel Publications, 2003.

Kappelman, Todd. "Dietrich Bonhoeffer: The Man and His Mission." *Probe Ministries* (July 14, 2002). http://www.leaderu.com/orgs/probe/docs/bonhoeffer.html (accessed January 2, 2009).

King, Karen L. *What Is Gnosticism?* Cambridge, London: Belknap Press of Harvard University Press, 2003. Quoted in Paul A. Mirecki, "What Is Gnosticism?" *The Catholic Biblical Quarterly* 67, no. 2 (April 2005): 1–2. http://newfirstsearch.oclc.org/images/@SPL/wsppdf1/HTML/03960/P5APQ/GFD.HTM (accessed August 11, 2007).

Kline, Bill. Field supervisor to the current author, Kline is cited in the work.

"The Knowledge of God." *Acts 17:11 Bible Study: Theology*. http://www.acts17-11.com/theology.html (accessed November 2, 2008).

LaRaviere, Richard. "Six Ways to Discern Between God's Voice and that of Satan." Part 3, *SermonCentral.com* (September 2007): 1–2. http://www.sermoncentral.com/sermons/

six-ways-to-discern-between-gods-voice-and-that-of-satan-part-3-richard-laraviere-sermon-on-growth-in-christ-111665.asp (accessed March 4, 2013).

Larsen, Timothy, David Bebbington, and Mark A. Noll, eds. *Biographical Dictionary of Evangelicals*. Downers Grove, IL: Inter-Varsity Press, 2003.

Larson, Christian D. *The Hidden Secret*. 1912. Reprint, Kila, MT: Kessinger Publishing, 2007. Quoted in Rhonda Byrne, *The Secret*, Hillsboro, OR: ATRIA Books/Beyond Words Publishing, 2006.

Lawrenz, Mel. *The Dynamics of Spiritual Formation*. Grand Rapids, MI: Baker Books, 2000.

Lawson, Christopher D. "The Moses Code Deception." *Spiritual Research Network, International* (February 11, 2008): 1–5. http://www.spiritual-research-network.com/themosescode.html (accessed August 13, 2008).

_______. "The Moses Code: A New Age Lie (An Overview)." *Beautiful Truth* (February 23, 2008). http://web.mac.com/beautifultruth/Beautiful-Truth/Podcasts_MP3/Entries/2008/2/25_The_Moses_Code_-_A_New_Age_Lie(An_Overview).html (accessed August 13, 2008).

_______. "'The Moses Code Deception.' The Moses Code: A New Age Lie (An Overview)." *Beautiful Truth* (February 25–27, 2008). http://web.mac.com/beautifultruth/Beautiful-Truth/Podcasts_MP3/Entries/2008/2/25_The_Moses_Code_-_A_New_Age_Lie(An_Overview).html. *www.spiritual-research-network.stirsite.com/podcasts.html* (accessed August 13, 2008).

"Lie." *Merriam-Webster Online Dictionary*, s.v. "Lie." http://www.merriam-webster.com/dictionary/truth (accessed September 1, 2008).

Loy, Jim. "The Law of Gravity." *General Physics* (2000). http://csep10.phys.utk.edu/astr161/lect/history/newtongrav.html (accessed March 11, 2008).

"Lucifer, The Garden of Eden, and The Tower of Babel." *Four Ways*

Christians Are Deceived (Modified September 10, 2005). http://procinwarn.com/fourways.htm (accessed April 1, 2008).

"Luke 4:7." *Biblos.com Parallel Bible.* http://bible.cc/luke/4-7.htm (accessed December 12, 2008).

MacArthur, John. *The Truth War: Fighting for Certainty in an Age of Deception.* Nashville, TN: Thomas Nelson Publishers, 2007.

Mandela, Nelson. "Education Quotations." *Brainy Quote, BrainyMedia.com.* http://www.brainyquote.com/words/ed/education158399.html (accessed December 17, 2008).

March, Eugene W. *Israel and the Politics of Land: A Theological Case Study.* Louisville, KY: Westminster John Knox Press, 1994.

McFall, Lynne. "Integrity." *Ethics* 98, no. 4 (1987): 5–20. John Deigh, ed. *Ethics and Personality.* Reprint, Chicago, IL: University of Chicago Press, 1992. Alan Montefiore. "Self-Reality, Self-Respect, and Respect for Others." *Midwest Studies in Philosophy* (1978). http://plato.stanford.edu/entries/integrity/ (accessed April 28, 2008).

______. "Integrity." *Ethics* 98, no. 4 (April 2001, revision May 2005): 5–20. http://plato.stanford.edu/entries/integrity/ (accessed August 4, 2007).

______. "Lynne McFall." *Philosophy at Syracuse* (2008): 1. http://plato.stanford.edu/entries/integrity/ (accessed April 28, 2008). Among her many accomplishments and awards, McFall is "Associate Professor, Emeritus, PhD, University of Pittsburgh, 1982, … [r]ecipient of a Wallace Stegner Fellowship from Stanford University," and "has written on integrity, bitterness, solitude, truth-telling, love, death, loyalty, and free will." Lynne McFall. "Integrity." *Stanford Encyclopedia of Philosophy* (April 9, 2001, revision May 26, 2005): 1–27. http://philosophy.syr.edu/FacMcFall.htm (accessed April 28, 2008).

Miller, Randolph Crump. *The Clue to Christian Education.* New York, NY: Scribner Publishers, 1950.

Monette, René. "What Is Deception?" *Overcoming Deception.* http://www.changingtimes.info/Overcoming.htm (accessed August 15, 2008).

Morris, Robert. Knowing if you are born of the Spirit is like knowing if you are married—you're either married, or you're not—there's no confusion. Author's paraphrase. ca. 2013.

Muggeridge, Malcolm. *The Green Stick: A Chronicle of Wasted Years.* Glasgow: William Collins and Sons, 1972. Quoted in Ravi Zacharias, *Can Man Live Without God,* Nashville, TN: W Publishing Group, a Division of Thomas Nelson, Inc., 1994.

"Naturalism." *Encarta Dictionary,* s.v. "Naturalism:" A system of thought that rejects all spiritual and supernatural explanations of the world and holds that science is the sole basis of what can be known.

Nichols, Lisa. Quoted in Rhonda Byrne, *The Secret,* Hillsboro, OR: ATRIA Books/Beyond Words Publishing, 2006.

Northup, Clark Sutherland, ed. *The Essays of Francis Bacon.* Boston, MA: Houghton Mifflin, 1936. Quoted in "Pilate as the Antithesis of Truth in Bacon's 'Of Truth,'" *Academon* (2002). http://online.colum.edu/antiword.php (accessed August 12, 2008).

Novak, Carole. "Interview with John L. Goodlad." *Technos Quarterly* 2, no. 3 (Fall 1993). http://www.ait.net/technos/tq_02/3goodlad.php (accessed February 16, 2008).

Orwell, George. *A Collection of Essays.* 1946. First Harvest ed. Orlando, FL: Houghton Mifflin Harcourt Publishing Company, 1981. George Orwell (1903–1950). English novelist and essayist. *ThinkExist.com.* http://thinkexist.com/quotation/during_times_of_universal_deceit-telling_the/193642.html (accessed March 5, 2013).

Pazmino, Robert W. "Teachings of Paul." In *The Evangelical*

Dictionary of Christian Education, Grand Rapids, MI: Baker Books, 2001.

Pearcey, Nancy R. "The Birth of Modern Science," *Bible-Science Newsletter* (October 1982). Nancy Pearcey. "How Christianity Gave Rise to the Modern Scientific Outlook." *Bible-Science Newsletter* (January 1989), states she "later expanded this material into a major theme throughout *Soul of Science*, especially chapter 1, 'An Invented Institution: Christianity and the scientific Revolution.'" Quoted in Nancy R. Pearcey, *Total Truth: Liberating Christianity from Its Cultural Captivity*, Study Guide edition, Wheaton, IL: Crossway Books, 2005.

_______. "Fact vs. Theory: Does Gould Understand the Difference?" *Bible-Science Newsletter* (April 1987).

_______. *Total Truth: Liberating Christianity from Its Cultural Captivity*. Study Guide edition. Wheaton, IL: Crossway Books, 2005.

"Perversion." *Merriam-Webster Online Dictionary*, s.v. "Perversion." http://www.merriam-webster.com/dictionary/perversion (accessed March 3, 2012).

"Philosophy." *Merriam-Webster Online Dictionary*, s.v. "Philosophy." http://www.merriam-webster.com/dictionary/philosophy (accessed October 31, 2008).

Plato. (427–347 BCE). Greek philosopher.

_______. Quoted in Augustus Hopkins Strong. *Systematic Theology*, N.d., Reprint, Valley Forge, PA: Judson Press, 1985.

_______. "Quotes on Truth." *What Is Truth?*: 1–10. http://www.whatistruth.org.uk/quotesontruth.php (accessed August 12, 2008).

Popkin, Richard H., and Avrum Stroll. *Philosophy Made Simple*. New York, NY: Made Simple Books, 1956. Quoted in Michael J. Anthony and Warren S. Benson, *Exploring the History and Philosophy of Christian Education: Principles for the 21st Century*, Grand Rapids, MI: Kregel Publications, 2003.

Price, John Milburn. Quoted in Michael J. Anthony, and Warren S. Benson, *Exploring the History and Philosophy of Christian Education: Principles for the 21st Century*, Grand Rapids, MI: Kregel Publications, 2003.

"Proverbs 29:25." *Parallel Bible, Biblos.com*. http://bible.cc/proverbs/29-25.htm (accessed March 5, 2009).

Pullias, Earl V., with Ronald E. Cottle. *A Teacher: Models of Excellence*. Columbus, GA: TEC Publications, 2005.

"Quotes on 'Truth.'" *What Is Truth*?: 1. http://www.whatistruth.org.uk/quotesontruth.php (accessed August 12, 2008).

Rano, Marsha Scudder. "Confronting Error among the Christian Populace: A Case Study of 'The Secret.'" DMin diss., Beacon University, 2009.

Riskin, Shlomo. Interview of "The Six Day War—Was It A Miracle?" (ca. 2008). Ancient Secrets of the Bible Collection II. Grizzly Adams® Productions Library, Baker City, OR.

Ritenbaugh, John W. "The Fruit of the Spirit: Meekness." *Forerunner* (November 1998). http://cgg.org/index.cfm/fuseaction/Library.sr/CT/PERSONAL/k/237/The-Fruit-of-Spirit-Meekness.htm (accessed April 24, 2008).

Roberts, Jon, and James Turner. *The Sacred and the Secular University*. Princeton, NJ: Princeton University Press, 2000. Quoted in Nancy R. Pearcey, *Total Truth: Liberating Christianity from Its Cultural Captivity*, Study Guide edition, Wheaton, IL: Crossway Books, 2005.

Robertson, Pat. *The Greatest Virtue: The Secret to Living in Happiness and Success*. Virginia Beach, VA: Christian Broadcasting Network, 2007.

Robison, James. "We Have A Choice: Humility or Humiliation." *Dallas Morning News*. October 24, 2006. http://www.wehaveachoice.org/ (accessed March 1, 2008).

Rogers, Cleon. "The Charismatic Movement—35 Doctrinal Issues." *Biblical Discernment Ministries* (December

1997): 1–34. http://www/rapidnet.com/-jbeard/bdm/Psychology/char/35.htm (accessed March 1, 2008).

______. "The Great Commission." *Bibliotheca Sacra* 130, no. 519 (July 1973): 259–260. Rogers is "Field Director for Germany, Greater Europe Mission, President, German Bible Institute, Seeheim, Germany." http://www.galaxie.com/article/php?article-id=1827 (accessed February 29, 2008).

______. "Moses: Meek or Miserable?" *Journal of Evangelical Theological Society* 29, no. 3 (March 1, 2008): 257–263. http://www.galaxie.com/article.php?article_id=5364 (accessed February 21, 2008).

Saldarini, Anthony J. *Pharisees, Scribes, and Sadducees in Palestinian Society: A Sociological Approach.* Wilmington, DE: Michael Glazer, 1988. Quoted in Michael J. Anthony and Warren S. Benson, *Exploring the History and Philosophy of Christian Education: Principles for the 21st Century*, Grand Rapids, MI: Kregel Publications, 2003.

Schaeffer, Francis. *True Spirituality.* Wheaton, IL: Tyndale House, 1972. Quoted in Nancy R. Pearcey, *Total Truth: Liberating Christianity from Its Cultural Captivity*, Study Guide edition, Wheaton, IL: Crossway Books, 2008.

Schultz, Thom. Founder and publisher of Group Publishing, Inc., Loveland, Colorado. Employs Biblical topics in curriculum lessons formulated with the active learning methodology.

"Science." *Merriam-Webster Online Dictionary*, s.v. "Science." http://www.merriam-webster.com/dictionary/science (accessed October 9, 2008).

Seift, Fletcher H. "Education in Ancient Israel from Earliest Times to 70 A.D." In *History of Christian Education*, Charles B. Eavey, Chicago, IL: Moody Press, 1964. Quoted in Michael J. Anthony, and Warren S. Benson, *Exploring the History and Philosophy of Christian Education: Principles for the 21st Century*, Grand Rapids, MI: Kregel Publications, 2003.

Sellier, Charles. Email message to current author, October 26, 2007. Sellier is president and founder of Grizzly Adams® Productions, Baker City, Oregon.

Shamblin, Gwen. "Constant Encouragement." *The WeighDownWorkshop Official Library* 31, no. 2: 1–2. http://store.weighdown.com/Constant-Encouragement-Year-Two-C34.aspx?p=2 (accessed April 1, 2008).

Shreve, Mike. Email message to current author, August 27, 2008. Bill Kline, field supervisor to the current author, added the parenthetic thoughts and Scripture references.

_______. *In Search of the True Light.* Rev. ed. 2006. Reprint, Cleveland, TN: Deeper Revelation Books, 2007.

Silver, Daniel J. *A History of Judaism.* New York, NY: Basic Books, 1974, 88. Quoted in Michael J. Anthony and Warren S. Benson, *Exploring the History and Philosophy of Christian Education: Principles for the 21st Century,* Grand Rapids, MI: Kregel Publications, 2003, 29.

Simpson, Sandy. "Every Man Did That Which Was Right in His Own Eyes." Apologetics Coordination Team, *deceptioninthechurch.com* (January 1, 2006): 1. http://www.deceptioninthechurch.com/everyman.html (accessed December 6, 2010).

Sizer, Ted. Quoted in John I. Goodlad and Timothy J. McMannon, eds., *The Public Purpose of Education and Schooling,* San Francisco, CA: Jossey-Bass, 1997, 127.

Smith, Mark K. "Friedrich Froebel and Informal Education." *The Informal Education Homepage* (1997, updated February 5, 2009). http://www.infed.org/thinkers/et-froeb.htm (accessed May 4, 2009).

Splendor, Veritatis. "Quotes on Truth." *What Is Truth?*: 1–10. http://www.whatistruth.org.uk/quotesontruth.php (accessed August 12, 2008).

Sproul, R. C. "Before the Face of God." *A Daily Guide for Living from Ephesians, Hebrews, and James* 4, no. 4 (2000 c1994): 416. http://jubilee-church.org/sermons/notes/2003/02/

meekness-not-weakness.html (accessed February 21, 2008).

Stafford, Tim. "The Pentecostal Gold Standard." *Christianity Today* 49, no. 7 (July 2005). http://search.ebscohost.com/login.aspx?direct=true&db=15h&AN=1741581&site=ehost-live (accessed July 30, 2007).

Stanley, Charles. "Building Truth Into Your Life." *In Touch Ministries* (March 16, 2013): 1–3. http://www.intouch.org/you/sermon/outlines/content?topic=building_truth_into_your_life_outline (accessed March 17, 2013). Dr. Charles F. Stanley is senior pastor of First Baptist Church Atlanta, founder of In Touch Ministries, and a *New York Times* best-selling author. He demonstrates a keen awareness of people's needs and provides Christ-centered biblically based principles for everyday life. http://www.intouch.org/about/about-dr.-charles-stanley.

Stephens, James. *Francis Bacon and the Style of Science.* Chicago, IL: Chicago University Press, 1975.

Stevens, R. Paul. *The Other Six Days: Vocation, Work, and Ministry in Biblical Perspective.* Grand Rapids, MI: Wm. B. Eerdmans Publishing Co., 2000.

Strang, Steve. Quoted in Tim Stafford, "The Pentecostal Gold Standard," *Christianity Today* (July 2005): 1. http://search.ebscohost.com/login.aspx?direct=true&db=15h&AN=1741581&site=ehost-live (accessed July 30, 2007).

Strong, Augustus Hopkins. *Systematic Theology.* N.d. Reprint, Valley Forge, PA: Judson Press, 1985.

"Substitute." *Merriam-Webster Online Dictionary,* s.v. "Substitute." http://www.merriam-webster.com/dictionary/substitute (accessed March 3, 2012).

Sylva, Ken. "New Bible Translations to Drop 'Father' and 'Son.'" *Apprising Ministries* (January 28, 2012): 1–2. http://apprising.org/2012/01/28/new-bible-translations-to-drop-father-and-son/ (accessed March 16, 2013).

ten Boom, Corrie, John Sherrill, and Elizabeth Sherrill. *The Hiding Place*. New York, NY: Bantam Books, 1984.

Thatcher, Margaret. "Compromise." *brainyquote.com*: 1. http://www.brainyquote.com/words/co/compromise146379.html (accessed April 9, 2013).

"Theology." *Merriam-Webster Online Dictionary*, s.v. "Theology." http://www.merriam-webster.com/dictionary/theology (accessed October 31, 2008).

Thiselton, Anthony C. *New Horizons in Hermeneutics*. Grand Rapids, MI: Zondervan Publishing House, 1992.

Thrasher, William L. Jr. *Basics for Believers: Foundational Truths to Guide Your Life*. Vol. 1. Chicago, IL: Moody Press, 1998.

Todd, S. C. "A View from Kansas on That Evolution Debate." *Nature* 401 (September 30, 1999): 423. Quoted in Nancy R. Pearcey, *Total Truth: Liberating Christianity from Its Cultural Captivity*, Study Guide edition, Wheaton, IL: Crossway Books, 2005.

Tolle, Eckhart. *A New Earth: Awakening to Your Life's Purpose*. New York, NY: Plume/Penguin Group, 2006.

"Truth." *Merriam-Webster Online Dictionary*, s.v. "Truth." http://www.merriam-webster.com/dictionary/truth (accessed March 27, 2008).

Twist, Lynn. "The Big Give: Reality TV, Oprah Style, $ Million Dollars as Prize Money? Cool!" *Pass It Forward—Australia* (March 4, 2008). http://pifaustralia.org/tag/philosophy/ (accessed December 27, 2008).

"United States Conference of Catholic Bishops-New American Bible." *Confraternity of Christian Doctrine, Inc.* (December 2002). http://www.usccb.org/nab/bible/matthew/matthew5.htm (accessed March 5, 2008).

Vine, W. E., Merrill F. Unger, and William White Jr. *Vine's Complete Expository Dictionary of Old and New Testament Words*. Nashville, TN: Thomas Nelson Publishers, 1996.

Wadmed, Sid. "There Are No Degrees of Integrity: You Either Have

It or You Don't." *The Little Red Book of Wisdom* (2011): 1–2. Under "Chapter 15." www.littleredbookofwisdom.com (accessed March 3, 2013).

Walker, James K. Interview of "The Enigma of the Dead Sea Scrolls." (ca. 2002). Grizzly Adams® Productions Library, Baker City, OR.

_______. Interview of "There Is More to the Secret." (2008). Grizzly Adams® Productions Library, Baker City, OR.

_______. "The Truth Behind the Secret." *Watchman Fellowship* (2006). http://www.watchman.org/ (accessed October 3, 2008).

Walker, James K., and Bob Waldrep. *The Truth Behind the Secret: A Reasoned Response to the Runaway Bestseller.* Eugene, OR: Harvest House Publishers, 2007.

Walsh, Neal Donald. Quoted in Rhonda Byrne, *The Secret.* Hillsboro, OR: ATRIA Books/Beyond Words Publishing, 2006.

Wattles, Wallace D. *The Science of Getting Rich: Financial Success Through Creative Thought.* 1910. Reprint, New York, NY: Barnes & Noble, 2007.

Westerhoff III, John H., ed. *A Colloquy on Christian Education: A Socialization Model.* Philadelphia, PA: United Church Press, 1972.

"Western philosophy." *Encyclopedia Britannica*: 25. http://www.britannica.com/ed/article-8640/Western-philosophy#365691.hook (accessed March 27, 2008).

"What is Chrislam?" *Got Questions Ministries* (ca. 2013): 1–2. http://www.gotquestions.org/Chrislam.html (accessed March 16, 2013). Question: "What is Chrislam?" Answer: "Chrislam is an attempt to syncretize Christianity with Islam. While it began in Nigeria in the 1980s, Chrislamic ideas have spread throughout much of the world. The essential concept of Chrislam is that Christianity and Islam are compatible, that one can be a Christian and a Muslim at the same time. Chrislam is not an actual religion of its own, but a blurring of the differences and distinctions between Christianity and Islam." Read more: http://www.gotquestions.org/Chrislam.html#ixzz2NhbmjioP.

"What Is the Difference Between Ethics and Morals?" *WiseGeek: Clear Answers for Common Questions*: 1. http://www.wisegeek.org/what-is-the-difference-between-ethics-and-morals.htm (accessed March 18, 2013).

"What Is Truth?" *havdalahdrasha.org* (2009): 1–2. http://www.havdalahdrasha.org/page_emet.html (accessed March 11, 2013).

Wigram, George V. *The Englishman's Hebrew Concordance of the Old Testament.* Peabody, MA: Hendrickson Publishers, Inc., 2003.

Wilson, Bill. *Metro Ministries.* www.metroministries.org. Quoted in Michael J. Anthony and Warren S. Benson, *Exploring the History and philosophy of Christian Education: Principles for the 21st Century*, Grand Rapids, MI: Kregel Publications, 2003.

Wilson, Bishop Thomas. "Quotes on Truth." *What Is Truth?*: 1–10. http://www.whatistruth.org.uk/quotesontruth.php (accessed August 12, 2008).

Wilson, Larry. "Yea, Hath God Said …" *New Horizons Magazine* (June 2003). http://www.opc.org/new_horizons/NH03/06a.html (accessed December 12, 2008). "The author is the general secretary of the Committee on Christian Education and editor of *New Horizons* magazine."

Wilson, Mike. "Liars, Thieves, Cheats—An Upcoming Generation of Christians." *AFA Journal, The Daily Jot Daily Reporting and Analysis of Current Events from a Biblical Perspective* (December 2, 2008): 4. www.dailyjot.com (accessed December 2, 2008).

Wirtschafter, C. L. "Families in a Fractured World." *Proceedings of the Center for Jewish-Christian Learning* 11 (Fall 1996): 34. Quoted in Michael J. Anthony, and Warren S. Benson,

Exploring the History and Philosophy of Christian Education: Principles for the 21st Century, Grand Rapids, MI: Kregel Publications, 2003.

Wulfestieg, Rick. The loin is the seat of our ability to procreate and reproduce Truth. Author's paraphrase. ca. 2008.

Wycliffe, John. Quoted in Charles B. Eavey, *History of Christian Education*, Chicago, IL: Moody, 1964. Quoted in Michael J. Anthony and Warren S. Benson, *Exploring the History and Philosophy of Christian Education: Principles for the 21st Century*, Grand Rapids, MI: Kregel Publications, 2003.

Yale Faculty. *Education in the United States*. 1445. N.d. Reprint, Cohen. Quoted in John L. Goodlad and Timothy J. McMannon, eds., *The Public Purpose of Education and Schooling*, San Francisco, CA: Jossey-Bass, 1997, 12.

Zacharias, Ravi. *Can Man Live Without God*. Nashville, TN: Word Publishing, a division of Thomas Nelson Publishers, 1994.

Zodhiates, Spiros, ed. *The Complete Word Study Dictionary: For a Deeper Understanding of the Word*. Word Study Series. Rev. ed. Chattanooga, TN: AMG Publishers, 1993.

_______. *Hebrew-Greek Key Word Study Bible*. New International Version. Chattanooga, TN: AMG Publishers, 1996.

Zucker, David J. "Conflicting conclusions: The hatred of Isaac and Ishmael." *Judaism* 39, no. 1 (Winter 1990). http://newfirstsearch.oclc.org/ (accessed October 10, 2007).

NOTES

A Word from the Author

1. Plato, (427–347 BCE), Greek philosopher.
2. W. E. Vine, Merrill F. Unger and William White Jr., *Vine's Complete Expository Dictionary of Old and New Testament Words* (Nashville, TN: Thomas Nelson Publishers, 1980), 645.
3. Ibid.
4. Marsha Scudder Rano, "Confronting Error Among the Christian Populace: A Case Study of 'The Secret'" (doctoral dissertation, Beacon University, 2009).
5. Vine et al., *Vine's Complete Expository Dictionary of Old and New Testament Words*, 645.
6. James Walker, Interview of "There Is More to the Secret," (2008), Grizzly Adams® Productions Library, Baker City, OR, Interview of "The Enigma of the Dead Sea Scrolls," (ca. 2002), Grizzly Adams® Productions Library, Baker City, OR. On Rhonda Byrne's *The Secret* (Hillsboro, OR: ATRIA Books/Beyond Words Publishing, 2006), Walker makes the observation that according to Byrne, "the real secret is you. It's your true identity. And, like a good author, Rhonda Byrne saves that part of the secret to the very last section [where she avers] the sacred secret is that you are God."

Introduction: Truth That Safeguards

7. Charles Stanley, "Building Truth Into Your Life," *In Touch Ministries* (March 16, 2013): 1–3, http://www.intouch.org/you/sermon/

outlines/content?topic=building_truth_into_your_life_outline (accessed March 17, 2013). Dr. Charles F. Stanley is senior pastor of First Baptist Church Atlanta, founder of In Touch Ministries, and a *New York Times* best-selling author. He demonstrates a keen awareness of people's needs and provides Christ-centered biblically based principles for everyday life. http://www.intouch.org/about/about-dr.-charles-stanley.

8. Corrie ten Boom, John Sherrill and Elizabeth Sherrill, *The Hiding Place* (New York, NY: Bantam Books, 1984).

Part I: Truth or Consequences

9. Author's paraphrase of television commercial broadcast ca. 1990s.

Chapter 1
And You Shall Be as Gods: The Lie of the Ages

10. Rano, "Confronting Error Among the Christian Populace."
11. William L. Thrasher, Jr., *Basics for Believers: Foundational Truths to Guide Your Life*, vol. 1 (Chicago, IL: Moody Press, 1998), table of contents. Thrasher is the associate editor of Moody Press, Chicago, Illinois, and author of manifold works on Biblical theology. Thrasher identifies the foundational truths of Christianity as: "God; The Trinity; Names and Attributes of God; The Lord Jesus Christ; The Holy Spirit; The Bible; Doctrine; The Fall; Sin; The Incarnation; The Crucifixion; The Resurrection; The Gospel; and The New Birth."
12. Douglas R. Groothuis, "New Age Movement: New Age or Old Occult?" *Biblical Discernment Ministries* (Revised November 2001): 1–16, http://www.rapidnet.com/~jbeard/bdm/Cults/newage.htm (accessed February 25, 2009). "The New Age Movement is a modern revival of very ancient, divergent, religious traditions and practices. The actual original root is squarely centered in Genesis 3:1–5, and reverberates throughout the movement's continued historical expressions. In the original lie, Satan questions God's word, His authority and benevolent rule (v. 1), disputes that death results from

disobedience (v. 4, and claims that through the acquisition of secret or Gnostic wisdom man can be enlightened and can be 'like God' (v. 5)."

13. Ibid.
14. Rhonda Byrne, *The Secret* (Hillsboro, OR: ATRIA Books/Beyond Words Publishing, 2006).
15. "Now the serpent was more subtle and crafty than any living creature of the field which the Lord God had made. And he [Satan] said to the woman, Can it really be that God has said, You shall not eat from every tree of the garden? And the woman said to the serpent, We may eat the fruit from the trees of the garden, Except the fruit from the tree which is in the middle of the garden. God has said, You shall not eat of it, neither shall you touch it, lest you die. But the serpent said to the woman, You shall not surely die, For God knows that in the day you eat of it your eyes will be opened, and you will be like God, knowing the difference between good and evil and blessing and calamity" (Gen. 3:1–5, AMP).

Chapter 2
Induction to Truth: Equipping the Saints

16. The events of this case study are factual with some narrative license and took place in the 1990s. Linda Crawford is a fictitious name that has been assigned to the real person to protect her privacy.
17. *Alēthinos* (S228) refers to "real, ideal, genuine, it is used of God, John 7:28; 17:3; 1 Thess. 1:9; Rev. 6:10;" these declare that God fulfills the meaning of His Name; He is "very God," in distinction from all other gods, false gods … signifies that He is veracious, "true" to His utterances, He cannot lie.
18. *Alētheia* (S225) is used objectively, signifying "the reality lying at the basis of an appearance; the manifested veritable essence of a matter (Cremer), e.g., Rom. 9:1; 2 Cor. 11:10;" … especially of Christian doctrine … where "the truth of God" may be "the truth concerning God" or "God whose existence is a verity"… [and] … is indicative of His faithfulness in the fulfillment of His promises as exhibited

in Christ. … Not just ethical "truth," but "truth" in all its fullness and scope, as embodied in Him.

19. *Pseudos* (S5579) (some mss. have *dolos*, "guile," KJV); 2 Thess. 2:9, where "lying wonders" is, lit., "wonders of falsehood," i.e., wonders calculated to deceive (cf. Rev. 13:13–15), the purpose being to deceive people into the acknowledgment of the spurious claim to deity on the part of the Man of Sin. … Note: In Rom. 1:25 the "lie" or idol is the outcome of pagan religion; in 1 John 2:21, 22 the "lie" is the denial that Jesus is the Christ; in 2 Thess. 2:11 the "lie" is the claim of the Man of Sin.
20. Groothuis, "New Age Movement: New Age or Old Occult?"
21. Ravi Zacharias, *Can Man Live Without God* (Nashville, TN: Word Publishing, a division of Thomas Nelson Publishers, 1994), 101.
22. Vine et al., *Vine's Complete Expository Dictionary of Old and New Testament Words*, 645.
23. Ibid., 367.
24. Ibid., 645.
25. Ibid., 366.
26. "What is Chrislam?" *Got Questions Ministries*: 1–2, http://www.gotquestions.org/Chrislam.html (accessed March 16, 2013). Question: "What is Chrislam?" Answer: "Chrislam is an attempt to syncretize Christianity with Islam. While it began in Nigeria in the 1980s, Chrislamic ideas have spread throughout much of the world. The essential concept of Chrislam is that Christianity and Islam are compatible, that one can be a Christian and a Muslim at the same time. Chrislam is not an actual religion of its own, but a blurring of the differences and distinctions between Christianity and Islam." Read more: http://www.gotquestions.org/Chrislam.html#ixzz2NhbmjioP.
27. Ken Sylva, "New Bible Translations to Drop 'Father' and 'Son,'" *Apprising Ministries* (January 28, 2012): 1–2, http://apprising.org/2012/01/28/new-bible-translations-to-drop-father-and-son/ (accessed March 16, 2013).
28. John Stocker, ca. 2010.

29. E. W. Bullinger, *Number in Scripture* (New York, NY: Cosimo Classics, 2005), 135.
30. Author Unknown.
31. Rick Wulfestieg, ca. 2008.
32. Jack Hayford, ca. 1980s.
33. "Proverbs 29:25," *Parallel Bible, Biblos.com* (2009), http://bible.cc/proverbs/29-25.htm (accessed March 5, 2009).
34. Paul J. Bucknell, "Developing a Fear of God, Joshua 1:10," *Biblical Foundations for Freedom*, under "Fear of God: Living in the Awe of the Holiness of God, Fear not man," under "The Godly Man: When God touches a man's life," http://www.foundationsforfreedom.net/Topics/FearGodMan/FearGod019.html (accessed March 5, 2009).
35. Spiros Zodhiates, *Hebrew-Greek Key Word Study Bible*, New International Version (Chattanooga, TN: AMG Publishers, 1996).
36. "1 John 4:18," *Jamieson-Fausset-Brown Bible Commentary*, http://bible.cc/1_john/4-18.htm (accessed March 5, 2009).
37. W. Guy Delaney, "Obedience is Better Than Sacrifice," *Sermon Teaser.com* (2011): 1–2, http://www.sermonteaser.com/obedience-is-better-than-sacrifice/ (accessed March 11, 2013).
38. Thrasher, *Basics for Believers*, table of contents.
39. Julia Duin, "Statistics: Moral Values, America a Christian Nation, and More," *The Washington Times* (December 31, 2004), under "Public Christian Symbols Backed," http://www.ucmpage.org/news/barna_report1.html (accessed September 24, 2008).
40. Byrne, *The Secret.*
41. Groothuis, "New Age Movement: New Age or Old Occult?"
42. Bullinger, *Number in Scripture*, 89.
43. Ibid., 90–91.
44. "What is truth?," *havdalahdrasha.org* (2009): 1–2, http://www.havdalahdrasha.org/page_emet.html (accessed March 11, 2013).
45. Ibid.
46. Ibid.
47. Zacharias, *Can Man Live Without God*, 126.
48. Ibid.
49. Ralph Waldo Emerson, "Quotes on Truth," *What Is Truth?* (ca.

2008): 1–10, http://www.whatistruth.org.uk/quotesontruth.php (accessed August 12, 2008).

50. Vine et al., *Vine's Complete Expository Dictionary of Old and New Testament Words*, 366.

51. W. J. Dumbrell, *Covenant and Creation: An Old Testament Covenantal Theology* (Nashville, TN: Thomas Nelson Publishers, 1984), 38, quoted in R. Paul Stevens, *The Other Six Days: Vocation, Work and Ministry in Biblical Perspective* (Grand Rapids, MI: Wm. B. Eerdmans Publishing Co., 2000), 93.

52. "Lucifer, The Garden of Eden, and The Tower of Babel," *Four Ways Christians Are Deceived* (Modified September 10, 2005): 1–4, under "The Repackaged Lie," http://procinwarn.com/fourways.htm (accessed April 1, 2008).

53. R. Paul Stevens, *The Other Six Days: Vocation, Work, and Ministry in Biblical Perspective* (Grand Rapids, MI: Wm. B. Eerdmans Publishing Co., 2000), 99.

Part II: God of All Truth

54. Jack W. Hayford, "Integrity of Heart," *Jack Hayford Ministries* (2013): 1–2, http://www.jackhayford.org/teaching/articles/integrity-of-heart/ (accessed February 8, 2013).

Chapter 3
Man Embraces the Truth: Authentic Life and Purpose

55. Zacharias, *Can Man Live Without God*, 93.

56. *Merriam-Webster Online Dictionary*, s.v. "Truth," http://www.merriam-webster.com/dictionary/truth (accessed March 27, 2008).

57. Paul Jonathan Hollander, quoted in Norman Swartz, "The Myth of the Flat Earth," Department of Philosophy, *Simon Fraser University* (August 8, 1995): 1, http://www.sfu.ca/philosophy/swartz/flat_earth.htm (accessed December 27, 2008). In his response to logic-l of the PHILOSOP email discussion group initiated by Swartz, Hollander replies: "If I remember my Western Civ. correctly, the

comment Aristotle makes at *De Caelo* II.14 298a9-15, that the ocean to the west (i.e. the Atlantic) quite possibly connects with India, was known to Columbus and helped convince him that the Earth was round. Such terms as 'West Indies' and 'Indian' (meaning Native American) would seem to be due in part to Aristotle."

58. *Merriam-Webster Online Dictionary*, s.v. "Science," http://www.merriam-webster.com/dictionary/science (accessed October 9, 2008).
59. Francis Bacon, "The Essays," *Oregon State University* (1601), under "Of Truth," oregonstate.edu/instruct/phl302/texts/bacon/bacon_essays.html (accessed August 12, 2008). Francis Bacon is credited for ushering in modern science with his assertion that knowledge is power.
60. Marsha Craig, Debra Lester, Connie Henderson, and Mary Granderson, "Discovering Gravity: What Goes Up Must Come Down," Smile Program Chemistry Index, Basic Tools and Principles, *Illinois Institute of Technology* (N.d.): 1, http://www.iit.edu/~smile/cheminde.html (accessed October 28, 2008).
61. Tom Henderson, "Newton's Third Law of Motion," *The Physics Classroom Tutorial* (2007): 1, http://www.glenbrook.k12.il.us/GBSSCI/PHYS/CLASS/newtlaws/u2l4a.html (accessed October 28, 2008).
62. Frances Herbert Bradley, (1846–1924), British philosopher.
63. *Merriam-Webster Online Dictionary*, s.v. "Philosophy," http://www.merriam-webster.com/dictionary/philosophy (accessed October 31, 2008).
64. Ray Bradley, "Is Everything Relative, Including Truth?" Department of Philosophy, *Simon Frazier University*, http://www.sfu.ca/content/dam/sfu/philosophy/docs/bradley/relative.pdf (accessed October 30, 2008). Bradley is Emeritus Professor of Philosophy, Simon Fraser University; former Professor of Philosophy, University of Auckland, and author of articles like, "Does the moon exist only when someone is looking at it?"
65. Bradley Dowden and Norman Swartz, "Truth," *Internet Encyclopedia of Philosophy*, http://www.iep.utm.edu/t/truth.htm (accessed October 30, 2008).

66. Ibid.
67. Winston Churchill, "Winston Churchill quotes," *TruthExist.com Quotations* (ca. 2013): 1, http://thinkexist.com/quotation/the_truth_is_incontrovertible-malice_may_attack/220093.html (accessed March 19, 2013).
68. Oliver Wendell Holmes Jr., "Law in Science and Science in Law," *Harvard Law Review* 12, no. 443 (1899), in *The Essential Holmes*, edited with an introduction by Richard A. Posner (Chicago, IL: University of Chicago Press, 1996), 188–190. *See* also E. Donald Elliott, "The Evolutionary Tradition in Jurisprudence," *Columbia Law Review* 85, no. 38 (1985): 52–53. This article provides a good overview of legal theories that draw explicit metaphors to evolution.
69. Nancy R. Pearcey, *Total Truth: Liberating Christianity From Its Cultural Captivity*, Study Guide edition (Wheaton, IL: Crossway Books, 2005), 84. Born and raised in a nominal Christian home, Nancy Pearcey became an atheist in her high school years, and through a series of events that only God could orchestrate, Pearcey found herself under the personal tutelage of Dr. Francis Schaeffer in the Alps of Switzerland, which would forever change her life and the lives of the untold thousands of people whom she would influence through her life, her ministry, and her writings.
70. *Merriam-Webster Online Dictionary*, s.v. "Theology," http://www.merriam-webster.com/dictionary/theology (accessed October 31, 2008).
71. Vine et al., *Vine's Complete Expository Dictionary of Old and New Testament Words*, 645.
72. Ray S. Anderson, *The Soul of Ministry: Forming Leaders for God's People*, 1st ed. (Louisville, KY: Westminster John Knox Press, 1997), 6.
73. Ibid., 18.
74. Winston Churchill, "Quotes On Truth," *What Is Truth?*: 1–10, http://www.whatistruth.org.uk/quotesontruth.php (accessed August 12, 2008).

75. Vine et al., *Vine's Complete Expository Dictionary of Old and New Testament Words*, 645.

76. Veritatis Splendor, "Quotes on Truth," *What Is Truth?*: 1–10, http://www.whatistruth.org.uk/quotesontruth.php (accessed August 12, 2008).

77. Bishop Thomas Wilson, "Quotes on Truth," *What Is Truth?*: 1–10, http://www.whatistruth.org.uk/quotesontruth.php (accessed August 12, 2008).

78. "Francis Schaeffer Library," *The Pulpit Page, Visionary Gallery*: 1–14, under "Philosophy Page," http://www.tillwehavefaces.net/the%20pulpit%20page.html (December 18, 2008). His lifetime of influence through two dozen works and a heart seeking truth, Schaeffer addressed the Christian faith through works like *Escape From Reason*. Upon his death President Ronald Reagan eulogized, "It can rarely be said of an individual that his life touched many others and affected them for the better; it will be said of Dr. Francis Schaeffer that his life touched millions of souls and brought them to the truth of their Creator."

79. Pearcey, *Total Truth*, 18.

80. Ibid., 354.

81. Emerson, "Quotes on Truth," *What Is Truth?*: 1–10, http://www.whatistruth.org.uk/quotesontruth.php (accessed August 12, 2008).

82. Vine et al., *Vine's Complete Expository Dictionary of Old and New Testament Words*, 645.

83. The events of this case study are factual with some narrative license and took place in 2004. Jessica Foster is a fictitious name that has been assigned to the real person to protect her privacy.

84. Ed Gungor, interview of "There Is More to The Secret," (2008), Grizzly Adams® Productions Library, Baker City, OR. Ed Gungor, *There Is More to the Secret: An Examination of Rhonda Byrne's Bestselling Book the Secret* (Nashville, TN: Thomas Nelson Publishers, 2007), 72.

Chapter 4
God's Very Nature: Truth

85. Zacharias, *Can Man Live Without God*, 93.
86. Plato, "Quotes On Truth," *What Is Truth?* (ca. 2008): 1–10, http://www.whatistruth.org.uk/quotesontruth.php (accessed August 12, 2008).
87. Plato, quoted in Augustus Hopkins Strong, *Systematic Theology*, 261.
88. Augustus Hopkins Strong, *Systematic Theology* (N.d.; repr., Valley Forge, PA: Judson Press, 1985), 261.
89. "David Friedrich Hollaz," *Studium Exitar: The Journal of Confessional Language Studies at MLC* (2002, 2006), http://www.studiumexcitare.com/content/67 (accessed November 8, 2008). "The history of Lutheranism ascribes Hollaz, pastor and theologian, the title of the last great dogmatician of the period of Lutheran orthodoxy, a designation which modern students of Lutheran dogmatics recognize." However, "Pastor Hollaz, God's humble servant … unceasingly preached Christ crucified."
90. David Friedrich Hollaz, quoted in Thomasius, *Christi Person und Werk*, 1:137, quoted in Augustus Hopkins Strong, *Systematic Theology*, 261.
91. "Western Philosophy," *Encyclopedia Britannica* (2008): 25, http://www.britannica.com/ed/article-8640/Western-philosophy#365691.hook (accessed March 27, 2008).
92. Ibid.
93. Author Unknown.
94. "What is the Difference Between Ethics and Morals?" *WiseGeek: Clear Answers for Common Questions* (2013): 1, http://www.wisegeek.org/what-is-the-difference-between-ethics-and-morals.htm (accessed March 18, 2013).
95. Augustine, cited in Henry Chadwick, *Augustine: A Very Short Introduction* (Oxford, England: Oxford University Press, 2001), 54.
96. Ronald T. Habermas, "Catechism," in *The Evangelical Dictionary of*

Christian Education, ed. Michael J. Anthony (Grand Rapids, MI: Baker Books, 2001), 111–113.

97. Stanley Fleming, "On Truth," *Gate Breakers Ministries* (Spring 2008): 1, http://www.gatebreakers.com/On_Truth.pdf (accessed November 3, 2008).
98. Ibid.
99. Jack W. Hayford, quoted in Tim Stafford, "The Pentecostal Gold Standard," *Christianity Today* (July 2005): 1, http://search.ebscohost.com/login.aspx?direct=true&db=15h&AN=1741581&site=ehost-live (accessed July 30, 2007).
100. Jack W. Hayford, *Pastors of Promise: A Practical and Passionate Call for Faithful Shepherds* (Ventura, CA: Gospel Light Publications, 1997), 6.
101. Jack W. Hayford, *The Church on the Way: Learning to Live in the Promise of Biblical Congregational Life* (Old Tappan, NJ: Chosen Books, 1983), 17.
102. Mel Lawrenz, *The Dynamics of Spiritual Formation* (Grand Rapids, MI: Baker Books, 2000), 144.
103. Mark DeMoss, *The Little Red Book of Wisdom* (Nashville, TN: Thomas Nelson, 2007), 104. Mark DeMoss is president of The DeMoss Group, a public relations firm he founded in 1991 to serve Christian organizations and causes. A number of the largest non-profit organizations in America are counted among The DeMoss Group's clients. Mark has spent his life around wise people and has worked closely with some of the most prominent religious leaders of the past several decades. Mark and his wife April live in Atlanta, Georgia, with their three teenagers.
104. Sid Wadmed, "There are no degrees of Integrity: You either have it or you don't," *The Little Red Book of Wisdom* (2011): 1–2, under "Chapter 15," www.littleredbookofwisdom.com (accessed March 3, 2013).
105. *Merriam-Webster Online Dictionary*, s.v. "Integrity," http://www.merriam-webster.com/dictionary/integrity (accessed February 27, 2009).
106. Pearcey, *Total Truth*, 51.

107. Francis Schaeffer, *True Spirituality* (Wheaton, IL: Tyndale House, 1972), quoted in Pearcey, *Total Truth*, 355.
108. Ibid.
109. Lawrenz, *The Dynamics of Spiritual Formation*, 40–41.
110. Mark Halfon, "Integrity," *Stanford Encyclopedia of Philosophy* (April 9, 2001, revised May 26, 2005): 1–27, (1976): 54, http://plato.stanford.edu/entries/integrity/#6 (accessed February 21, 2008).
111. Mark Halfon, "Integrity," *Stanford Encyclopedia of Philosophy* (April 9, 2001), http://plato.stanford.edu/entries/integrity/#4 (accessed February 21, 2008).
112. Lynne McFall, "Integrity," *Ethics* 98, no. 4 (April 2001, revised May 2005): 5–20, http://plato.stanford.edu/entries/integrity/ (accessed August 4, 2007).
113. McFall, "Integrity," 5–20. Lynne McFall, "Lynne McFall," *Philosophy at Syracuse*: 1, http://plato.stanford.edu/entries/integrity/ (accessed April 28, 2008). Among her many accomplishments and awards, McFall is "Associate Professor, Emeritus, PhD, University of Pittsburgh, 1982, … recipient of a Wallace Stegner Fellowship from Stanford University," and "she has written on integrity, bitterness, solitude, truth-telling, love, death, loyalty, and free will." Lynne McFall, "Integrity," *Stanford Encyclopedia of Philosophy* (April 9, 2001, revised May 26, 2005): 1–27, http://philosophy.syr.edu/FacMcFall.htm (accessed April 28, 2008).
114. R. C. Sproul, "Before the face of God," *A Daily Guide for Living from Ephesians, Hebrews, and James* 4, no. 4 (2000, ca. 1994): 416, under "Meekness," http://www.jubilee-church.org/sermons/notes/2003/02/meekness-not-weakness.html (accessed February 21, 2008).
115. Augustine, "Saint Augustine Quotes and Biography," *QuoteDB*: 1, http://www.quotedb.com/authors/saint-augustine (accessed November 10, 2008).
116. Earl V. Pullias with Ronald E. Cottle, *A Teacher: Models of Excellence* (Columbus, GA: TEC Publications, 2005), 74.
117. Ibid.
118. E. M. Bounds, "Prayer and Importunity," *The Necessity of Prayer*, under "Chapter 6 and 7," www.jesus-is-savior.com/Books,%20

Tracts%20&%20Preaching/Printed%20Books/NOP/nop-chap_06.htm (accessed March 21, 2008).

119. Jack W. Hayford, *Prayer Is Invading the Impossible* (Gainesville, FL: Bridge-Logos Publishers, 2002), 11.
120. Ibid., 186.
121. Pearcey, *Total Truth*, 44–45.
122. James Robison, "We Have a Choice: Humility or Humiliation," *Dallas Morning News*, October 24, 2006, 1, http://www.wehaveachoice.org/ (accessed March 1, 2008).
123. Tony Evans, quoted in James Robison, "We Have a Choice: Humility or Humiliation," *Dallas Morning News*, October 24, 2006, 1, http://www.wehaveachoice.org/ (accessed March 1, 2008).
124. Gwen Shamblin, "Constant Encouragement," *The WeighDownWorkshop Official Library* 31, no. 2 (2008): 1, http://store.weighdown.com/Constant-Encouragement-Year-Two-C34.aspx?p=2 (accessed April 1, 2008).
125. Ibid.
126. W. T. Jones and Robert J. Fogelin, *A History of Western Philosophy: The Medieval Mind*, 2nd ed. (New York, NY: Harcourt Brace Jovanovich, 1969), 146–147.
127. M. G. Easton, *Illustrated Bible Dictionary*, 3rd ed. (Washington, DC: Thomas Nelson, 1897).
128. Hayford, *The Church on the Way*, 17.
129. Anthony J. Saldarini, *Pharisees, Scribes, and Sadducees in Palestinian Society: A Sociological Approach* (Wilmington, DE: Michael Glazer, 1988), 52, quoted in Anthony and Benson, *Exploring the History and Philosophy of Christian Education*, 34.
130. Michael J. Anthony, "Synagogue Schools," Michael J. Anthony, ed., *The Evangelical Dictionary of Christian Education*, 677.
131. Shamblin, "Constant Encouragement," 2.
132. Michael J. Anthony and Warren S. Benson, *Exploring the History and Philosophy of Christian Education: Principles for the 21st Century* (Grand Rapids, MI: Kregel Publications, 2003), 36.
133. Severe F. Frost, *Historical and Philosophical Foundations* (Columbus,

OH: Charles E. Merrill, 1966), 36, quoted in Anthony and Benson, *Exploring the History and Philosophy of Christian Education*, 30.

134. Ibid.
135. Anthony and Benson, *Exploring the History and Philosophy of Christian Education*, 37.
136. Frost, *Historical and Philosophical Foundations*, 36, quoted in Anthony and Benson, *Exploring the History and Philosophy of Christian Education*, 30.
137. John W. Ritenbaugh, "The Fruit of the Spirit: Meekness," *Forerunner* (November 1998): 1, http://cgg.org/index.cfm/fuseaction/Library.sr/CT/PERSONAL/k/237/The-Fruit-of-Spirit-Meekness.htm (accessed April 24, 2008).
138. Fletcher H. Seift, "Education in Ancient Israel from Earliest Times to 70 A.D.," in Charles B. Eavey, *History of Christian Education* (Chicago, IL: Moody Press, 1964), 59, quoted in Anthony and Benson, *Exploring the History and Philosophy of Christian Education*, 30.
139. Cleon Rogers, "The Charismatic Movement: 35 Doctrinal Issues," *Biblical Discernment Ministries* (December 1997): 1–34, http://www.rapidnet.com/~jbeard/bdm/Psychology/char/35.htm (accessed March 1, 2008).
140. Ritenbaugh, "The Fruit of the Spirit: Meekness."
141. Cleon Rogers, "Moses: Meek or Miserable?" *Journal of Evangelical Theological Society* 29, no. 3 (March 1, 2008): 257–263, http://www/galaxie.com/article/php?article_id=5364 (accessed February 21, 2008).
142. Wilbur Dwight Dunkel, "The Meek Shall Inherit the Earth: A Study in Shakespearean Tragedy," *Theology Today* 15, no. 3 (October 1958): 359–365, http://www.theologytoday.ptsem.edu.oct1958/v15-3-article7.htm (accessed February 21, 2008).
143. Carole Novak, "Interview with John I. Goodlad," *Technos Quarterly* 2, no. 3 (Fall 1993): 1–5, http://www.ait.net/technos/tq_02/3goodlad.php (accessed February 16, 2008).
144. Immanuel Kant, quoted in Anthony and Benson, *Exploring the History and Philosophy of Christian Education*, 246.
145. Hayford, "Integrity of Heart—Honest to God."

146. Kant, quoted in Harold H. Titus, *Living Issues in Philosophy*, 364–365.
147. June Nichols, The Church on the Way, ca. 1971.
148. Jim Elliot, quoted in Anthony and Benson, *Exploring the History and Philosophy of Christian Education*, 39.
149. Anthony and Benson, *Exploring the History and Philosophy of Christian Education*, 225–226.
150. Bill Wilson, Metro Ministries, quoted in Anthony and Benson, *Exploring the History and Philosophy of Christian Education*, 276–278. (All of the materials related to the description of Metro Ministries come from their Website located at www.metroministries.org.)
151. Author Unknown.
152. Richard LaRaviere, "Six ways to discern between God's voice and that of Satan," Part 3, *SermonCentral.com* (September 2007): 1–2, http://www.sermoncentral.com/sermons/six-ways-to-discern-between-gods-voice-and-that-of-satan-part-3-richard-laraviere-sermon-on-growth-in-christ-111665.asp (accessed March 4, 2013).
153. William Barclay, *Educational Ideals in the Ancient World* (Grand Rapids, MI: Baker, 1959), 209, quoted in Anthony and Benson, *Exploring the History and Philosophy of Christian Education*, 124.
154. Anthony and Benson, *Exploring the History and Philosophy of Christian Education*, 279.
155. Stevens, *The Other Six Days*, 16.

Chapter 5
Benefits of the Truth: Light, Clarity, Clear Vision

156. Pearcey, *Total Truth*, 42.
157. Anthony and Benson, *Exploring the History and Philosophy of Christian Education*, 24.
158. Ibid.
159. *Gates of Prayer* (New York, NY: Central Conference of American Rabbis, 1955), 191, quoted in Anthony and Benson, *Exploring the History and Philosophy of Christian Education*, 23.
160. C. L. Wirtschafter, "Families in a Fractured World," *Proceedings of*

the Center for Jewish-Christian Learning 11 (Fall 1996): 34, quoted in Anthony and Benson, *Exploring the History and Philosophy of Christian Education*, 23.

161. Daniel J. Silver, *A History of Judaism* (New York, NY: Basic Books, 1974), 88, quoted in Anthony and Benson, *Exploring the History and Philosophy of Christian Education*, 29.
162. Anthony and Benson, *Exploring the History and Philosophy of Christian Education*, 39.
163. Anderson, *The Soul of Ministry*, 69.
164. Ibid., 76.
165. Ibid., 82.
166. Ibid.
167. Ibid., 91.
168. Ibid., 90.
169. Larry Wilson, "Yea, Hath God Said…" *New Horizons Magazine* (June 2003), http://www.ope.org/new_horizons/NH03/06a.html (accessed December 12, 2008). "The author is the general secretary of the Committee on Christian Education and editor of *New Horizons* magazine."
170. Ibid.
171. John Milburn Price, quoted in Anthony and Benson, *Exploring the History and Philosophy of Christian Education*, 362. Price's contributions in the field of religious education at Southwestern are nothing short of monumental, especially given the liberal cultural and theological context of America at this time. Price continued to serve as the dean of the school for forty-one years. For a more detailed accounting of the many accomplishments of Price at Southwestern Baptist Theological Seminary, see the article by Rick Yount, *Evangelical Dictionary of Christian Education*, s.v. "John Milburn Price."
172. John Wycliffe, quoted in Eavey, *History of Christian Education*, 132, quoted in Anthony and Benson, *Exploring the History and Philosophy of Christian Education*, 177.
173. Anthony and Benson, *Exploring the History and Philosophy of Christian Education*, 177.
174. Anderson, *The Soul of Ministry*, 113.

175. Ibid., 124.
176. Ibid., 125.
177. Ibid., 140.
178. I. M. Fraser, "Theology and Action," *Scottish Journal of Theology* 2, no. 4 (December 1949): 414–415; 411–423), quoted in Stevens, *The Other Six Days*, 16.
179. Anderson, *The Soul of Ministry*, 149.
180. Ibid., 151.
181. Ibid., 155.
182. Cleon Rogers, "The Great Commission," *Bibliotheca Sacra* 130, no. 519 (July 1973): 259–263, http://www.galaxie.com/article/php?article_id=1827 (accessed February 29, 2008).
183. Pullias and Cottle, *A Teacher: Models of Excellence*, 199.
184. "Education quotes," *ThinkExist.com*: 1, http://thinkexist.com/quotations/education/ (accessed March 27, 2008).
185. Thom Schultz, founder and publisher of Group Publishing, Inc., Loveland, Colorado, employs Biblical topics in curriculum lessons formulated with the active learning methodology.
186. Pearcey, *Total Truth*, 56.
187. Anthony and Benson, *Exploring the History and Philosophy of Christian Education*, 37.
188. Ibid., 356.
189. Ibid., 93.
190. Ibid., 337–338.
191. Ibid., 106.
192. Robert W. Pazmino, "Teachings of Paul," in Anthony, ed., *The Evangelical Dictionary of Christian Education*, 686–688.
193. Ibid.
194. Anthony and Benson, *Exploring the History and Philosophy of Christian Education*, 99.
195. Ibid., 17.
196. Ibid.
197. Ibid., 43.
198. Ibid.
199. Ibid., 76.

200. Elwood P. Cubberley, *The History of Education* (Boston, MA: Houghton Mifflin, 1948), 77, quoted in Anthony and Benson, *Exploring the History and Philosophy of Christian Education*, 88.
201. Anthony and Benson, *Exploring the History and Philosophy of Christian Education*, 98.
202. Ibid.
203. Fredrick Eby and Charles F. Arrowood, *The History and Philosophy of Education: Ancient and Medieval* (Englewood Cliffs, NJ: Prentice-Hall, 1940), 713, quoted in Anthony and Benson, *Exploring the History and Philosophy of Christian Education*, 147.
204. Anthony and Benson, *Exploring the History and Philosophy of Christian Education*, 180.
205. Ibid., 171.
206. Charles B. Eavey, *History of Christian Education*, (Chicago, IL: Moody, 1964), 215, quoted in Anthony and Benson, *Exploring the History and Philosophy of Christian Education*, 263–264.
207. Anthony and Benson, *Exploring the History and Philosophy of Christian Education*, 188.
208. Eavey, *History of Christian Education*, 215, quoted in Anthony and Benson, *Exploring the History and Philosophy of Christian Education*, 263–264.
209. Mark K. Smith, "Friedrich Froebel and Informal Education," *The Informal Education Homepage* (1997, updated February 5, 2009), http://www.infed.org/thinkers/et-froeb.htm (accessed May 4, 2009). "Invented in the 1830s by German educator Friedrich Froebel, kindergarten was designed to teach young children about art, design, mathematics. … Froebel's philosophy of education rested on four basic components: free self activity, creativity, social participation, and motor expression." www.geocities.com/Athens/Forum/7905/fblkind.html (accessed May 4, 2009).
210. Ibid.
211. Oliver P. Chitwood, *History of Colonial America* (New York, NY: Harper and Row, 1961), 640, quoted in Anthony and Benson, *Exploring the History and Philosophy of Christian Education*, 309–310.
212. R. Freeman Butts, *A Cultural History of Education* (New York,

NY: McGraw Hill, 1947), 449, quoted in Anthony and Benson, *Exploring the History and Philosophy of Christian Education*, 316.

213. Anthony and Benson, *Exploring the History and Philosophy of Christian Education*, 321.
214. George Albert Coe, quoted in Anthony and Benson, *Exploring the History and Philosophy of Christian Education* 348–349.
215. George Albert Coe, quoted in Mary C. Boys, *Educating in Faith* (San Francisco, CA: Harper and Row, 1980), 51.
216. Anthony and Benson, *Exploring the History of Christian Education*, 300–360.
217. John H. Westerhoff III, ed., *A Colloquy on Christian Education: A Socialization Model* (Philadelphia, PA: United Church Press, 1972), 66.
218. Kenneth O. Gangel and Howard G. Hendricks, eds., *The Christian Handbook on Teaching: A Comprehensive Resource on the Distinctiveness of True Christian Teaching* (Grand Rapids, MI: Baker Books, 1998), 68.
219. Anthony and Benson, *Exploring the History and Philosophy of Christian Education*, 404.
220. Ibid., 416.
221. John Dewey, quoted in Jim Loy, "The Law of Gravity," *General Physics* (2000), under "Physics and Chemistry," http://csep10.phys.utk.edu/astr161/lect/history/newtongrav.html (accessed March 11, 2008).
222. Sir Isaac Newton, quoted in Loy, "The Law of Gravity," (2000).
223. David Gough, "Johann Heinrich Pestalozzi," in Anthony, ed., *The Evangelical Dictionary of Christian Education*, 531–532.
224. John Dewey, *Democracy and Education*, quoted in Goodlad and McMannon, eds., *The Public Purpose of Education and Schooling*, 45.
225. Jones and Fogelin, *A History of Western Philosophy*, 146–147.
226. Leslie E. Carlson, Lowell Coolidge, Earl L. Core, Huber L. Drumwright and Virtus E. Gideon, *The Expositor's Study Bible* (N.d.; repr., Baton Rouge, LA: Jimmy Swaggart Ministries, 2005).
227. Ibid.

Part III: Father of Lies

228. The events of this case study are factual with some narrative license and took place in 1982. Rita Frye is a fictitious name that has been assigned to the real person to protect her privacy.

Chapter 6
Man Rejects the Truth: Disingenuous Life and Purpose

229. Christopher Lawson, "The Moses Code: A New Age Lie (An Overview)," *Beautiful Truth* (February 23, 2008): 1, http://web.mac.com/beautifultruth/Beautiful-Truth/Podcasts_MP3/Entries/2008/2/25_The_Moses_Code_-_A_New_Age_Lie(An_Overview).html (accessed August 13, 2008). According to Lawson, an example of the deceiving spirits and doctrines of demons to which Paul refers in 1 Timothy 4:1–2 is "The Moses Code." This is a New Age perversion of God's declaration, "I AM that I AM," when identifying Himself to Moses on Mount Sinai. The perversion deceives its adherents into believing that by invoking God's declaration in conjunction with occult incantations and techniques, they can control their lives and their environments.
230. Neil T. Anderson, "Christ, Our Ruler," *Neil Anderson's Daily in Christ, Freedom in Christ Ministries* (October 13, 2008): 1–2, www.crosswalkmail.com (accessed October 13, 2008). Pastor and teacher, former chairman of the Department of Practical Theology at Talbot School of Theology, Biola University, U.S.A.; and founder and president emeritus of *Freedom in Christ Ministries*, Dr. Neil Anderson is author of works on issues like spiritual warfare and spiritual bondage.
231. Francis J. Beckwith and Gregory Koukl, *Relativism: Feet Firmly Planted In Mid-Air* (Grand Rapids, MI: Baker Books, 2006), 55.
232. James K. Walker, interview of "There Is More to the Secret," (2008), Grizzly Adams® Productions Library, Baker City, OR.
233. Groothuis, "New Age Movement: New Age or Old Occult?"

234. Byrne, *The Secret*, 175–183.

235. Gungor, interview of "There Is More to The Secret," (2008), Grizzly Adams® Productions Library, Baker City, OR. Gungor is a forward thinking pastor and author whose passion it is to see believers walk in truth and light through spiritual formation and personal experience. Gungor is quoted as describing Christianity this way: "Christianity is like a cough. Standing at a safe distance and imitating someone else's cough is nothing like getting close and catching it yourself." Some of his works include *Religiously Transmitted Diseases: Finding a Cure When Faith Doesn't Feel Right*, and his work released in early 2008 by Thomas Nelson, *The Vow: An Ancient Path of Spiritual Formation That Still Transforms Today.*

236. Neil T. Anderson, "According to the Spirit," *Neil Anderson's Daily in Christ, Freedom in Christ Ministries* (October 2, 2008): 1–2, http://www.crosswalkmail.com (accessed October 2, 2008).

237. Neil T. Anderson, "Highlights In Today's Reading, Luke 23–24," *Bible Pathways Devotional*: 1–2, http://www.crosswalk.com (accessed October 31, 2008).

238. Faith in Action, "Pilate: What is Truth? *The Passion of the Christ,*" *The Passion of the Christ,*" *Our Faith in Action* (February 2004), http://222.catholiceducation.org/articles/lesson_plans/1p0089.html (accessed August 12, 2008).

239. Clark Sutherland Northup, ed., *The Essays of Francis Bacon* (Boston, MA: Houghton Mifflin, 1936), quoted in "Pilate as the Antithesis of Truth in Bacon's 'Of Truth,'" *Academon* (2002): 1, http://online.colum.edu/antiword.php (accessed August 12, 2008).

240. James Stephens, *Francis Bacon and the Style of Science* (Chicago, IL: Chicago University Press, 1975).

Chapter 7
Satan's Very Nature: Deception

241. Malcolm Muggeridge, *The Green Stick: A Chronicle of Wasted Years* (Glasgow, England: William Collins and Sons, 1972), 16–17, quoted in Zacharias, *Can Man Live Without God*, 96.

242. The events of this case study are factual with some narrative license and took place in 2008. Molly Henderson is a fictitious name that has been assigned to the real person to protect her privacy.
243. Lynn Twist, "The Big Give: Reality TV, Oprah style, $ million dollars as prize money? Cool!" *Pass It Forward—Australia* (March 4, 2008), under "Turning kindness into one million dollars," http://pifaustralia.org/tag/philosophy/ (accessed December 27, 2008).
244. Esther Hicks and Jerry Hicks, *The Law of Attraction: The Basics of the Teachings of Abraham* (Carlsbad, CA: Hay House, Inc., 2006), 21.
245. Fleming, "On Truth."
246. Ibid.
247. "Luke 4:7," *Biblos.com Parallel Bible* (2008): 1, http://bible.cc/luke/4-7.htm (accessed December 12, 2008).
248. Byrne, *The Secret*, 57.
249. Ibid.
250. Ibid., 175.
251. Ibid., 148.
252. Neal Donald Walsh, quoted in Byrne, *The Secret*, 177. In her work *The Secret* Byrne describes Walsh as "author, International speaker, and spiritual messenger."
253. Byrne, *The Secret*, 164.
254. Ibid., 65.
255. Hicks and Hicks, *The Law of Attraction*, 205.
256. Ibid.
257. Ibid., 64–65.
258. Ibid., 82.
259. Byrne, *The Secret*, 73.
260. Mike Shreve, *In Search of the True Light*, rev. ed. (Cleveland, TN: Deeper Revelation Books, 2007), 3.
261. Ibid., 4.
262. Ibid., 119.
263. Byrne, *The Secret*, 71.
264. Christian D. Larson, *The Hidden Secret* (1912; repr., Kila, MT: Kessinger Publishing, 2007), quoted in Rhonda Byrne, *The Secret.*
265. Ibid.

266. Wallace D. Wattles, *The Science of Getting Rich: Financial Success Through Creative Thought* (1910; repr., New York, NY: Barnes and Noble, 2007), 7–8.
267. Ibid., 17–18.
268. Shreve, *In Search of the True Light,* back cover. In his bio-sketch, Shreve describes his conversion this way: "Seeking Ultimate Reality, Mike Shreve turned to eastern religions. Eventually he became a teacher of Hundalini Yoga at four universities. Then a supernatural encounter with the Lord Jesus Christ dramatically changed his heart, life and belief system. Since 1971, he has traveled worldwide sharing his life-transforming insights."
269. Ibid.
270. Bill Kline, field supervisor of the current author.
271. Christopher Lawson, "'The Moses Code Deception,' The Moses Code: A New Age Lie (An Overview)," *Beautiful Truth* (February 25–27, 2008): 1, http://web.mac.com/beautifultruth/Beautiful-Truth/Podcasts_MP3/Entries/2008/2/25_The_Moses_Code_-_A_New_Age_Lie(An_Overview).html. www.spiritual-research-network.stirsite.com/podcasts.html (accessed August 13, 2008).
272. Lawson, "The Moses Code Deception," http://www.spiritual-research-network.com/themosescode.html (accessed August 13, 2008).
273. Eckhart Tolle, *A New Earth: Awakening to Your Life's Purpose* (New York, NY: Plume/Penguin Group, 2006).
274. Byrne, *The Secret,* 13.
275. Ibid.
276. Ibid.
277. Ibid., 41.
278. Ibid., 54.
279. Beckwith and Koukl, *Relativism,* 55.
280. René Monette, "What Is Deception?," *Overcoming Deception*: 1, http://www.changingtimes.info/Overcoming.htm (accessed August 15, 2008). Pastor and author René Monette is responsible for works like "Breaking Strongholds That Destroy the Family," and "The Need for True Repentance."

281. Lisa Nichols, quoted in Byrne, *The Secret*, 13.
282. Ibid., 47.
283. Ibid., 48.
284. Ibid., 52.
285. "Hebrews 11:1," *Matthew Henry's Concise Commentary, God's Word to the Nations* (Copyright 1995), http://bible.cc/hebrews/11-1.htm (accessed December 14, 2008). GOD'S WORD® is a copyrighted work of God's Word to the Nations. Quotations are used by permission. All rights reserved. God's Word to the Nations.
286. Ibid.
287. Ibid.
288. Wilson, "Yea, Hath God Said…," http://www.opc.org/new_horizons/NH03/06a.html (accessed December 12, 2008).
289. Kline, field supervisor of the current author.
290. Phil Enlow, "How Do You Know You Are Right?" *Midnight Cry Ministries*: 1, http://midnightcry.org/howknow2.htm (accessed December 14, 2008).
291. Ibid.
292. Ibid.
293. Byrne, *The Secret*, 177.
294. Ibid., 165.
295. Ibid., 184.
296. Ibid., 175.
297. Neil T. Anderson, "Taking Every Thought Captive," *Neil Anderson's Daily in Christ, Freedom in Christ Ministries* (November 2, 2008): 1–2, www.crosswalkmail.com (accessed November 2, 2008).
298. Ibid.
299. Ibid.
300. Ibid.
301. "The Knowledge of God," *Acts 17:11 Bible Study: Theology* (2008): 1, http://www.acts17-11.com/theology.html (accessed November 2, 2008.)
302. Beckwith and Koukl, *Relativism*, 55.
303. Shreve, *In Search of the True Light*.
304. Walker, interview of "There Is More to the Secret." Walker is co-author of *The Truth Behind the Secret: A Reasoned Response to the*

Runaway Bestseller (Eugene, OR: Harvest House Publishers, 2007). James Walker is president of *Watchman Fellowship*, "an independent, nondenominational Christian research and apologetics ministry focusing on new religious movements, cults, the occult and the New Age," http://www.watchman.org/ (accessed October 3, 2008).

305. James K. Walker and Bob Waldrep, *The Truth Behind the Secret: A Reasoned Response to the Runaway Bestseller* (Eugene, OR: Harvest House Publishers, 2007), 142.
306. Ibid., 145.
307. Ibid., 141.

Chapter 8
Detriments of the Lie: Darkness, Confusion, Cloudy Vision

308. Zacharias, *Can Man Live Without God*, 15.
309. Larry John, "Morals vs Ethics—According to the Pragmatic Thinker," *Enzine Articles* (October 26, 2007): 1, http://EnzineArticles.com/?Morals-vs-Ethics-According-to-the-Pragmatic-Thinker&id=802720 (accessed December 6, 2010).
310. Sandy Simpson, "Every man did that which was right in his own eyes," Apologetics Coordination Team, *DeceptionInTheChurch.com* (January 1, 2006): 1, http://www.deceptioninthechurch.com/everyman.html (accessed December 6, 2010).
311. Bullinger, *Number in Scripture,* 88–89. *Number in Scripture* originally published by Eyre and Spottiswoode in 1894.
312. Duin, "Statistics: Moral Values, America a Christian Nation, and More."
313. Charles Sellier, Email message to current author, October 26, 2007. Sellier is president and founder of Grizzly Adams® Productions, Baker City, Oregon.
314. Carlson et al., *The Expositor's Study Bible.*
315. Stevens, *The Other Six Days*, 23.
316. Nelson Mandela, "Education Quotations," *Brainy Quote, BrainyMedia.com* (2008): 1, http://www.brainyquote.com/words/ed/education158399.html (accessed December 17, 2008).

317. Nancy Pearcey, "The Birth of Modern Science," *Bible-Science Newsletter* (October 1982), Nancy Pearcey, "How Christianity Gave Rise to the Modern Scientific Outlook," *Bible-Science Newsletter* (January 1989), states she "later expanded this material into a major theme throughout *Soul of Science*, especially chapter 1, 'An Invented Institution: Christianity and the scientific Revolution,'" quoted in Pearcey, *Total Truth*, 155.
318. Ibid.
319. Nancy Pearcey, "Fact vs. Theory: Does Gould Understand the Difference?" *Bible-Science Newsletter* (April 1987), "The Required rapidity of the changes implies either a few large steps or many and exceedingly rapid smaller ones. Large steps are tantamount to saltations and raise the problems of fitness barriers; small steps must be numerous and entail the problems discussed under microevolution. The periods of stasis raise the possibility that the lineage would enter the fossil record, and we reiterate that we can identify none of the postulated intermediate forms. Finally, the large numbers of species that must be generated so as to form a pool from which the successful lineage is selected are nowhere to be found. We conclude that the possibility that species selection is a general solution to the origin of higher taxa is not great, and that neither of the contending theories of evolutionary change at the species level, phyletic gradualism or punctuated equilibrium, seem applicable to the origin of new body plans," J. Valentine and D. Erwin, "Interpreting Great Developmental Experiments: The Fossil Record," in Rudolf A. Raff and Elizabeth C. Raff, eds., *Development as an Evolutionary Process* (New York, NY: Alan R. Liss, 1987), 96, quoted in Pearcey, *Total Truth*, 167.
320. *Encarta Dictionary*, s.v. "Naturalism": A system of thought that rejects all spiritual and supernatural explanations of the world and holds that science is the sole basis of what can be known.
321. *Encarta Dictionary*, s.v. "Creationism": The belief that God created the universe.
322. S. C. Todd, "A View from Kansas on That Evolution Debate," *Nature* 401 (September 30, 1999): 423, quoted in Pearcey, *Total*

Truth: Liberating Christianity from Its Cultural Captivity, Study Guide ed. (Wheaton, IL: Crossway Books, 2005), 168.

323. John L. Elias, *A History of Christian Education: Protestant, Catholic, and Orthodox Perspectives* (Malabar, FL: Krieger, 2002), 127–128, quoted in Anthony and Benson, *Exploring the History and Philosophy of Christian Education*, 233.
324. Anthony and Benson, *Exploring the History and Philosophy of Christian Education*, 232.
325. Richard Dawkins, "Genetics: Why Prince Charles Is So Wrong," *Checkbiotech.org* (January 28, 2003): 1, http://www.checkbiotech.org/root/index.cfm?fuseaction=news&doc_id=4575&start=1&control173&page_nr=101&pg=1, quoted in Nancy R. Pearcey, *Total Truth*, 191.
326. Mandela, "Education Quotations."
327. Yale Faculty, "Education in the United States," (N.d.; repr., Cohen): 1445, quoted in Goodlad and McMannon, eds., *The Public Purpose of Education and Schooling*, 12.
328. Goodlad and McMannon, eds., *The Public Purpose of Education and Schooling*, 82.
329. Ibid., 58.
330. Ibid., 60.
331. Ibid., 61.
332. David C. Berliner and Bruce J. Biddle, *The Manufactured Crisis: Myths, Fraud, and the Attack on America's Public Schools* (Reading, MA: Addison-Wesley, 1995), 12.
333. Goodlad and McMannon, eds., *The Public Purpose of Education and Schooling*, 29.
334. Ibid., 133.
335. Ted Sizer, quoted in Goodlad and McMannon, eds., *The Public Purpose of Education and Schooling*, 127.
336. Ibid.
337. Goodlad and McMannon, eds., *The Public Purpose of Education and Schooling*, 29, 156.
338. Chicago (AP), "Mental illness on campus sometimes leads to violence," *Loveland Reporter-Herald*, December 2, 2008. This article

discusses current emotional maladies and severe psychological disorders among a vast number of students enrolled in the public school system.

339. Ibid.
340. Ibid.
341. Ibid.
342. George Barna, "Only Half of Protestant Pastors Have a Biblical Worldview," *Barna Update* (January 12, 2004), http://www.barna.org/FlexPage.aspx?Page=BarnaUpdate&BarnaUpdateID=156 (accessed May 7, 2006), quoted in Arley S. Enloe, "The Efficacy of Ministerial Training: an Assessment of Accredited and Non-accredited Theological Education from a Pastoral Perspective" (doctoral dissertation, Beacon University, 2008), 4.
343. Todd Kappelman, "Dietrich Bonhoeffer, The Man and His Mission," *Probe Ministries* (July 14, 2002), under "Leadership U," http://www.leaderu.com/orgs/probe/docs/bonhoeffer.html (accessed January 2, 2009).
344. Mike Wilson, "Liars, Thieves, Cheats—An Upcoming Generation of Christians," *AFA Journal, The Daily Jot Daily Reporting and Analysis of Current Events from a Biblical Perspective* (December 2, 2008): 4, www.dailyjot.com (accessed December 2, 2008).
345. Amber Baker, "Faithful Friends," *Loveland Reporter-Herald*, November 8, 2008. This article discusses current negative trends regarding truth in Christianity over against other world religions.
346. Ibid.
347. Ibid.
348. Ibid.
349. Sharon Lubkemann Allen, "Dispossessed Sons and Displaced Meaning in Faulkner's Modern Cosmos," *Mississippi Quarterly* 50, no. 3 (Summer 1997): 1, http://wf21a2.webfeat.org/ (accessed September 21, 2007).
350. Shlomo Riskin, interview of "The Six Day War—Was It A Miracle?," (ca. 2007), Ancient Secrets of the Bible Collection Season II, Grizzly Adams® Productions Library, Baker City, OR.
351. "Ishmael and Isaac," *Christian Science Monitor* 229, no. 92 (2007):

469–470, http://wf21a2.webfeat.org/sRoYI125/url=http://web.ebscohost.com/ehost/detail?vid=2&hid.htm (accessed September 21, 2007).
352. Colson, quoted in Zacharias, *Can Man Live Without God*, 9.
353. Dietrich Bonhoeffer, *The Cost of Discipleship*, trans. R. H. Fuller, rev. ed. (New York, NY: Macmillan, 1960), 30.
354. Stanley, "Building Truth into Your Life."
355. Ibid.

Part IV: The Gospel Truth

356. The events of this case study are factual with some narrative license and took place in 1973. Carol Roberts is a fictitious name that has been assigned to the real person to protect her privacy.

Chapter 9
But, I Would Never Do That: The Truth About the Truth

357. Paul Hackett, ca. 1980s.
358. Margaret Thatcher, "Compromise," *brainyquote.com*: 1, http://www.brainyquote.com/words/co/compromise146379.html (Accessed April 9, 2013).
359. Hackett, ca. 1980s.
360. Jack W. Hayford, ca. 1970s.

Chapter 10
Implementing Truth in Daily Life: Beginning at the Beginning

361. Robert Morris, ca. 2013.
362. Donald Colbert, interview, *getv.org* (January 18, 2013), John Hagee Ministries, San Antonio, TX. Don Colbert, MD, one of the country's foremost authorities on the integration of natural and conventional health care, brings a twenty-first-century approach to a timeless message of healthy lifestyle habits. Dr. Colbert conducts

comprehensive seminars in churches…and is a board-certified family practice physician, a best-selling author, and a dynamic public speaker. Over the past twenty years, he has treated more than 25,000 patients, integrating body, mind, and spirit into each of his health care strategies.

Part V: A Closer Look

363. George Orwell. *A Collection of Essays*, 1946, First Harvest ed. (Orlando, FL: Houghton Mifflin Harcourt Publishing Company, 1981). George Orwell (1903–1950). English novelist and essayist. *ThinkExist.com*, http://thinkexist.com/quotation/during_times_of_universal_deceit-telling_the/193642.html (accessed March 5, 2013).
364. Ibid.
365. Cheryl K. Chumley, "Good Samaritans: Teens return lost bag with 85K inside," *The Washington Times*, April 11, 2013. This article epitomizes what truth and honesty looks like in daily life. http://www.washingtontimes.com/news/2013/apr/11/good-samaritans-teens-return-lost-bag-cash-85k-ins/#ixzz2QwuUkn6o (accessed April 19, 2013).

Chapter 11
Twenty-One Days to Truth: Read, Pray, Live

366. *The Karate Kid*, "wax on wax off" scene, *movieclips.com* (1984), http://movieclips.com/9iWog-the-karate-kid-movie-wax-on-wax-off/ (accessed April 15, 2013).
367. Adapted from Jack W. Hayford's formula for praying from The Lord's Prayer, Matthew 6:9–13," (Lecture, Calvary Temple, Denver, CO, ca. 1986).
368. Adapted from Cleansing Stream Ministries, The Church on the Way, Van Nuys, CA, 1993.

Glossary Endnotes

369. "What is Chrislam?," Got Questions Ministries (ca. 2013): 1–2. http://www.gotquestions.org/Chrislam.html#ixzz2NhbmjioP (accessed March 16, 2013).
370. William L. Thrasher, Jr., Basics for Believers: Foundational Truths to Guide Your Life, vol. 1 (Chicago, IL: Moody Press, 1998), table of contents. Thrasher, the associate editor of Moody Press, Chicago, Illinois, and author of manifold works on Biblical theology, identifies the foundational truths of Christianity.
371. *Merriam-Webster Online Dictionary*, s.v. "Counterfeit," http://www.merriam-webster.com/dictionary/counterfeit (accessed March 3, 2012).
372. W. E. Vine, Merrill F. Unger and William White, Jr., *Vine's Complete Expository Dictionary of Old and New Testament Words* (Nashville, TN: Thomas Nelson Publishers, 1996), 145.
373. Vine et al., *Vine's Complete Expository Dictionary of Old and New Testament Words*, 151.
374. Ibid.
375. William L. Thrasher, Jr., *Basics for Believers: Foundational Truths to Guide Your Life*, vol. 1 (Chicago, IL: Moody Press, 1998), table of contents. Thrasher is the associate editor of Moody Press, Chicago, Illinois, and author of manifold works on Biblical theology. Thrasher identifies the foundational truths of Christianity as: "God; The Trinity; Names and Attributes of God; The Lord Jesus Christ; The Holy Spirit; The Bible; Doctrine; The Fall; Sin; The Incarnation; The Crucifixion; The Resurrection; The Gospel; and The New Birth."
376. *Vine's Expository Dictionary of New Testament Words*, Bible Study Info, http://studybible.info/vines/Humble%20(Adjective%20and%20Verb) (accessed March 3, 2013).
377. *Merriam-Webster Online Dictionary*, s.v. "Integrity," http://www.merriam-webster.com/dictionary/integrity (accessed March 3, 2012).
378. Vine et al., *Vine's Complete Expository Dictionary of Old and New Testament Words*, 366.

379. Ibid., 367.
380. Ibid., 369–370.
381. *Vine's Expository Dictionary of New Testament Words*, Bible Study Info, http://studybible.info/vines/Meek,%20Meekness (accessed March 3, 2013).
382. Groothuis, "New Age Movement: New Age or Old Occult?"
383. *Merriam-Webster Online Dictionary*, s.v. "Perversion," http://www.merriam-webster.com/dictionary/perversion (accessed March 3, 2012).
384. *Vine's Expository Dictionary of New Testament Words*, Bible Study Info, http://studybible.info/vines/Perverse,%20Pervert (accessed March 3, 2013).
385. *Merriam-Webster Online Dictionary*, s.v. "Substitute," http://www.merriam-webster.com/dictionary/substitute (accessed March 3, 2012).
386. Vine et al., *Vine's Complete Expository Dictionary of Old and New Testament Words*, 645.
387. Ravi Zacharias, *Can Man Live Without God* (Nashville, TN: Word Publishing, 1994), 101.
388. Vine et al., *Vine's Complete Expository Dictionary of Old and New Testament Words*, 645.
389. Ibid., 367.
390. Ibid., 369–370.
391. Ibid., 645.
392. Ibid., 16.

CPSIA information can be obtained at www.ICGtesting.com
Printed in the USA
LVOW13s2359261113

362876LV00002B/2/P

9 781462 727803